Unspoken

Unspoken

A Rhetoric of Silence

Cheryl Glenn

Southern Illinois University Press
Carbondale

Library of Congress Cataloging-in-Publication Data
Glenn, Cheryl.
      Unspoken : a rhetoric of silence / Cheryl Glenn.
          p. cm.
      Includes bibliographical references and index.
    1. Silence. I. Title.
BJ1499.S5G54 2004
808—dc22
ISBN 0-8093-2583-7 (hardcover : alk. paper)
ISBN 0-8093-2584-5 (pbk. : alk. paper)   2004001932

Printed on recycled paper. ♲

The paper used in this publication meets the minimum requirements of
American National Standard for Information Sciences—Permanence of Paper
for Printed Library Materials, ANSI Z39.48-1992. ∞

For Jon

The silences, the empty spaces, the language itself, the excision of the female, the methods of discourse tell us as much as the content, once we learn to watch for what is left out, for the unspoken.

—Adrienne Rich, *Blood, Bread, and Poetry*

Contents

Preface

Unspoken: A Rhetoric of Silence is the first study to offer a rhetoric of silence, to explore the ways silence can be as powerful as speech, the ways that silence and silencing deliver meaning. Over fifty years ago, Swiss philosopher Max Picard broke new ground with his *World of Silence* (1948), which asked readers to consider the virtues of silence as an ontological principle, from its resonance in language to its power in religion. Some thirty years later, Bernard Dauenhauer's *Silence: The Phenomenon and Its Ontological Significance* (1980) would again interrogate silence, with the author systematizing and clarifying the fundamental features of silence as a phenomenon. In 1994, George Kalamaras's *Reclaiming the Tacit Tradition* authenticated silence as a mode of knowing that complements language and thus enhances the teaching of writing. More recently, Frank Farmer's Bakhtinian-influenced *Saying and Silence* (2001) offers ways to hear and employ silences in the composition classroom and beyond. Robin Patric Clair's *Organizing Silence* (1998) provides a speech-communication study that investigates the ways dominant groups silence marginalized groups and the ways marginalized groups can band together and speak out. My own *Rhetoric Retold: Regendering the Tradition from Antiquity Through the Renaissance* (1997) provided me a 2,000-year span in which to negotiate and listen to both imposed and tactical silences and thus sparked this new project.

Just as these books provided a basis for my deeper understanding of silence, they also provided me a reason to write: I build on this scholarship to expand our understanding, construction, and production of silence *as a rhetoric*, as a constellation of symbolic strategies that (like spoken language) serves many functions. This is not to say that silence is always strategic, empowering, or patently engaging. Not all silence is particularly potent. However, silence is too often read as simple passivity in situations where it has actually taken on an expressive power. Employed as a tactical strategy or inhabited in deference to authority, silence resonates loudly along the corridors of purposeful language use. Whether choice or im/position, silence can reveal positive or negative abilities, fulfilling or withholding traits, harmony or disharmony, success or failure. Silence can deploy power; it can defer to power. It all depends.

Current explorations into silence thus work to remind us of how much more we have to learn about women's and men's delivery of silence, especially when history, rhetoric, linguistics, politics, and culture offer us so many silent passages, some eventually (some never) spoken or heard. *Unspoken* addresses these needs. No other work organizes, contextualizes, and analyzes silence in a way that connects it with the construction and production of human communication—or conceives of it as a rhetoric, per se. I foresee *Unspoken* as extending in necessary ways the ongoing scholarly conversation about the power of conscientious speaking out and of silence, about power and control, and especially about who remains silent and who silences.

Few documented accounts explicitly demonstrate the usefulness and sensibility of silence, particularly in our talkative Western culture, where speech is synonymous with civilization itself and where silence-as-obedience is frequently rewarded. Despite its inaudibility, silence is "everywhere," existing in overlapping states: environmental, locational, cultural, communal, and personal. It can be self- or other-initiated, self- or other-derived. Whatever its shape, the form of silence (its delivery) is always the same. But the function of silence—that is, its effect upon people—varies according to the social context in which it occurs. Therefore, *Unspoken* listens to silence in a number of mutually productive and sometimes contradictory ways. "Defining Silence" (chapter 1), charts the range of spaces inhabited by silence, using the views provided by linguistics, phenomenology, rhetoric, and anthropology; the chart accounts for previous unseen and unmeasured contours of the silent landscape as well as for the paradoxical irregularities of intention and perception.[1] "Engendering Silence" (chapter 2) investigates silence and voice as gendered positions, setting forth a grammar of silence, a way to think about the complexity and multiple variations of silence as it relates to systems of power (race, sex, sexuality, age, class, clan, ethnicity, status, and so on)[2]; "Witnessing Silence" (chapter 3) and "Attesting Silence" (chapter 4) extend the gender analysis of chapter 2 to the highly politicized silences and words of Anita Hill, Lani Guinier, President Clinton, and the sequence of figures known as "all the President's women," which starts with Gennifer Flowers and ends with Chelsea Clinton.[3] "Commanding Silence" (chapter 5), a representative methodological application, carries my analysis into a specific cultural site perceived as silent by dominant U.S. culture. This chapter interrogates the cultural silence allegedly commanded by various American Indian groups (among them, Navajo, Apache, Hopi, and pueblo), few of whom are tethered to a Western rhetorical tradition of individual public display and argumentative prowess, most of whom have been described by Anglo researchers.[4] "Opening Silence" (chapter 6) offers specific venues for further research into rhetorics of silence. In this final chapter, I offer some potential sources for rhetorics of silence: listening, religion, music, ethnic-specific communication, and, most prominently, the circulation of silence as a creative or ethical resource within the college classroom and for college writers. Thus, this final chapter offers additional theoretical and methodological implications for further research into silence as a rhetorical art.

Acknowledgments

Unspoken came to voice with substantial support. I am grateful to the Pennsylvania State University Department of English and Don Bialostosky, then department head, for providing me a semester to begin drafting this book; to the Research and Graduate Studies Office of the College of the Liberal Arts for providing me travel money to conduct research at the University of New Mexico's Center for Southwest Studies; to the Tracy Winfree McCourtney and Ted H. McCourtney Endowed Fund in the Humanities, which allowed me to interview American Indians in the Southwest; to the Institute for Arts and Humanistic Studies for making possible two research trips to Gallaudet University and a return to the Southwest; and to the Human Subjects Institutional Review Board for approving the research proposal and design that anchors my interviews with a number of Southwest Indians. A National Endowment for the Humanities Summer Stipend provided a full summer of research and writing. I also want to thank interim department head Marie Secor for her necessary support and the Pennsylvania State University for granting me a sabbatical leave in order to finish this book.

Without the research assistance of Jessica Enoch and Wendy B. Sharer and of student interns Robin Hatfield, Christine Mahady, Jennifer Monahan, and Danielle Luzzo, who spent hours on LIAS and in the Pattee Library tracking down hard-to-locate sources of every kind having to do with silence, I could not have completed this book. I am grateful for their contributions as well as those of Rosalyn Collings Eves, Keith Gibson, Vorris Nunley, and Kakie Urch. I also want to thank the undergraduate students who took "Rhetorics of Silence" with me and taught me more about the rhetorical power of silence and silencing than all the books we read.

My gratitude also extends to the many people who so graciously allowed me to interview them. Among them, Louisa Baca, C. Maurus Chino, Todd Epaloose, Evelyn Fredericks, Laura Kaye Jagles, Kathryn and Lee Marmon, Leila Moquino O'Neal, Earl Ortiz, Annette Romero, Kevin Saavedra, Andrew Todacheene, Danielle Victoriano, and Billie Wanya, in particular, talked with me at length about their notions and uses of silence as members of various Indian pueblos or tribes. Each of them made certain that I knew them first as individuals who use silence in their own idiosyncratic ways and then as representatives of their culture.

Maurus and Andrew were especially adamant that I turn from reading what whites said about Indians to what Indians write and say about Indians. "What you read is not always what's happening in the real world," they warned me. "Sometimes," Andrew told me, "you listen to a white person tell about Indians; you turn around and think, 'Where in the hell did they read that shit?'" Over the course of my research, Maurus called me a number of times with reading suggestions, and Andrew sent me articles and citations. Both these men stressed the importance of letting Indians speak for themselves. For their interest and frankness, I remain grateful—and forever changed.

My biggest debt remains with my family, friends, and colleagues. Jon, Anna, Darrin, Eddie, Helen, Mom, and Terry all understood my need to make silence speak, and their support for my writing helped sustain me. Over many a meal and bottle of wine, Pat Shipman and Alan Walker, neighbors extraordinaire, pushed (and pushed) me to apply for grants, keep writing, and give my compulsion a name; hence, the title, *Unspoken*. I am grateful for the friendships and intellectual respect for this project demonstrated by Jamie Barlowe, Dale Bauer, Robin Becker, Pat Belanoff, Shari Benstock, Ann Berthoff, Jane Bradley, Jim Brasfield, Brenda Jo Brueggemann, Veronica Burk, Karlyn Kohrs Campbell, Lisa Ede, Bob Edwards, Richard Leo Enos, Karen Foss, James Fredal, George Kalamaras, Anne Ruggles Gere, Sandra Mortola Gilbert, Keith Gilyard, Joe Harris, Anita Plathe Helle, Charlotte Holmes, Sue Hum, Shirley F. Wilson Logan, Andrea Lunsford, Margaret Marshall, Jaime Mejia, Joyce Irene Middleton, Marilyn Moller, Roxanne Mountford, Dickson Musslewhite, Bob Nye, Michell Phifer, Kris Ratcliffe, Elaine Richardson, Jacqueline Jones Royster, Marie Secor, Jack Selzer, Sandy Spanier, Sandy Stelts, Carolyn and Fred Swearingen, C. Jan Swearingen, John Vickrey Van Cleve, Kathleen Welch, Jim West, and Lynn Worsham—all of whom responded to my requests for stories of silence and silencing; sent me relevant articles, essays, books, or good cheer; participated in conference panels on silence; or read yet another version of yet another grant proposal or drafted chapter. Not only are they Cato's good people speaking well, but they are good people delivering and experiencing silence and silencing as well.

In addition I want to thank George Kalamaras and Kris Ratcliffe, who gave my manuscript an insightful and generous read. For their invaluable criticism, suggestions, and praise, I remain infinitely grateful. Gary and Sandy Scharnhorst were extraordinary resources for me, especially during my early research trips to Albuquerque, making sure I found Zimmerman Library, the Center for Southwest Research, the best new and used bookstores, good restaurants, and suitable people to interview. My cousin Lee Marmon continues to meet with me several times a year to discuss his seventy-some years on Laguna Pueblo, our relatives, and his amazing talents as a professional photographer. His vast knowledge of pueblo culture, literature, U. S. history, and family history continues to inspire me. Margaret Johnson and Sid Davis were another couple, whose friendship and generosity have long supported me in my Southwest travels. I wish Margaret had lived to read the culmination of my research and writing, for she would have giggled with delight in detecting her firm influence on my thinking and have phoned me immediately upon discovering places where her influence hadn't held fast but should have. I'm also grateful to Karl Kageff, executive editor of Southern Illinois University Press, for his intellectual leadership, his smart publishing sense, and his enduring dedication to rhetoric and composition. We are all fortunate to have him in our profession. The Coalition of Women Scholars in the History of Rhetoric and Composition continues to provide me a safe venue for trying out my latest ideas within the good company of intellectual sisters. Rarely silent or unspoken, these are good women speaking (writing, signing, laughing, advising, and joking) well.

For permission to reprint certain material, I gratefully acknowledge the following:

From "Against Silence," *The Horse Fair*, by Robin Becker, © 2000. Reprinted by permission of the University of Pittsburgh Press.

From "Silence," *The Collected Poems of Langston Hughes* by Langston Huges, copyright © 1994 by The Estate of Langston Hughes. Used by permission of Alfred A. Knopf, a division of Random House, Inc.

From "Silence: A Rhetorical Art for Resisting Discipline(s)," part of chapter 3 that was previously published in *JAC* 22.2 (Spring 2002): 261–92.

A Word (or Two) on Terms and Categories

As I worked on *Unspoken*, I faced numerous decisions for the terms I would use to refer to or categorize people or groups of people. Often, a variety of terms seems to refer to the same or closely related groups or conditions—especially to an outsider like me, who wants to talk about the hearing impaired or Native Americans. While my semantic decisions are based on my experiences preparing this book, those same decisions were based ultimately on my own social and physical attributes: I am white, female, heterosexual, feminine, feminist, hearing, well-educated at a Big Ten school, fully employed at another Big Ten school. Thus it is that this volume bears the ideological weight of my own perspective, and while I cannot reduce it, I can acknowledge it.

Given that I came to this project thinking of gender as the power differential playing out in concepts of masculine and feminine, it was an easy stretch to imagine silencing and silence as gendered sites of rhetorical delivery or invention. Often, silencing is an imposition of weakness upon a normally speaking body; whereas silence can function as a strategic position of strength. In gendered terms, then, this means that silencing can be "feminine," while purposeful silence can be "masculine"—depending, of course, on the power differential in play. For instance, the pervasive and strong pro-oralism stance (learn to speak, learn to read lips) of the hearing-impaired community lends itself to this same attitude: nonpurposeful silence must surely be a weakness or a feminization because it is more powerful (i.e., more masculine) to "speak" to the hearing world. Thus, the now-militant stance in the "Deaf" community (with "Deaf" differing from "deaf," a term closer in meaning to "hearing-impaired") is that signing is every bit as powerful (masculine) as speaking and that American Sign Language (ASL) is indeed a language. No need to feel weakened by deafness or signing; instead, one can be empowered by the ASL community.

Initially, I considered categories of gender (masculine and feminine) as having more to do with power than with sexed bodies (male and females). But I rethought those categories in light of Judith Butler's thorough interrogation of those biological categories (*Bodies That Matter*), an argument that biological categories are made apparent in exactly the same ways that masculine and feminine are constructed—through repeated performances and iterations. I respect the ways Butler has enriched scholarly thinking on the concepts of gender and sex, but I decided to remain with my initial terminology for gendered power differentials: "masculine" and "feminine" work well to indicate sites of strength and weakness in this study, just as they have in my previous work.

But when I came to making a decision about the many other options for referring to various groups of people, I became even more uncomfortable. How can any one term—"white," "black," "Indian," "deaf"—capture the wildly rich diversity of any social, cultural, ethnic, or bodily group? How can any one term capture their group identity, let alone their individual humanity? How can "white," for example, speak to the various categories it supposedly constitutes, when only a hundred years ago, Slavs, Celts, Italians, and Jews were not "white"?

And what about the politics of naming native peoples? How could I—a white woman—choose a name? Would I refer to them as "Amerindans," "Natives," "aboriginals," "Native Americans," "American Indians," "Native People," "Indigenous Americans," "Indians," or a term that I have not yet heard? Should I refer to them only in terms of their tribe or pueblo? Or, given the postcultural narratives of U.S. culture, should I refer to them as postindian?[1] What choices did I have, particularly given Gerald Vizenor's biting insights in *Manifest Manners*:

> The word Indian, and most other tribal names, are simulations in the literature of dominance. . . . The word *Indian* . . . is a colonial enactment, not a loan word, and the dominance is sustained by the simulation that has superseded the real tribal names.
>
> The Indian was an occidental invention that became a bankable simulation; the word has no referent in tribal languages or cultures. The postindian is the absence of the invention, and the end of representation in literature; the closure of that evasive melancholy of dominance. . . .
>
> The postindian warrior is the simulation of survivance in new stories. Indians, and other simulations, are the absence of tribal intimation; the mere mention of blunders in navigation undermines the significance of discoveries and the melancholy of dominance. The contrivance of names, however, endures in the monologues of manifest manners and the literature of dominance. (10–11)

When I began my visits and my interviews to the homes, places of work, and reservations of these indigenous peoples, I stumbled with terminology. Initially, I referred to myself and "my people" as "Anglo" or "Euroamerican" and to my interviewees as "Native Americans."

Fortunately, one of the men stopped me and corrected me: "'Native American,'" he told me, "is a term made up by white people." I doubt he self-identifies as postindian, but he surely does not identify as Native American. He told me that whatever I called him did not change who he was, but that I should probably refer to him by name, pueblo, and only then as an "Indian."

So I did.

In his answers to my many questions, in the course of our conversation, he often referred to "whites" and "white people," never using the term "Anglo." I told him that I was using the term "Anglo" because "white" had become such a contested term. In fact, I mentioned to him that there was a new area of research called "Whiteness Studies," and that scholars, mostly white themselves, argued that whiteness was a construct, changing over time and space, no way transhistorical. The Indian man laughed and said, "Yeah, right—there's no such thing as 'white'? You've never been Indian."[2]

In terms of categories, particularly racialized ones, there is simply too much to consider. We all unname even as we rename. As Patricia Williams, in *The Alchemy of Race and Rights*, tells us:

> On the one hand, race isn't important because it isn't important; most of us devoutly wish this to be a colorblind society, in which removing the words "black" and "white" from our vocabulary would render the world, in a miraculous flash, free of all division. On the other hand, real life isn't that simple. Often we have to use the words in order to acknowledge the undeniable psychological and cultural power of racial constructions upon all our lives; we have to be able to call out against the things that trouble us, whether racism or other forms of suffering. (83–84)[3]

So I decided to use the terms "white" and "black." I would have used the term "nonwhite" throughout, but I have too many instances for referring to Indians, who are, indeed, nonwhite. However, when I'm referring to the raced power differentials that Anita Hill and Lani Guinier inhabited, the invisible racial privilege neither of them enjoyed, and what Joyce Irene Middleton refers to as the "power-concealing rhetoric" of the white men who opposed each of these women, I use the term "nonwhite" as my semantic option (438–39). Middleton frequently reminds her readers of Richard Dyer's compelling argument for using "nonwhite":

> Where I need to see whiteness in relation to all peoples who are not white, "black" will not do. The other option would be "people of colour," the preferred US term (though with little currency in Britain). While I have always appreciated this term's generosity, including in it all those people that "black" excludes, it none the less reiterates the notion that some people have colour and others, whites, do not. We need to recognize white as a colour too, and just one among many, and we cannot do that if we keep using a term that reserves

colour for anyone other than white people. Reluctantly, I am forced back on "non-white." (11)

Keeping Dyer's argument in the forefront of my thinking, I nonetheless went with Williams's argument, for the most part. I also decided to use the term "Indian" generically, though that, too, is an imprecise naming category.[4] And when I worked with the hearing-impaired and members of the D/deaf communities (materials that are not developed in this project), I found myself using "hearing-impaired" as a physical description, "deaf" as a social description, and "Deaf" as a political one. My semantic choices are definite yet tentative as they will evolve as I continue to learn, come to recognize, and respect the resonance of any name.

Even though I have learned a great deal in the course of writing *Unspoken*, much still remains for me to learn. In fact, if I have learned anything, it comes down to "two or three things I know for sure," to paraphrase Dorothy Allison. First of all, the complexity and difficulty of naming, ascribing, and identifying roles is beyond me, beyond any one of us. Whatever attributions I associate with myself resonate with some sort of an overarching governing narrative by which I figure and refigure my bodily, social, and intellectual selves. If I cannot handily identify myself, can I claim to identify others? The second thing I know for sure is that "white," "black," "nonwhite," "Indian," "hearing," "hearing-impaired" are "false" categories. They are socially constructed, historically located categories, to be sure, but they are not grounded in material reality. Yet despite their "falseness," these are operative categories in U. S. culture, each with a gatekeeping function in terms of treatment, opportunity, hope, and—most important—racial perspective. Although none of these seemingly monolithic categories accurately accounts for the very real and different people within it, each category does lend itself to a measure of generalization, as Williams makes clear. For instance, my whiteness has allowed me more educational and thereby material opportunity than the Indianness of some of my friends. Thus, each of these categories works for and against its constituents as a social force. The third thing I have learned for sure is that the complexity of identification, the politics of gender and sexuality, and the infinite inflections of scholarly discourses all describe and circumscribe my own life, even as they contribute to ever-unfolding spirals of bewilderment, confrontation, refusal, and dream.

Unspoken

1
Defining Silence

Silence can be a plan
rigorously executed
the blueprint to a life
It is a presence
it has a history a form
Do not confuse it
with any kind of absence.
             —Adrienne Rich, "Cartographies of Silence"

In *Rhetoric Retold: Regendering the Tradition from Antiquity Through the Renaissance,* I worked to write women into histories and theories of rhetoric. Since rhetoric always inscribes the relation of language and power at a particular moment (including who may speak, who may listen or who will agree to listen, and what can be said), canonical rhetorical history has represented the experience of males, powerful males, with no provision of allowance for females. My goal was to broaden the view of rhetoric, to regender the rhetorical landscape in order to bring male—and female—rhetoricians clearly into sight. At every turn of that project, I faced the central problem of our collective, feminist project: silence and silencing. As I knitted together material to write Sappho, Aspasia, Diotima, Hortensia, Fulvia, Julian of Norwich, Margery Kempe, Margaret More Roper, Anne Askew, and Elizabeth I into rhetorical history, I witnessed the centuries of male-controlled education, politics, law, and religion that had written them out—silenced them—in the first place. But I also witnessed the pockets of female rhetorical activity that punctuated those long stretches of silence.

Much of the past is, of course, irrevocably silenced: gestures, conversations, and original manuscripts can never be recaptured. Silence and silencing still greet us in every library, every archive, every text, every newscast—at every turn. As Max Picard tells us, "There are eventless periods in human history, periods in which history seems to carry silence—nothing but silence—around her; periods in which [wo/]men and events are hidden beneath the silence" (83). Still, while most of the female and male tradition has been regrettably lost, enormous amounts of material survive that can be used to re-create those traditions within our histories.

1

The rediscovery of these words and voices has become an important scholarly industry as has the turn to studies in silence.[1]

Rhetoric Retold provided me a venue for piercing the "silence" of gendered silences that speak through women and men. For instance, I first became aware of the paradoxical properties of silence (its powers and limitations) when I worked on the rhetorical display of Protestant Reformer Anne Askew. In 1546, the aristocratic Askew was arrested on grounds of radical Protestantism, making her the first gentlewoman to be judged by a jury. Accordingly, she was forced out of the feminine private sphere and thrust directly into masculine public view, where she refused to tell her own secrets. Under harsh religious interrogation, Askew refused to talk about anything but her Protestant faith, refusing to share the names of any other members of her sect, and revealing no concealed information besides her extraordinary mastery of Scripture. In other words, even under torture, Askew delivered *silence* rather than the called-for, expected, self-disclosing answers: "God has given me the gift of knowledge, but not of utterance. And Solomon says, that a woman of few words, is a gift of God, Proverbs 19." Her delivery suits perfectly her aims: it is unrevealing, a rhetoric of concealment, of silence. Therein lies the importance of Anne Askew to my current project: she shows me how recorded silence can "work," how truly powerful and empowering it can be, even as she loses her life. She demonstrates the power of silence but also its dangers.

After naming Askew's practice a "rhetoric of silence," I came to believe that silence may well be the most undervalued and *under*-understood traditionally feminine site and concomitant rhetorical art. After all, St. Paul's first-century censure held for millennia: "Let a woman learn in silence with all submissiveness. I permit no woman to teach or to have authority over men; she is to keep silent" (*Holy Bible,* 1 Tim. 2:11–12). Not surprisingly, silence has long been considered a lamentable essence of femininity, a trope for oppression, passivity, emptiness, stupidity, or obedience.

The rhetorical tradition, long preoccupied with written and spoken rhetorics, has for too long ignored the rhetorical powers of silence. Though rhetorical handlists still mention *silence* and its generations *(aposiopesis, interpellatio, obticentia, praecisio,* and *reticentia),* the contemporary rhetorical scene, for the most part, assumes silence to be simply an absence of text or voice. *Unspoken* argues otherwise. Throughout this book, I will argue that silence is a specific rhetorical art, one that merits serious investigation within rhetoric and composition studies. In this chapter, I will provide a broad historical overview of the reasons silence has long remained an unappreciated rhetorical art, foreground several important scholarly investigations into silence, and supply a tentative grammar of silence as a rhetoric.

Speech vs. Silence

In ancient times, speech was perceived as a gift of the gods and thus as a distinguishing characteristic of humans; therefore, speech became the authorized medium of culture and power, and its seeming obverse a sign of "animality." The primacy of the spoken word characterizes Greek and Judaic genius and carried over into Christianity: "In the beginning was the Word, and the Word was with God, and the Word was God" (John 1.1). Thus, language has long represented the specifically human way of transcending biology and achieving humanity, culture. In *Language and Silence,* George Steiner writes,

> That articulate speech should be the line dividing man from the myriad forms of animate being, that speech should define man's singular eminence above the silence of the plant and the grunt of the beast . . . is classical doctrine well before Aristotle. We find it in Hesiod's *Theogyny* (584). Man is, to Aristotle, a being of the word (ζῷον λόγον ἔχον [2]). How the word came to him is, as Socrates admonishes in the *Cratylus,* a question worth asking . . . but it is not a question to which a certain answer lies in human reach.
>
> Possessed of speech, possessed by it, the word having chosen the grossness and infirmity of man's condition for its own compelling life, the human person has broken free from the great silence of matter. Or, to use Ibsen's image: struck with the hammer, the insensate ore has begun to sing. (36)

Little wonder, then, that speaking or speaking out continues to signal power, liberation, culture, or civilization itself. That seeming obverse, silence, signals nothingness.

Steiner goes to argue that silence is nothing, nowhere to find anything, for silence "surrounds the naked discourse" (21). Silence is subordinate to speech; it is speech that points out silence and points to the silence within itself. Without speech, silence would be invisible, nothing. In *The World of Silence,* Picard, who reveres silence, writes, nonetheless, that "it is language and not silence that makes man truly human. The word has supremacy over silence" (15). Wilhelm von Humboldt (1767–1835) writes that language is the distinguishing blessing immediately conferred on humans. For him, speech and understanding, different products of the power of language, depend upon the spiritual forces of humanity, and language is "the most radiant sign and certain proof that man does not possess intrinsically separate individuality" (qtd. in "Humboldt" 73). Thomas Mann tells us that "speech is civilization itself. The word . . . preserves contact—it is silence which isolates" (518). In other words, speech—and only speech—keeps us humanly together. Most language users agree: language is all, silence is nothing.

I do not agree. As I will argue throughout this book, it is silence that reveals speech at the same time that it enacts its own sometimes complementary rhetoric.

I am not alone in my conviction that silence is every bit as important as speech, that the unspoken offers us an as yet underexamined rhetorical art. Even though language and humanity have thus come to be conflated, with nearly all humans demonstrating some facility with spoken language, and even though silent humans are suspect if not discounted altogether, silence continues to tug at our civilized consciousness. Picard explains our dilemma:

> One cannot imagine a world in which there is nothing but language and speech, but one *can* imagine a world where there is nothing but silence.
>
> Silence contains everything in itself. It is not waiting for anything; it is always wholly present in itself and it completely fills out the space in which it appears. (17, emphasis added)

Containing everything in itself, silence is meaningful, even if it is invisible. It can mean powerlessness or emptiness—but not always. Because it fills out the space in which it appears, it can be equated with a kind of emptiness, but that is not the same as absence. And silencing, for that matter, is not the same as erasing. Like the zero in mathematics, silence is an absence with a function, and a rhetorical one at that.

THE PRESENCE OF SILENCE, THE ABSENCE OF WORDS

The stupendous reality is that language itself cannot be understood unless we begin by observing that speech is not only surrounded by silence but consists most of all in silences:

> Silence is not simply what happens when we stop talking. It is more than the mere negative renunciation of language; it is more than simply a condition that we can produce at will.
>
> When language ceases, silence begins. But it does not begin *because* language ceases. The absence of language simply makes the presence of Silence more apparent. (Picard 15, emphasis added)

Picard asks us to educate ourselves to the fact that silence and language work together, each shaping and generating the other in a natural dynamism of meaning making:

> Speech came out of silence, out of the fullness of silence. The fullness of silence would have exploded if it had not been able to flow out into speech. . . . There is something silent in every word, as an abiding token of the origin of speech. And in every silence there is something of the spoken word, as an abiding token of the power of silence to create speech. (24)

Speech often fails us, though, and silence rarely does, a basic truth I wish I had realized earlier in my life. Silence—not the spoken word—is the only phenomenon that is always at our disposal. Silence permeates our every moment, its identity a stretch of time perforated by sound. Thus silence remains inescapably one form of speech and an element in every dialogue.

The Art and Practice of Conversation

The ratio between silence and language reconfirms a Western notion of language as positive, and silence as negative; silence as foreground, silence as background; language as melody, silence as harmony. Thus speaking and silence remain tied to our civilizing tendencies, which play out expressly in conversation.

Conversation remains our social glue, the coin of the realm, the way to win friends and influence people—where silence and speech hang in a delicate balance. Too much silence is rarely tolerated from those who are expected to speak: "The cat got your tongue?" "Why are you so quiet?" "Is everything OK?" Silence is rewarded only when signifying obedience or proper subordination: The subaltern should not speak but feign rapt listening with their silence. "Children should be seen and not heard." "Silence gives grace to a woman—though that is not the case likewise with a man" (Aristotle, *Politics* 1.5.9).

Yet whether to speak or remain silent (who gets to speak; who should remain silent) always depends on the rhetorical situation. In "Dialectical Tensions of Speaking and Silence," an eloquent Socratic dialogue with Foucauldian overtones, Robert L. Scott explains,

R: . . . To speak is to assert one's position. To remain silent is to defer to the position of another. One must do both thoughtfully and carefully.

Q: I defer to one who is older and wiser . . . . I defer also to the person of superior power.

R: In each case your desire is the same and different. You desire to receive. In the first, to receive knowledge; in the second, to receive power. . . .

Q: A prince has power; a sage, wisdom. But what have common people to give? One must know if one is to govern silence and speech in their presence.

R: You are correct. Power and wisdom are both necessary if the state is to be well governed. Common people have power, also, the power of their numbers and their needs. . . . Power is focused at the top, but the state, as does all earthly things, draws power from the bottom. . . .

Q: So one must remain silent before superiors and speak before the common people?

R: Yes. And one must remain silent before the common people and speak to superiors.

Q: Can one do both?

R: The key is one's sense of order. One must maintain and enhance one's position. One's position depends on order. Without order, no one has position. . . . (3–4)

Scott's dialectic lays out the patterning of order and power, of maintaining—and yet enhancing—one's position.

Conversation has always been a medium for establishing oneself as an intellectual, social, or financial player—but not, or so the rules allege, at the expense of any one listener.[3] Conversation continues to imply the equality among participants: no one interrupts, no one remains silent, everyone takes turns.[4] The equality ideal is just that, for most often, "people who come into a conversation with the most real-world power tend to display the signs of power within the conversation: they monopolize the floor and topics" (Tannen 49)—or, I might add, use the prerogative of remaining silent, which can rattle their conversation partner.

Ideally, there should be no gaps and no overlaps, no competition for speaking, no worries about silences. We learn early on to fill up social space and compress silence, to use words for phatic communication, small talk, and idle conversation. Thus, for the most part, we Westerners are accustomed to sustained conversation and notice with dismay disruptive gaps or unexpected silences. We have not yet come to understand that the rhetorical significance of the unspoken often resonates with that of the spoken. A brief silence or conversation gap can occur for several reasons: the speaker has deliberately inserted it; it signifies the invitational space between turn taking; or the topic at hand has been exhausted. These companionable gaps are anticipated by the other and closed by merely moving on. But the longer the gap, the colder it is and the more awkward it can be to repair, especially given our cultural belief in the importance of a streamed conversation. Instead of opening up a space for hearing something new, that longer gap usually signifies that something or someone is out of kilter. But rather than signifying an oddity, perhaps that longer gap carries with it what should be easily recognized rhetorical meaning, such as notification of *differend:* one party simply cannot voice his or her complaints or point because the other party insists on speaking within a different language game or genre of discourse. The talker could then use the rhetorical information to make a change in her or his own speech pattern, rather than considering such silence to be static, empty, annoying, even threatening.

Noticeably silent people, we have been led to believe, are either psychologically inhibited or inappropriate in their deliveries of silence; they are not performing the role of conversant. Only an already-accomplished conversationalist, writes Martin Heidegger, can produce appropriate and effective silences:

"Keeping silent authentically is possibly only in genuine discoursing. . . . In that sense one's reticence makes something manifest, and does away with 'idle talk'" (208). Conversationalists who deliberately use silence, then, should have already established their conversational skill and their rhetorical and real-world power. Expert conversationalists know how to deliver whatever is unsayable (the inexplicable and inexpressible) with verbal assurance or with a silence that signifies their power. Nonskilled and always/already disempowered conversationalists, on the other hand, render silence that seemingly signifies their subordination.

Therefore, most of us talk and talk, even though we know that it is usually speech—not silence—that gets us into trouble. (And few so-called accomplished conversationalists can control their unconscious, especially if they are determined to draw people together.) After all, as Susan Sontag tells us, "Words are too crude" (22). Speech gets us into trouble, yet it holds us together. Silence can be troubling, but yet it too holds us together, too. In fact, I would argue, sometimes the deepest human bond of all is wordless:

Speech is one symptom of Affection
And Silence one—
The perfectest communication
Is heard of none.

(Dickinson 1681).

Given how our language works, then, speech and silence are not mutually exclusive; they are inextricably linked and often interchangeably, simultaneously meaningful. Speech and silence depend upon each other: behind all speech is silence, and silence surrounds all speech. As linguists Deborah Tannen and Muriel Saville-Troike tell us, "The significance of silence can usually be interpreted only in relation to sound, but the reverse is also the case, with the significance of sound depending on the interpretation of silence" (3). Poet José Ortega y Gasset points out that because one cannot say everything, speech consists above all in silences (246). He goes on to write that "a being who could not renounce saying many things would be incapable of speaking. . . . Each people leaves some things unsaid *in order to* be able to say others" (246, emphasis added). Thus it is that all speakers alternate speech with silence; "silence never ceases to imply its opposite and depend on its presence . . . any given silence has its identity as a stretch of time being perforated by sound" (11). Silence relies on the impending perforation of speech, and speech depends on its own renunciation. Thus it is that I imagine an interpretative framework of speech and silence in a reciprocal rather than an oppositional relationship. The spoken and the unspoken reciprocate as they deliver often complementary rhetorical significance. Each of these rhetorical arts carries with it a grammar, value, and most of all meaning.

The Art and Practice of Silence

Silence as a topic of intellectual pursuit has been ongoing for nearly sixty years. Picard's major speculative investigation into silence as an ontological principle, from its resonance in language to its power in religion and philosophy, stimulated Bernard Dauenhauer's examination some thirty years later. Dauenhauer calls Picard's work "the most explicit and concrete detailing of the great variety of ways in which silence phenomenally appears," although the book does not pretend to be "systematic" (vii). Dauenhauer's *Silence: The Phenomenon and Its Ontological Significance* interrogates silence, with the author systematizing and clarifying the four fundamental features of silence as a phenomenon with ontological significance:

> (1) Silence is a founded, active intentional performance which is required for the concrete clarification of the sense of intersubjectivity. In its pure occurrences, (2) it does not directly intend an already fully determinate object of any sort. Rather, motivated by finitude and awe, (3) silence interrupts an "and so forth" of some particular stream of intentional performances which intend determinate objects of some already specified sort. As such, (4) silence is not the correlative opposite of discourse, but rather establishes and maintains an oscillation or tension among the several levels of discourse and between the domain of discourse and the domains of nonpredicative experience. (82)

Not mutually exclusive categories, these four characteristics coalesce to sustain the tenuous connection of silence with speech, of silence with human production and intention. These considerations enable Dauenhauer to clarify the ontological significance of the positive and negative phenomenon known as silence: "Silence, as well as discourse, is ingredient in both the initiative and the responsiveness which is required for man to manifest the meaning of being" (107).

In the spirit of Dauenhauer's concentration on silence as a state of being, Kalamaras authenticates silence as a "mode of knowing" in *Reclaiming the Tacit Tradition* (1). Especially pertinent for writers and writing teachers, *Reclaiming* echoes previous assertions of the reciprocity between speech and silence yet expands those assertions with the author's vast knowledge of Eastern philosophies of meditation. Natural silences, Kalamaras tells us, are not opposed to language but help shape it in dynamic and generative ways: "Silence is not opposed to language, which I define as the human capacity for vocal and written utterance. Rather, silence and language act in a reciprocal fashion in the construction of knowledge" (5, 8). Kalamaras refutes a Western history that equates silence with emptiness or unworthiness and pushes continuously to establish silence as a site of knowing, composing, generation.

Like Kalamaras, Frank Farmer recognizes the possibilities hinged on silence and, using a Bakhtinian framework rather than an Eastern philosophical one, offers a rich analysis of "voice" in terms of saying, silence, and, of course, dialogism. His work also has important implications for the writing classroom.

In *Organizing Silence,* Clair also connects speech and silence: "language (i.e., both gestural and verbal) is born in the expression of silence and silence is heard through language" (15). And because speech and silence are "born of the same breath, these expressive activities give significance to each other" (21). Clair's two-fold argument concerns silencing and coming to voice. She writes that dominant groups silence marginalized groups in a variety of ways: through coercion, hegemony, discursive practices that privilege some and abandon others, systematic structuring of institutions, informal impositions of conversation, or noisy(er) discourse. And she investigates the ways marginalized groups (can) organize and speak out, through resistance, demonstrations, alternative aesthetics, defiance, even self-contained silence. Like speech itself, silence actively participates in our lives, taking on varied forms and fulfilling a variety of functions.

All of these works ground my own study and support my argument that silence—the unspoken—is a rhetorical art that can be as powerful as the spoken or written word. Like speech, the meaning of silence depends on a power differential that exists in every rhetorical situation: who can speak, who must remain silent, who listens, and what those listeners can do.

A Shape Unseen, but Recognized

Silence exists in overlapping states: environmental, locational, communal, personal. It can be self- or other-initiated, self- or other-derived. Silence can be something one does, something that is done to someone, or something one experiences. However it takes shape, the form of silence (the delivery) is always the same, but the function of specific acts, states, phenomena of silence—that is, its interpretation by and effect upon other people—varies according to the social-rhetorical context in which it occurs.

Whether silence breaks a stream of conversation, awaits the end of a ceremony, demonstrates respect, faces off with power, punctuates the sounds of music or poetry, or conserves energy, silence sounds the same: it is an absence of sound. We think of silence as an absence of sound, yet silence never exists in the physical absolute: "There is no such thing as absolute silence, something is always happening that makes a sound" (Cage 9). And, besides, silence itself is not silent: it is the origination of sound, the sound or creative flow of being (bodies being beating bodies, fires being crackling fires, rain being pattering rain, computers being humming computers, and so on.)

Thus it is that even when we imagine that we are experiencing environmental silence, something makes a sound. If the washing machine is not running, then the furnace or water softener is. Traffic moves along streets, cushioning the sounds of walkers and talkers. Birds signal one another as they fly overhead or roost in trees. When we experience the locational silences of funeral homes, libraries, or courtrooms, environmental sounds—even speech—leak into the silence. When we share silence communally with others, when two or more solitudes come together, at religious or musical events, someone always coughs, sneezes, or clears the throat. And when we practice silence on a personal level, our own breathing and beating hearts accompany us wherever we are, no matter how silent we try to be. Yet according to our Western culture, in each of these settings, we say we are experiencing silence when we are conscious of these silences.

Wherever it is delivered, however it is directed, silence is recognized as silence—if it is recognized at all. Saville-Troike makes the important distinction between "the absence of sound when no communication is going on, and silence which is part of communication. Just as not all noise is part of 'communication,' neither is all silence" (4). On the whole, silences go unnoticed when they serve as short pauses between words or between speakers' exchange, as does the locational silence that I referred to earlier. Silence is expected (and therefore goes unnoticed) from people who wield power, be it religious, therapeutic, bureaucratic, or legal: it is the silent listener who judges, and who thereby exerts power over the one who speaks (Foucault, *History* 61–62).[5]

Silence also goes unnoticed (or, if noticed, then appreciated) in those whose words are not valued, which makes for a kind of communal silence. Aristotle celebrated the connection between silence and women; John Bunyan told wives to "take heed of an idle, talking or brangling tongue" and to be silent in the presence of their husbands (33); and Anatole France quips that "We have medicine to make women speak; we have none to make them keep silence" (2.4). Throughout Western social history, all people gendered feminine (or weaker) have been systematically muted if not silenced. Silence has been the ornament of the female sex; the Virgin Mary served as the model of feminine silence, for the Bible mentions no more than five times that she spoke during her entire life.[6]

In response to these beliefs in women's natural silence, Jean Bethke Elshtain challenges us to consider that

> those silenced by power—whether overt or covert—are not people with nothing to say but are people without a public voice and space in which to say it.
>
> Of course, years and years of imposed inaction and public silence strangle nascent thoughts and choke yet-to-be spoken words, turning the individuals thus constrained into reflections of the sorts of beings they were declared to be in the first place. (15)

Thus, women's silence or the silence of any traditionally disenfranchised group often goes unremarked upon if noticed at all. In "Notes on Speechlessness," Michelle Cliff admonishes us to realize "the alliance of speechlessness and powerlessness; that the former maintains the latter; that the powerful are dedicated to the investiture of speechlessness on the powerless" (5).

Expected silences—those of females, children, servants, lesser beings of every kind—are just that: expected. All silence has a meaning. In a courtroom, we must stand silently when the judge enters, when people are testifying, when the attorneys are talking, or we will be charged with contempt of court. At the funeral home, we cannot chat and laugh; we are supposed to speak in hushed tones, if at all. In every case, we are expected to deliver the silence of respect. Expected silence can carry meaning, and unexpected silences, silences delivered instead of language, carry meaning too. Expected silences can go unrecognized, but unexpected silences are quickly labeled.

That is the problem: unexpected silences unsettle us, often making us anxious about the specific meaning. If I telephone you, and you do not help carry forward the conversation, I wonder why. I consider all the reasons you have not fulfilled my predictions. Maybe I have called at a bad time; maybe you are in the middle of something and are disconcerted by my call. Maybe you do not like to talk on the phone. Maybe you do not like me. If I know that you have had a bad day at the office, I will be able to frame your silence within a context. But if I am puzzled by your silence, then it delivers ambiguity. If you are supposed to be home from the hospital and you are not answering your telephone, your silence also delivers ambiguity and no small measure of anxiety. But even when I know the reason for silence, when, for instance, my adolescent son is angry with me for not allowing him to stay out all night, I am no longer anxious. I know he is performing what Perry Gilmore calls "stylistic sulking," but even in the face of that understanding, I still long for the silence to be replaced by speech (139).

Our own unexpected silences (one of the many speech blunders known as paraphasias) can throw us off as well. We are embarrassed when our conversation partner's name suddenly evaporates from our consciousness, when we cannot recite our own telephone number or address, when we mangle sentences, or face strange lapses of memory. Most frustrating is our wondering what exactly we were about to say. My mother refers to her experiences with paraphasias as "senior moments," but she, just like the rest of us, has suffered occasionally from such moments throughout her life. Often the person's name we need is silenced, but only temporarily: in the evening, while we are watching television, the name comes to us seemingly out of the blue.

Any kind of stress can intensify paraphasias, the silencing of words, from the stress of the social moment to external stresses. More than a decade ago, Pat

Shipman's house burned to the ground, destroying everything she and her husband owned, save three Christmas balls, one aluminum baking dish, and the gold mounts from a few bits of jewelry. She was devastated and took six months' leave from her position as Associate Dean of Medicine at Johns Hopkins. Recouping their vast losses became her full-time job. But the deluge of insurance forms, with their insistence on lists, infinite description, and replacement-cost analyses, drowned one of the few things that the fire had not burned: her normal (which is to say extraordinary) language capacity. This productive publishing scholar began to experience paraphasias; more specifically, she suffered from aphasia, a loss of nouns. The pressure of producing a comprehensive list of a lifetime of objects, from safety pins and clothing to books and artwork, submerged her capacity to produce the nouns that represented those objects. It was a dual loss, first of the material manifestations of a lifetime and then of the words to describe them. Psychiatrist Kurt Goldstein writes that this "lack of ability of naming objects is often connected with a very characteristic change of the whole personality" (301). Shipman was no exception.

It was the loss of words that was the most terrifying for her, a self-described word person (and author of more than ten books and more than fifty scholarly articles) for whom writing and speaking were essential personal and professional skills. This was a loss so profound that the silence left behind by the absence of nouns was deafening. She feared her essence—her ability to think and express those thoughts in words—was irreparably damaged. The fire caused an acute psychic disequilibrium, a series of alarms and disturbances, which triggered the mechanism for acute language disequilibrium, which, in turn, intensified the initial psychic disequilibrium. Goldstein continues by explaining that not only is language use changed in such people but behavior is as well: all of their acting and thinking becomes concentrated on their own personality and its relationship to the world; they are "persons acting in the world rather than thinking and speaking about the world" (302). What a terrible position for someone whose thoughts and speech were essential actions for recovering her material and psychic possessions.

Recovery was not easy, but Shipman's loss was not permanent. As she rebuilt and refurnished her home, she rebuilt and refurnished her psychic self as well (with the help of an extraordinary therapist). After recovery, she realized that she wanted to quit academia to follow an ambition she had long harbored: she wanted to write full time. She is now an internationally known science writer, the recipient of prestigious prizes (the Phi Beta Kappa science book prize and the Rhône-Poulenc prize for science writing, to name just two), her books widely praised for their articulate intelligence. Nouns, verbs, adjectives—all the parts of speech—are once again at her disposal now that she is living within a normal range of stress, released from an almost unimaginable psychic tension.[7] Indeed, silence is a shape unseen but clearly recognized. And its delivery is always the same.

CHOICES AND IM/POSITIONS

Daily, on both an interpersonal and personal level, each of us experiences or participates in silence and silencing: silence as a strategic choice, or silence as an enforced position. Whether consciously or unconsciously, we inhabit silence constantly—as we think, in the spaces between our words, as we wait for others to finish their speaking, in our preoccupation. I want to extend Aristotle's antistrophic salvo that "rhetoric is the counterpart of dialectic" to argue that rhetoric and dialectic are both spoken arts, closely allied (*Rhetoric* 1.1.1354a). Therefore, the true counterpart of verbal rhetoric can be only the nonverbal—silence. In "Rhetoric and Silence," Robert L. Scott writes that "every decision to say something is a decision not to say something else, that is, if the utterance is a *choice*. In speaking we remain silent. And in remaining silent, we speak" (146).

In much the same way we inhabit spoken discourse, we inhabit silence: in a kaleidoscopic variety of rhetorical situations. Ever sensitive to *kairos,* to the appropriateness and timeliness of the occasion, of words, or of silence, we attempt to fashion our communication successfully. Neither speech nor silence is more successful, communicative, informative, revealing, or concealing than the other. Rhetorical success depends upon the rhetorical situation. Just as a blurted-out statement or an alleged misstatement can reveal us, so can our silence, whether controlled or instinctive. Just as we use words to obfuscate meaning or to buy time, we use silence. The question is not whether speech or silence is better, more effective, more appropriate. Instead, the question is whether our use of silence is our choice (whether conscious or unconscious) or that of someone else.

When silence is our choice, we can use it purposefully and effectively. In recent years, for example, the United States witnessed as former Oklahoma University law professor Anita Hill broke her silence. On 11 October 1991, Hill seized the national consciousness with "It would have been more comfortable to remain silent. I took no initiative to inform anyone. But when I was asked by a representative of this committee to report any experience [with Supreme Court Justice nominee Clarence Thomas], I felt I had to tell the truth. I could not keep silent" (qtd. in Morrison, *Race-ing* vii). Very quickly, Hill—and all her listening and watching audience—would see that her silence (as Audre Lorde so firmly put it) would not protect her. But until that moment, her silence had worked to protect her from becoming a public spectacle. She had not been afraid to speak; silence had not been imposed upon her: Anita Hill chose silence. Years later, she chose to speak.

Which form of communication—silence or words—was better? It depends—better for whom?

When Hill raised her voice to those fourteen white men on the Senate Judiciary Committee, she helped sensitize Americans to the pervasiveness and difficulty of sexual harassment:

> in the nine months following Hill's testimony to the Senate Judiciary Committee, inquiries about sexual harassment to the Equal Employment Opportunity Commission . . . increased by 150 percent and a record-breaking number of charges (7,407) were filed, a 50 percent increase over the same period a year earlier. (Bystrom 268)

Two years later, the U.S. Supreme Court would rule that sexual harassment is intolerable—not to be sanctioned—in the contemporary workplace, whether it is the Stanford Medical School, the United States Navy, Franklin High School, Stroh's Brewery, the New York City Police Department, or Forklift Systems, Inc. (Ross).

Hill's coming to voice out of silence galvanized the attention of the U.S. public—but at whose expense, and to whose advantage? In some circles, Hill is celebrated as a feminist civil rights hero; in others, she is remembered as only a lying, conniving opportunist. Regardless of her reputation, Hill was relieved from her Oklahoma University tenured faculty position not long after Thomas was seated on the Supreme Court.

During the years that Hill chose to remain silent, her reputation was not at issue, her faculty appointment not at stake. Whatever her reasons, silence was her self-determined choice. But silence as a strategic choice, one growing directly out of *kairos*, works differently from silence as a position enforced by others, as in the case of Lani Guinier.

University of Pennsylvania law professor Lani Guinier soon followed Hill onto the public, political stage, where she too was expected to negotiate silence, but in this case, the silence was her position, her silencing. President Clinton's nomination of Guinier to head the Justice Department's civil rights division was hailed by U.S. Attorney General Janet Reno as "the best possible choice" for the position (qtd. in West 38). But as soon as Guinier became politicized by right-wing conservatives, "the White House . . . banned Guinier from talking to reporters and from most public speaking engagements, to avoid preempting formal confirmation proceedings" (West 39).

In *Lift Every Voice*, Guinier writes that "the press was 'off-limits' to me, while I was fair game to it. . . . I was not allowed to speak to the public, whether through formal interviews or at public events held in local communities" (133). "I was being humiliated by words and condemned to wordless silence simultaneously" (57).

Guinier obeyed (and perhaps trusted) the administration, which was warning her: "'Don't engage the opposition . . . . Just wait. You'll get a hearing, and then you can respond'" (134). Guinier's (self-en)forced silence, her deliberate silencing, did not work to her advantage, because the media's killer epithet "Quota Queen" (with its resonance of welfare, quotas, and uppity black women) destroyed her political opportunities (West 39).[8]

The day after President Clinton withdrew her nomination, Guinier broke her silence and asked the American people to learn some "positive lessons" from her ordeal "about the importance of public dialogue on race in which all perspectives are represented and in which not one viewpoint monopolizes, distorts, caricatures, or shapes the outcome" (*Tyranny* 190). A year later, Guinier told the graduating class at Hunter College that her experience had deepened her conviction that "silence is not golden" and that we have an obligation to use language to "confront rather than to condemn our problems" (Newman).

Hill and Guinier inhabited their silences differently: Hill made a choice; Guinier responded to her position. Eventually, they both spoke beyond their silence, addressing the issues at hand—for a short time. Paradoxically, they have resumed their silence about the particulars that everyone in their audience remembers and, instead, speak out on general issues of sexual harassment, civil rights, race, the American democratic process, and the Capitol Hill process. Guinier writes that "what had silenced me as a Clinton nominee now gave me a chance, and even more a reason, to speak out" with both a new voice and a renewed faith in the ongoing struggle for civil rights (*Lift* 276). And Guinier now admits, "To some extent . . . I had acquiesced [in] my own silencing. I was temporarily swept away by the promise of the 'big job'" (141).

Employed as tactical strategy or inhabited in deference to authority, silence resonates loudly along the corridors of purposeful language use, of rhetoric. Whether choice or im/position, silence can reveal positive or negative abilities, fulfilling or withholding traits, harmony or disharmony, success or failure. Just like speech, silence can deploy power; it can defer to power. It all depends.

The Signs of Silence

As absence of the spoken word, as presence of nonverbal communication, as strategic choice, or as imposition, silence takes many forms and serves many functions, particularly as those functions vary from culture to culture. From time to time, for example, the uses of silence in Asian, American Indian, and religious cultures have all been romanticized as the superhuman practices of special people. Some of these practices will be covered in later chapters. But for now, I want to concentrate on the widely held assumption that a person cannot *not* communicate (Watzlawick and Jackson 48–49). Given that assumption, all human silences are a form of communication; listeners and observers will attach various and individualized meaning(s) to the silence, regardless of the silent person's intent.

Several researchers have taxonomized the meanings and uses of silence in ways that I will refer to throughout this study. Richard L. Johannesen writes that "the personality, prior experiences, and cultural conditioning of an individual will influence how he perceives silence, what meaning he will attach to it" (29). Then he synthesizes a good deal of communication research to come up with an inexhaustive list of potential meanings for silence:[9]

1. The person lacks sufficient information to talk on the topic.
2. The person feels no sense of urgency about talking.
3. The person is carefully pondering exactly what to say next.
4. The silence may simply reflect the person's normal rate of thinking.
5. The person is avoiding discussion of a controversial or sensitive issue out of fear.
6. The silence expresses agreement.
7. The silence expresses disagreement.
8. The person is doubtful or indecisive.
9. The person is bored.
10. The person is uncertain of someone else's meaning.
11. The person is in awe, or raptly attentive, or emotionally overcome.
12. The person is snooty or impolite.
13. The person's silence is a means of punishing others, of annihilating others symbolically by excluding them from verbal communication.
14. The person's silence marks a characteristic personality disturbance.
15. The person feels inarticulate despite a desire to communicate; perhaps the topic lends itself more to intuitive sensing than to verbal discussion.
16. The person's silence reflects concern for not saying anything to hurt an other person.
17. The person is daydreaming or preoccupied with other matters.
18. The person uses silence to enhance his own isolation, independence, and sense of self-uniqueness.
19. The silence marks sulking anger.
20. The person's silence reflects empathic exchange, the companionship of shared mood or insight.

Johannesen's compilation of meaningful silences provides a general framework over which to stretch *Unspoken* and the following research studies as well.

Sidney J. Baker's psycholinguistic investigation into the nature of interpersonal silence, for instance, uncovers two basic forms, "when speech breaks down or words become irrelevant" (157). The first category, which he refers to as "negative silence," is best represented in situations where "fear, hatred, anger, or acute anxiety strike us dumb" (157). Whether the social situation is composed of lovers, friends, enemies, or strangers, the silent person is either too overwrought to speak or cannot find the words to express his or her feelings. Although words might usefully defuse the situation, the person cannot produce them. Baker calls the second form "positive silence." When words become irrelevant, people, whether intimate friends, lovers, or close family members, luxuriate in a mutually comfortable zone of silence of tranquility. Words are unnecessary because no tensions need to be resolved with conversation or words. Of course, between these two poles of silence lies the entire spectrum of rhetorical arts, human speech acts and behaviors that include practices of silence.

Thomas J. Bruneau categorizes silence into three types: psycholinguistic, interactive, and sociocultural. Psycholinguistic silence is part of the normal flow of speech. These "necessary and variable impositions of slow-time on the temporal sequence of speech" (23) manifest themselves in "non-lexical intrusive sounds"; "sentence corrections; word changes; repeats; phonemic or syllabic stutters; omissions of parts of words; sentence incompletions" (Blankenship and Kay 360–61). Bruneau breaks down this first category even further, into fast-time and slow-time psycholinguistic silences, allowing that slow-time psycholinguistic silences (often associated with artistic, aesthetic, and metaphoric silence) can be difficult to differentiate from his second category, interactive silences.

Often slow-time or slower, interactive silences are always/already understood by the small group or partners. This group uses silence in order to exchange information or solve problems, and each participant understands the "degree and manner in which he is expected to participate in communicative exchange" (Bruneau 28). However, if these silences are overlong, they strain, threaten, or ruin the interpersonal relationship at hand. So even though the necessity of silence has been accepted by the participants, the measure of silence is negotiated in the following ways: "speech certification and listener recognition of the completion of thoughts"; "questioning of the meaning of the previous speech"; "decisions about clarification or qualification of recent or past participant messages"; and "non-verbal jockeying to gain the burden of speech" (28). Participants can use silence to get attention, create anxiety in others, stifle any personal relationship, control or discipline others—in just the same ways people regularly use speech.

Sociocultural silences, the last of Bruneau's categories, are those "related to the characteristic manner in which entire social and cultural orders refrain from speech and manipulate both psycholinguistic and interactive silences" (36). Building on the work of Keith Basso and Dell Hymes, Bruneau pushes his taxonomy of silence beyond that familiar to mainstream (i.e., chatty, noisy) U.S. culture. Certain religious practices rest in silence, that of the Benedictines, Carthusians, Trappists, Quakers, Puritans, Amish, and Buddhists, for example. Some silence is used for contemplation, for self-improvement, while other silences, shunning, for instance, are used as a form of punishment. Nearly all religions practice silent contemplation or prayer: "entire systems of religious dogma seem to be built on either the control of silence as worship or the repetitive, chanting denial of silence" (38). Sociocultural silences include the locational silences of the courtroom, classroom, library, prison, church, and hospital. And such silences also inhabit acts of protest and control. In these ways, silence is used to preserve ideologies of all kind.

As the preceding broadly conceived research projects suggest, the functions of silence are diverse, as multifarious as the motives for silence. The functions and the motives for silence are inextricably linked, for silence can be used to threaten, show respect, demonstrate a language inadequacy, emphasize the spoken, connect, judge, or activate—just like speech. The preceding research represents an even larger (but still relatively small) body of research that helps me listen to, consider, and analyze the gendered, aesthetic, ascetic, cultural, and physical silences in the following chapters at the same time that I argue for silence as a rhetorical art, one that can be as powerful as the spoken or written word.

The studies of Picard, Dauenhauer, Kalamaras, Farmer, Clair, Johannesen, Baker, and Bruneau provided my deeper understanding of silence as well as my ability to identify and explain the pervasiveness and rhetorical effectiveness of silence in our talky culture. I built on this scholarship in order to analyze silence *as a rhetoric,* as a constellation of symbolic strategies that (like spoken language) serves many functions. This is not to say that silence is always empowering or patently engaging. Not all silence is particularly potent. However, silence is too often read as simple passivity in situations where it has actually taken on an expressive power: when it denotes alertness and sensitivity, when it signifies attentiveness or stoicism, and particularly when it allows new voices to be heard.

Employed as a tactical strategy or inhabited in deference to authority, silence resonates loudly along the corridors of purposeful language use. Whether choice or im/position, silence can reveal positive or negative abilities, fulfilling or withholding traits, harmony or disharmony, success or failure. Silence can deploy power; it can defer to power. It all depends.

Current explorations into silences are reminders of how much more we have to learn about women's and men's delivery of silence. In the following chapters, then, *Unspoken* will organize, contextualize, and analyze silence in ways that connect it with the construction and production of human communication—with rhetoric. *Unspoken* will extend the ongoing scholarly conversation about the power of conscientious speaking out and of silence, about power and control, and especially about who remains silent and who silences.

2
Engendering Silence

Moving from silence into speech is for the oppressed, the
colonized, the exploited, and those who stand and struggle side
by side, a gesture of defiance that heals, that makes new life and
new growth possible.

—bell hooks, *Talking Back*

"Between the sexes, the male is by nature superior and the female inferior, the
male ruler and the female subject" (*Politics* 1.2.12); "One quality of action is nobler
than another if it is that of a naturally finer being: thus a man's will be nobler
than a woman's" (*Rhetoric* 1.9.15). With these two unquestioned dicta, Aristotle
shaped Western culture and rhetorical practices for twenty-five hundred years.
For him, the "natural" deficiencies of women guaranteed their natural subordination to those naturally finer beings, men, Athenian citizens who were awarded
the right and privilege of a public voice. Quoting Sophocles, Aristotle writes,
"Silence gives grace to woman—though that is not the case likewise with a man"
(*Politics* 1.5.9).

The voices that founded the Athenian polis were male, only. "Athenian" meant
male citizen; there was no word for female citizen. Systematically excluded from
the polis (and therefore silenced) were women, foreigners, and slaves. Not even
the Macedonian-born Aristotle qualified for Athenian citizenship and the concomitant rights and responsibilities. Athenian citizens were wealthy, land-own-
ing, Athenian-born males from citizen-class families. For this elite group, public oratory fed the spirit of Panhellenism, a doctrine sorely needed to unify the
Greek city-states, just as it satiated the male appetite for public display. As a system, the polis implied "the extraordinary preeminence of speech over all other
instruments of power, [with speech becoming] the political tool par excellence,
the key to authority in the state, the means of *commanding* and *dominating* others" (Aristotle, *Politics* 49, emphasis added). Since antiquity, then, most women
and many men have been automatically disqualified from the public sphere of
speech as well as from positions of command and domination. Just as the rhetorical tradition has devalued these nonprestigious people, it has devalued the
silent rhetorical display.

In addition to Western politics, Western religion has also confirmed and perpetuated the inequality between the sexes with its mandate that God is male. So standard a belief provoked Mary Daly's apothegm, "when God is male, the male is god" (*Church* 38). In "What Became of God the Mother," Elaine H. Pagels investigates this fundamental feature of the God of Israel, who neither shares his power with a female divinity nor serves as her divine Husband or Lover (97). This independent, omnipotent male god has been translated into the three most influential religions in the Western hemisphere: Christianity, Judaism, and Islam. Theologians of these religions all say that God is not to be considered in sexual terms at all, yet "the actual language they use daily in worship and prayer conveys a different message and gives the distinct impression that God is thought of in exclusively *masculine* terms" (97). Despite their theology, then, the beliefs and practices central to all these religions demonstrate that "men form the legitimate body of the community, while women will be allowed to participate only insofar as their own identity is denied and assimilated to that of men" (98).[1] Thus, these age-old religions, still thriving and dominant in the United States, have gendered speech and silence, rendering feminine, or weaker, all women and many men.

Masculine discourse has been the monologue of a male-dominated ruling class, while feminine discourse has spoken the perspectives of the dominated: the poor, the disabled, the "raced," the foreign, and, of course, the female—except, of course, in the case of Oedipus, whose answer to the Sphinx helps us reconsider the politics of language use from the time of earliest recorded history. Muriel Rukeyser's "Myth" helps refocus our thinking:

Long afterward, Oedipus, old and blinded, walked the
Roads.   He smelled a familiar smell. It was
the Sphinx.   Oedipus said, "I want to ask one question.
Why didn't I recognize my mother?"   "You gave the
wrong answer," said the Sphinx.   "But that was what
made everything possible," said Oedipus.   "No," she said.
"When I asked, What walks on four legs in the morning,
two at noon, and three in the evening, you answered,
Man.   You didn't say anything about woman."
"When you say Man," said Oedipus, "you include women
too. Everyone knows that."   She said, "That's what
you think." (17)

Both the Sphinx and Oedipus are right: for years, "man" allegedly included "woman" in most languages, but for much longer than that, "woman" was considered inconsequential, not meriting cultural inclusion, let alone scholarly attention.

In this chapter, I will demonstrate the ways the uses of silence—just like speech—are gendered, with the already-empowered using silence to maintain their power and the already-weak performing simply another iteration of a regulatory norm. I will provide an overview of gender theory, linking it with theories of muting or silencing. Then, I will demonstrate the specific ways silence performs its rhetorical artistry, as a means to maintain power or admit subordination. Higher education provides some of the most compelling and moving examples of silence and silencing as rhetorical positions.

GENDER AS AGENDA

The terms "sex" (male, female) and "gender" (masculine, feminine) are often used interchangeably, with gender predicated on the "*conceptual* and rigid (structural) opposition of two biological sexes" (de Laurentis 5, emphasis in original). For two thousand years, humans have been conditioned to accept the opinions of "thinkers from Aristotle and Rousseau to Talcott Parsons and Erik Erikson . . . [who] have argued that women not only differ from men but are not as equipped mentally and physically to function in the spheres of society in which [certain] men *predominate* (Epstein 2, emphasis added).

In recent years, however, a number of scholarly projects have expanded common knowledge and linguistic practices. Anne Fausto-Sterling's "How Many Sexes Are There?" reminds us that babies arrive along a spectrum of biological sexes: male, male-female, hermaphrodite, female-male, and female. And Joan Wallach Scott reminds us that gender, a term borrowed from grammar to designate categories of nouns,[2] is nothing more or less than "a *social* category imposed on a sexed body" (32, emphasis added). Rather than being a biological sex or a state of nature, gender is, according to Teresa de Laurentis, "the representation of each individual in terms of a particular social relation which pre-exists the individual" (5).

Thus, gender can be released from the dualist lens of male-female biology that equates female with feminine and male with masculine. If gender is a social category, then it is a socially constructed one that describes the institution of power relations learned through and perpetuated by culture. Gender is a cultural role, a social rank, a "primary way of signifying relations of power," writes Thomas Laqueur (12). Hence, Scott's "more or less" directly relates to *power*—not to genitalia.

Current academic wisdom receives gender in at least these two ways: (1) as a hierarchy of power relations, and (2) as a horizontal axis of incommensurability (be it financial, academic, religious, or physical). Despite the academy's theorizing and push toward revitalizing our thinking about the appropriate or inappropriate roles for sexed bodies of all ages, races, and capabilities, the practical differences between the two concepts of gender have not quickly or easily translated into mainstream culture: men and women in both systems remain likely to experience their "gender" as a kind of fatalistic sex, bred in muscle and bone, with little chance for change. Thus even if, as Laqueur in his bolder moments argues, biology is also socially constructed and if, as the ever-bold Judith Butler argues, "gender is the social significance that sex assumes within a given culture" (*Bodies* 5), the distinction between gender and sex is not as important to this study as the distinctions people themselves might make between their so-called biological sex and their so-called social roles and the connections they might make between their social standing and their social roles.

That said, categories of sex and gender are neither mutually exclusive nor constantly overlapping. Race, sex, ethnicity, socioeconomic class, prestige, sexuality, and physical ability—power, performance, and societal expectations—all work to determine the amount of leakage between the two main categories of sex and gender, and, in turn, between fundamental rhetorical issues that bear repeating: who speaks, who remains silent, who listens, and what those listeners can do. Hence it becomes clear that regardless of the sexed bodies involved, "gender relations are created not only by a sexual division of labor and a set of symbolic images, but also through contrasting possibilities of expression for men and women" (Gal 175).

In other words, whether people are male or female, masculine or feminine, is not so important to their purposeful use of silence or speech as their willingness to use silence or speech to fulfill their rhetorical purpose, whether it is to maintain their position of power or resist the domination of others. As I have said before, rhetorical power is not limited to words alone, and for this reason, the study of silence has much to offer to the powerful and disempowered alike. Every rhetorical situation offers participants an opportunity to readjust or maintain relations of power.

Still, it is the difference that is reduced to sexual or racialized identity that has long been used to justify, exploit, and yet conceal gendered power differentials and regulate speech and silence. As Trinh T. Minh-ha reminds us, the body remains "the most visible difference between men and women," despite the healthy complication of sexual [and racial] categorization ("Difference" 32). Racist and sexist ideologies continue to play out in gendered power differentials, which evolve over time and place but always invite some people to speak and Others to remain silent.

SYSTEMATIC SILENCING (OR NONHEARING)

That women and other traditionally disenfranchised groups have been systematically and consciously excluded from public speaking and active listening comes as no surprise: these groups have, since before Aristotle's time, been excluded from full participation in the production of all Western canonized cultural forms, including the production of rhetorical arts. Power and authority in cultural production have customarily been the prerogatives of the male citizen. The work and experiences of Others have been entered into the general currency of thought on terms determined and approved by these male citizens, particularly in the United States, where there is no genderlect spoken only by the female population.[3]

Both Cheris Kramarae and Mary Daly have argued for a genderlect, as a way for women and Others to speak and be heard on their own terms, but their salvos have gone mostly unnoticed. Kramarae explains that she is "interested in pushing on words and their definitions, questioning and often mocking traditional practices in order to make possible new meanings and practices" that reflect and inform women's world and women's knowledge making (qtd. in Foss, Foss, and Griffin 55). In order to begin developing the necessary vocabulary, however, we "must look for women's language and communication in new ways and in new places" (Kramarae and Treichler 17):

> We need to look in such places as gynecological handbooks passed between women for centuries; in women's art; in folklore and oral histories; in graffiti and gossip; in journals; in letters and diaries; in songs, billboards and posters; in the cant and chant of witchcraft and voodoo; in slogans; in parodies and humor; in poetry; in graphics; in comics and symbols; and in the mass of work by "noncanonized" writers whose richness and diversity we are only just beginning to comprehend. (Kramarae and Treichler 17)

Daly, on the other hand, begins describing the ways that the pseudogeneric grammatical terms, such as "person" or "people," will continue to silence and erase women so long as the masculine remains the unmarked gender. For Daly, as well as for a number of sociolinguists, the generic masculine is both ambiguous and discriminatory. Daly moves quickly to explain why the rhetorical realm of the Background (where women and Others reside, talk, and listen) must be enhanced—at the expense of the foreground (which is dominated mostly by white men). In *Talking Back,* bell hooks provides a case in point when she describes a familiar childhood Background, the warm rooms of home, where

> heated discussions began at the crack of dawn, women's voices filling the air, giving orders, making threats, fussing. Black men may have excelled in the [foreground] art of poetic preaching in the male-dominated church, but in the church of the home, where everyday rules of how to live and how to act were established, it was black women who preached. There, black women spoke in a language so rich, so poetic, that it felt to me like being shut off from life, smothered to death if one were not allowed to participate. (5)

Such ideas for an English genderlect of the Background continue to be met with both consternation and enthusiasm. But despite any enthusiasm, no distinct genderlect has yet been totally accepted, implemented, or respected, not even within the Background itself.

Muted Groups

In an explanation that holds some thirty years later, Edwin Ardener describes the systematic estrangement of some groups from the production of cultural forms. Ardener's methodological framework could underpin research on any set of asymmetrical power relations, but given the division of the sexes on a global scale as well as the dominance of males in public life, women's mutedness is his focus:

> If we look at those classes which are usually considered to be the exploiting or dominant classes, and then we consider those others which are supposedly the exploited or suppressed classes, there is this dimension that hasn't been mentioned yet: which is [that] of relative articulateness. One of the problems that women presented was that they were rendered "inarticulate" by the male structure; that the dominant structure was articulated in terms of a male world-position. Those who were not in the male world-position were, as it were, "muted." . . .
>
> We may speak of "muted groups" and "articulate groups" along this dimension. There are many kinds of muted groups. We would then go on to ask: "What is it that makes a group muted?" We then become aware that it is muted simply because it does not form part of the dominant communicative system of the society—expressed as it must be through the dominant ideology, and that "mode of production" . . . which is articulated with it. (21).

Despite raising the issue of essentialism, Ardener's statements offer this study the reminder that in every human culture, women are in some way subordinate to men, and many men are in some way subordinate to certain other men. Or, to say it another way, "there is a Third World in every First World, and vice-versa" (Trinh, Introduction 3).

The dominant group in a social hierarchy renders "inarticulate" subordinate or muted groups (any of the traditionally disenfranchised) and excludes them from the formulation, validation, and circulation of meaning. Thus, the inability to speak fluently in certain social interactions can indicate mutedness, and silence itself becomes the language of the powerless. Dale Spender believes that women remain silent rather than to speak continually in a language not of their own making ("Defining"). Trinh, however, resists the *differend* of Spender's analysis, arguing that "silence can only be subversive when it *frees* itself from the male-defined context"; therefore, "silence as a *refusal* to partake in the story does sometimes provide us with a means to gain a hearing" (Introduction 9; "Difference" 15, emphasis added). Susan Gal maintains that if women want to speak at all, they must speak in the dominant language, which Trinh thinks is impossible as does Carol Gilligan, who writes that women are not actually speaking in the dominant language anyway, despite the fact that men and women may be "using similar words to encode disparate experiences of self and social relationships" (173). Gilligan adds that we have only recently begun to notice the silence of women and the difficulty of hearing what they say when they speak, for women do, she writes, speak in a "different voice." And hooks again complicates the preceding opinions with her statement that she "was taught that it was important to speak but to talk a talk that was in itself a silence" (*Talking* 7).

I am not suggesting that muted groups in the United States have a completely different language, no dominant language use at all, or only silence. Nor am I generalizing that muted groups are never heard or do not resist their domination. These groups demonstrate linguistic resistance to linguistic domination in a number of ways, from speaking out and "telling" to "talking back." Resistance can be nothing more (or less) than "talking back," a phrase bell hooks uses to mean "speaking as an equal to an authority figure" (*Talking* 5). She goes on to write that "back talk" or "talking back" has always meant for her "daring to disagree" or just "having an opinion" (5). "To speak when one was not spoken to was a courageous act—an act of risk and daring" (5). Speaking within and to the Background, hooks writes that

> it was in that world of woman talk (the men were often silent, often absent) that was born in me the craving to speak, to have a voice, and not just any voice but one that could be identified as belonging to me. To make my voice, I had to speak, to hear myself talk—and talk I did—darting in and out of grown folks' conversations and dialogues, answering questions that were not directed at me, endlessly asking questions, making speeches. Needless to say, the punishments for these acts of speech seemed endless. They were intended to silence me—the child—and more particularly the girl child. Had I been a boy, they might have encouraged me to speak, believing that I might someday be called to preach [in the foreground]. There was no "calling" for talking girls, no legitimized rewarded speech. The punishments I received for "talking back" were intended to suppress all possibility that I would create my own speech. That speech was to be suppressed so that the "right speech of womanhood" would emerge. (*Talking* 5–6)

The "right speech of womanhood" is clearly marked to differentiate it from the authorized speech of those in power. Expanding on that same point, hooks writes that "for black women, our struggle has not been to emerge from silence into speech but to change the nature and direction of our speech, to make a speech that compels listeners, one that is heard" (*Talking* 6), and she compares women's speech to that of

> the black male preacher whose speech was to be heard, who was to be listened to, whose words were to be remembered, [unlike] the voices of black women—giving orders, making threats, fussing—[which] could be tuned out, could become a kind of background music, audible but not acknowledged as significant speech. (*Talking* 6)

Thus, the authorization of some linguistic practices and not others appears to demonstrate the innate superiority of those who use authorized forms as it simultaneously demonstrates the inferiority of those who use unauthorized forms.

The logic of this continually reiterated social practice often inculcates a muted group as subaltern, inadequate if not worthless. As Pierre Bourdieu has argued persuasively in *The Logic of Practice,*

> the most fundamental social choices are naturalized and the body, with its properties and its movements, is constituted as an analogical operator establishing all kinds of practical equivalences among the different divisions in the social world—divisions between the sexes, between the age groups, between the social classes. (71)

In any advanced society, opportunities to speak (while others listen) reside in rituals, gestures, and ceremonial occasions. Alongside these speaking opportunities are formal rules, laws, and contracts. Together, the opportunities and rules comprise the continued divisions in the social world as well as one's personal identity, what Bourdieu refers to as one's "practical sense."

In operative terms, one's personal identity or practical sense becomes one's cultural capital, one's economic, political, and social power. One's cultural capital passes from place to place, from person to person; it can be accumulated, transferred, and bequeathed as and by means of the dominant discourse (those forces of dominance—behavior, voice, gesture, language, etiquette, possessions, credentials, accomplishments).

Who can speak and who must remain silent are basic rhetorical features of the dominant discourse, of one's practical sense. And for Bourdieu, the power implicit in cultural capital circulates explicitly as dominant discourse:

> The embodied cultural capital of the previous generations functions as a sort of advance (both a head-start and a credit) which . . . enables the newcomer [and his or her future generations] to start acquiring the basic elements of the legitimate culture from the beginning, that is, in the most unconscious and impalpable way. . . . Legitimate manners owe their value to the fact that they

manifest the rarest conditions of acquisition, that is, a social power over time which is tacitly recognized as supreme excellence. (*Distinction* 70–71)

Social power, language power, access to the dominant discourse can make many people appear supremely excellent and others appear to be profoundly inferior.

Given the androcentric sociolinguistic and anthropological research that has dismissed the concerns of muted groups, and despite the feminist research that has worked to challenge the authority and credibility of these male-biased accounts, I do not want to dismiss the epistemologies of muted groups. Rather, I want to accentuate the fact that they are often disadvantaged when it comes to articulating their experience and circulating their cultural capital to, through, and within the discourse of the dominant culture. The analysis of hooks is straight-on: "Certainly, for black women, our struggle has not been to emerge from silence into speech but to change the nature and direction of our speech, to make a speech that compels listeners, one that is heard" (*Talking* 6).

Members of these muted groups thus continue to find themselves in situations in which they are—in a practical sense—adapting, mediating, and subordinating their own ideas and forms of expression to that of the dominant discourse and in the dominant idiom. Sometimes they speak and are heard; sometimes they speak and are ignored; sometimes they remain silent.

Speaking Through the Dominant Idiom

> This is the oppressor's language yet I need to talk to you.
> —Adrienne Rich, "The Burning of Paper Instead of Children"

Ardener's muted-group theory proposes that language and norms for its articulation are controlled by the dominant group even though both the muted and dominant groups generate beliefs (or ordering ideas) of social reality at the unconscious level. All language, then, is the language of the dominant order, and if they speak at all, subordinate groups must speak through that language in what Elaine Showalter refers to as "double-voiced discourse," a discourse that reflects and refracts the social, literary, and cultural heritages of both the dominant and muted groups (263).

According to Carolyn G. Burke, double-voicing could only mean "when a woman writes or speaks herself into existence, she is forced to speak in something like a foreign tongue, a language with which she may be personally uncomfortable" (844). And Xavière Gauthier laments that double-voicing is yet another linguistic double-cross:

As long as women remain silent, they will be outside the historical process. But, if they begin to speak and write *as men do,* they will enter history subdued and alienated; it is a history that, logically speaking, their speech should disrupt. (162–63)

Since these arguments have appeared, scholars of every stripe have worked to disrupt the dominant discourse, the most well-known, perhaps, being Audre Lorde, in "The Master's Tools Will Never Dismantle the Master's House."[4] Lorde writes,

> Those of us who stand outside the circle of this society's definition of accept-able women; those of us who have been forged in the crucibles of difference—those of us who are poor, who are lesbians, who are Black, who are older—know that *survival* is *not an academic skill*. It is learning how to stand alone, unpopular and sometimes reviled, and how to make common cause with those others identified as outside the structures in order to define and seek a world in which we can all flourish. It is learning how to take our differences and make them strengths. *For the master's tools will never dismantle the master's house.* (112, emphasis in original)

Although some might argue that Lorde is speaking through double-voiced dis-course, her words nevertheless slice through the dominant discourse, taking little if any care to establish common ground with oppressors, male and female alike.

Still, Lorde's words reach across her location of oppression, from her mem-bership in a muted group, just as Daly's words often do: "The essential thing is to hear our *own* words, always giving prior attention to our *own* experience, never letting prefabricated theory have *authority* over us" (*Beyond* 189, emphasis in original). Daly's speech, delivered from her location of oppression and frustra-tion, occasionally resonates with the tone of Lorde's; other times, however, she speaks her feminine language, her genderlect, with words so unfamiliar, foreign, and disruptive to the patriarchal order that they do not always reach their mark:

> In the beginning was not the word. In the beginning is the hearing. Spinsters spin deeper into the listening deep. We can spin only what we hear, because we hear, and as well as we hear. We can weave and unweave, knot and unknot, only because we hear, what we hear, and as well as we hear. (*Gyn/Ecology* 424)

Krista Ratcliffe explains Daly's sometimes mystifying language as a kind of new speech, rather than a genderlect, new speech that is essential to radical feminist de/mystification. Such new speech leads to new questions, new words, talk, texts, and so on (*Anglo-American* 83). Daly's own ideolect could lead to a more widely distributed genderlect, of sorts, but as yet, it has not. Clearly it is not a double-voicing through patriarchal language so much as it is an ideolect performed in the presence of patriarchal language.

Although Ardener refers to mutedness rather than silence, and Lorde and Daly speak for and as women only, these theories hold wider application. As I have said before, but in a slightly different way, the alpha group in every social situation determines (and tries to control) the speech, speaking patterns, and silences for the women and men in the beta, gamma, (and lower) groups in every social situation. Given that most if not all social situations are framed in hierarchy, both women and men inhabit some measure of silence within a muted group, speak in double-voiced discourse, and consider their words and silence against the dominant system of communication. In every case, context (the combination of rhetorical situation plus the power differential) is the crucial factor for analyzing the discourse and the interlocutors.

The bald polarities of male-female rights and privileges are not as important to *Unspoken* as a more nuanced examination of power. This study relies much more on observing the asymmetrical power produced by cultural and social systems that construct and perpetuate value systems of speech and silence. These value systems equate speech and silence with so-called masculine and feminine performances, particularly when a corporeal body constitutes the stage for such spoken or silent, gendered performances.[5]

First I hear the bleep, bleep, bleep of a siren. Hmm, I look in my rear-view mirror and see red lights flashing behind me and immediately look at my speedometer. OK, so I am going 71 in a 55 m.p.h. zone—everyone is. The black car bears down on me, and I pull over to the berm. The highway patrol car pulls in behind me, and I can see the patrol talking over her radio. She walks up to my car, with her hand poised near her gun. Her gun?? Good lord, what have I done? Closer to the point, what does she think I've done?

I want to talk, to ask her, to hear her answers. Unfortunately, I know from experience that no amount of talking on my part will persuade her to talk to me beyond requesting my driver's license and my car registration. I rifle through my purse and the glove compartment to come up with what she wants, hand them to her, and she walks back to her car and to her radio, silently. Even though I have a good inkling why she pulled me over in the first place (I may have been driving slightly over the speed limit), I cannot help but wonder if I am guilty of anything else. Did I neglect to pay a parking fine? Have I forgotten to renew my driver's license or my plates? Has my used car ever been stolen? Still, I wait for her to return to my car window; I want her to talk to me. I want to break the silence. When she does, when she provides a reason for the ticket she is writing me, I am grateful: she has filled the void of ambiguity with something, a ticket.

Verbal or silent interactions are exercises and negotiations in power. One person acts (with words or silence), another reacts (ditto), and either interpersonal balance is achieved or imbalance is created. Such incidents occur so frequently that they often go almost unnoticed or unremarked. But even when they are noticed, they are often left unaddressed, for "many of us [have] develop[ed] default mechanisms for dealing with them without having to give too much thought. Giving thought takes too much time and energy" (Anonymous VIII).

So far in this chapter, I have talked about silence mostly in traditional terms of imbalance, of weakness, impotence, fear, and subordination in the face of dominance. But as the preceding example indicates, silence also enacts strength and power, ideas that make immediate sense to us when we remember our helplessness in the face of someone else's silence. In fact, we are so thoroughly used to negotiating power in verbal interaction that we become aware of doing so only when things go wrong, and it is at such points of imbalance in the interaction that silence becomes significant. No amount of talking on our part—whether to law enforcement personnel, judges, juries, preachers, parents, partners, children, or bosses—will catalyze their speaking or break their silence sooner than they want.

Back in the early 1970s, Erika Jong's *Fear of Flying* was touted among literary circles. Jong used the sexual revolution, the swinging seventies, as the backdrop for frustratingly stagnant sociolinguistic relations between men and women, as the following scene demonstrates:

He puts on his pajamas reproachfully. She stands in her stocking feet.
"Why do you always have to do this to me? You make me feel so lonely."
"That comes from you."
"What do you mean it comes from me? Tonight I wanted to be happy. It's Christmas Eve. Why do you turn on me? What did I do?"
Silence.
"What did I do?"
He looks at her as if her not knowing were another injury.
"Look, let's just go to sleep now. Let's just forget it."
"Forget what?"
He says nothing.
"Forget the fact that you turned on me? Forget the fact that you're punishing me for nothing? Forget the fact that I'm lonely and cold, that it's Christmas Eve and again you've ruined it for me? Is that what you want me to forget?"
"I won't discuss it."
"Discuss what? *What* won't you discuss?"
"Shut up! I won't have you screaming in the hotel." (118, empahisis in original)

The silence of those with power and authority over us, or with the power and authority invested in them by the institutionalized structures, which govern and control society (marriage, for example), often works to intensify our anxiety and our frustration. Whether they are beloved partners, children, or friends—or "merely" authority figures—they all hold a measure of power over us.

It is as though each of these people is thinking, "You need me to give you information, but I will not communicate—and you cannot make me." Thus, they use their silence to get our attention or to sustain it, or both. They can draw on our inquiry, our inferences, our projections. Or they can use their silence to cut us off and out.

When silence is a means for exerting control and managing the situation, silence originates with the dominant party, stimulating the subordinate party to explore options for breaking the silence, for rousing speech from the other, as evidenced in the excerpt from Jong. To maintain control of the situation, the dominant party must wield silence as a means to press the subordinate into taking on the burden of silence—or speech, whatever the case may be. After all, as Max Weber told us nearly forty years ago, the classic conception of power is the ability of one actor in a social relationship to impose his or her will on another (152).

Sociolinguists Pamela Fishman and Victoria DeFrancisco have both identified the ways husbands silence wives. Fishman writes that "the definition of what is appropriate or inappropriate conversation becomes the man's choice. . . . [Therefore, women] must be available to do what needs to be done in conversation, to do the shitwork and not complain" (98–99). DeFrancisco writes that although women talk more in marital conversations, they are interrupted more often, and their conversational topics are not often developed (417). The basic problem for all the wives in DeFrancisco's study was "getting a response at all" (417). Thus, many of the wives learned to remain silent rather than initiate fruitless conversation. For the subordinate, then, silence is not a means of exerting control; rather, it is a means of accepting that control, for it demonstrates silence-as-respect and a willingness to wait.[6]

Shifting responsibility for silence can be played out in a wide range of situations, from Jong's fictionalized marital dispute (and Fishman's and DeFrancisco's markedly similar research findings) to a U.S. courtroom, where the judge speaks initially and then remains silent (or mostly silent) while the opposing parties speak their respective cases. Any person in the courtroom who does not speak and remain silent according to the rules of dominance (the judge) and subordination (everyone else) violates the norm and will be threatened or charged with contempt of court. In this case, the judge, by order of her or his elected or appointed office, authorizes the use and enforcement of silence. Violators will indeed be prosecuted.

Silent Threats and Insults

From the top down. In "Silence and the Acquisition of Status in Verbal Interaction," Richard J. Watts writes that "inter-turn silences, particularly those of more than 1.7 seconds' duration, contribute in significant ways to the acquisition or loss of discourse status" (110).[7] The highway patrol officer's and the judge's silences extend much longer than 1.7 seconds, enhancing the status they already hold. But theirs is a situational (as well as institutional) silence, one that is always expected despite (or because of) the discomfort it causes others. Other authority figures, however, exert silence-as-control when silence is neither expected nor appropriate. Now while these uses of silence may be unintentional or unconscious, they, nevertheless, keep the subordinate figures in their place, particularly if theirs or the authority-figure's status is unresolved.

When a boss ignores an employee, treating that person as a nonperson, that silence can be threatening if not insulting to the other person. The reasons for the silence may vary: unsure bosses may be concentrating steadily on their own performance and on how best to establish or maintain their power; they may be thinking about the best way to respond to a complaint, a policy, or an employee's change in status; they may be overcome with stresses and doubts that render them inarticulate to the point of silence; or they may not realize that they are not speaking (enough) to their employee. But whatever their causes, whether the silences are conscious or unconscious, the effect is the same: the employee feels slighted, insulted, maybe even threatened and tortured, and always angry. Foucault's description of successful discipline and punishment applies easily to such a situation: the silent treatment can be a technique of torture, producing a certain degree of pain, forming part of a ritual, and creating a spectacle, seen by all almost as its [torture's] triumph (*Discipline* 33–34).

No matter what the situation, gendered power differentials—or gendered attempts at equilibrium—are played out with language and silence whenever a boss and an employee are involved and especially when the interactive silences are prolonged (longer than 1.7 seconds). Whether intermittent or constant, such silent treatment is torturous.

Not long ago, a female English professor at a mid-sized land-grant university was preparing her dossier for promotion and tenure. Naturally, she wanted her dossier to represent her and her work in the very best of light. She admits that she was uneasy and stressed as she prepared her dossier, but she refuses to tell a free-floating sociocultural narrative of her experience. She locates it at the center of a politicized, gendered context.

Her department chair had been recently appointed and, his bravado notwithstanding, was not performing his new status evenly or successfully. The assistant professor went to him for advice on putting together a successful, persuasive dossier. He put her off. Both people in this social situation were suffering from stress of figuring out the tenure process, but only the assistant professor could (was not afraid to?) articulate it.

The chair ignored her e-mails, her notes, and her voice mails except to let her know in an off-hand way that the tenure process was to be a unilinear flow in which all the communication, like the power, was to be initiated and controlled from one side, his side. Since his assumption contrasted markedly from the university-wide communiqués on the tenure process that encouraged discussion and exchange, she was confused, frustrated, and angry. She says now that she did not especially want to talk with her chair, that had he still been her colleague, he would have been one of her last choices for advice. But he was her chair, and the tenure process created a need for exchange between them. What materials should go in a tenure dossier? What order should they go in? What professors from other universities (the outside reviewers) should review the materials? How might reviewers be determined?

Beyond being told straight-out that her reviewers would be "randomly selected" for the sole purpose of preventing her from knowing who they would be, she received little advice and less information. When she heard conflicting information from others going through the process in other departments, she had no way to untangle the information. She was always "stopped," she writes, "somewhere between the head secretary's office and the chair's office, and my questions were just not answered" (Anonymous 1).

One time, and one time only, her chair told her to check with his administrative assistant (the head secretary, who had assisted a number of department chairs over the years), but he never mentioned what was obviously true: this assistant professor's tenure and promotion case would be the first one he had ever been responsible for, and his administrative assistant was more knowledgeable about the dossier and the process than he was. He never mentioned his insecurities or inexperience; in fact, he never mentioned anything at all. He remained silent, to the point that when he passed this assistant professor in the hallways, he deflected his gaze and did not speak, as though she were not there.

Remembering back on this weird professional experience, she wrote to me that she

> thought a great deal during this period about the situation I was finding myself in. I thought about it as a situation in which human needs are created—one needs to go through a tenure process—but in which all possibilities of exchange were blocked off. Depending on the importance of the need, what happens when exchange is impossible? Here, the exigency was actually insti-

tutional—in other words, at that point, I wouldn't have "chosen" to communicate based upon need; it was that the need to communicate was created by the process, then abrogated.

I found myself confronting what was, by closest analogy, a kind of existential void . . . . [M]uch of my life seemed up for grabs, and indeed, any sense of problem-solving, any of the logical routes one would use, any of the powers of language that might be summoned in any other situation to make any kind of common sense or procedural sense were simply cut off. It was, indeed, a situation in which the only thing one can do is learn not to care.

I thought a great deal during that time about how autism of a sort might develop: it astonished me often to know that the assumption so constantly made in my field, in my profession, that language matters, didn't matter one iota. The process I was going through was teaching me that language DIDN'T matter, that in effect NO ONE IS THERE. So I think that what I'd have to say is that silence in this sense acquired for me an important palpable material presence of nothingness.

On the other hand, the sense of voice meant also that I might as well say anything. I filled the gaps with hallucinatory images of myself with shorn hair, in some kind of total non-speaking state for the rest of my life in the institution.

Don't speak to me now? Why speak to me later? What would be the point, anyway?[8]

This woman's tenure and promotion went through without a hitch, but this now-associate professor of English has been wary of silence-as-power ever since. Her relationship with her chair remains uneasy. She says that he now acts as though he is "afraid" of her, which might explain why he still seems hesitant to speak to her.

Protection of hierarchy is not the only use of silence. Punishment or retribution is yet another common use for it. A historian with a richly deserved endowed professorship describes "a particularly galling" use of silence. At his former institution, his chair was supposed to nominate and shepherd through appointments to research professor, a status that brings more pay and less classroom teaching—a genuine perquisite for the renowned researcher. The problem was that this professor thought his scholarly record and international reputation would speak for itself, that he would not have to rely on a personal relationship with his lesser-known chair. The department chair thought otherwise. Despite fifteen years of good relations, the chair had heard a (true) rumor that the professor had criticized him. Nevertheless, the chair solicited letters for the recommendation but said nothing to the professor, not a syllable about the rumor or about how the nomination process was moving along: "He said nothing to me, knowing full well that I wanted to see some sign, and in spite of numerous opportunities [to show a sign]" (Anonymous IV). The professor did not know what to do except wait—and then attend the awards ceremony:

> Because I was in doubt, I had to go, but . . . no award. He had used silence to make me sweat and ultimately to force me into the humiliation of going to the ceremony and witness others getting awards. He used silence as a weapon against me very effectively indeed. Getting the award two years later has never erased the brutal uncertainty of the silent treatment he gave me.

I went into this study thinking that silence used against "people" always meant silence used against traditionally disenfranchised groups. But this is an example of silence being manipulated by one well-educated white male to hurt another equally well-educated white male. The department chair used his cultural capital *as department chair* to inflict silent punishment. His silence was a kind of supremely strategic and successful passive-aggressive move—its effect has lasted more than a decade.

Across the discourse community. Authority figures are not the only ones who can use silence to keep others under control. Peers use it as well, to imply disapproval of a person's behavior, of the issue under consideration—all without having to say anything that anyone else could quote or remember exactly. Thus, silence can translate into an attitude, most often of censure or reprimand. In another of my interviews, a woman told me that she "doesn't like being given the silent treatment," though she admits that she has occasionally "been offended enough not to want to run into someone for a while" (Anonymous II). She continues by saying

> On one occasion I received an offensive anonymous note in my mailbox from a colleague in another department. I knew who it was from some sleuthing and from previous knowledge of this person's peculiarities, but for various reasons I could not make the incident public. . . . So the next time I saw this person, I administered a very obvious and stern silent treatment, and the person was clearly flustered and hasn't said much to me since—which suits me exactly. I couldn't confront directly because I had no proof.

In this situation, she uses silence ("a very obvious and stern silent treatment") in order to regain her social status, which had been threatened by the anonymous note. And she maintains her status by keeping the other person flustered and at bay. Yet even in the face of her deliberate tack and successful outcome, she says, without the slightest trace of irony, "I guess . . . I'll be silent when I think I have nothing to gain from confrontation . . . . I'll usually try to avoid direct unpleasantness."

The silent treatment is not limited to women or by women. A well-established male professor at a large urban university wrote to me about the silent treatment he received, which he suspected arose out of the subdisciplinary turf battles within his department, in this case between composition and theory.[9] He writes,

The defacto leader of the theorists . . . opposed all hires in composition and mine in particular. I remember trying to start a couple of conversations with him when I first [arrived] and being more or less politely rebuffed. Then, two or three years into my job there, [he] and I had an open disagreement during a search committee meeting about a candidate for a job in composition, during which I thought [he] was pretty high-handed. I went to his office the next day and told him so, and he told me that he thought the entire field of composition was a fraud.

After that conversation, [he] never spoke to me again—at least not outside of the context of a public department meeting. What made this particularly odd was that we often rode the elevator together . . . . I'd say, "Hi [xxx]" or "Good morning, [xxx]," and he'd stare through me like I wasn't there—this whether there were other people in the elevator or not. In fact, he'd sometimes talk to another person who stepped into the elevator with me while acting as if I wasn't there.

While I'd like to say that this didn't bother me, and while I can say that I never gave up on greeting [him] whenever we met, I have to admit that his silence began to take a psychic toll. I can remember, for instance, coming into the building, seeing him at the elevator and thinking, maybe I should just take the stairs, but not allowing myself to do so and instead walking up and saying, "Hello [xxx]"—only to play through the same non-script once more. (Anonymous IX)

Having since moved on to another university, this male professor writes to assure me that despite these intermittent silences, his life in that department was, for the most part, very good. He has kept in good contact with many of his former colleagues and friends. But my asking him about uses of silence in the professional sphere made him

realize that much of the strain of working at [that specific university] came not only from (the fairly routine) hallway arguments and committee confrontations, but also from the ways hierarchies were policed silently and almost continuously. (Anonymous IX)

Since much profession-related stress comes from the silent enforcement of hierarchies, I do wonder if Professor X, who refused to speak, suffered at all.

Both of these examples demonstrate how silence can be used tactically, purposefully, but without the kind of spoken, one-to-one confrontation that can be witnessed by others or regretted later. This kind of silent treatment can also be transferred to small-group interactions.

When small groups come together, there is often one person (the overtalker) who wants to push a particular agenda item at the expense of the overall agenda and the designated leader. The overtalker's reasons for pushing her or his own agenda might be politics, of course, but it might also be nervousness, insecurity, frustration, fear, or medication. Whatever the reason or motive, the result is the same: one ever-dependable group member interrupts, deflects, and pushes while the other group members punctuate this loquaciousness with individual attempts to get back on track—or with silence. Sometimes the others will stop to address the overtalker's concerns, but only as a way to move on and forward. Rarely does a peer cut off, shut down, or confront the overtalker verbally.

Everyone else is too polite, too well-schooled in group behavior, too much in control of his or her own words. An English department committee chair described the trouble she was having working with a young overtalker as follows:

> The radical politics of some younger members of the department and how those views interact awkwardly, meeting mostly silence rather than articulated opposition, interests me though I have no answers. . . . However, I saw something in [John Edgar] Wideman's *Hoop Roots* where he's talking about playground basketball (serious non-pro men playing) that spoke to part of the issue: "A [new] player must learn, then respect the unspoken rules, respect opponents, himself, his teammates, the sanctity and fragility of the shared enterprise" (46). [She], in particular, has no sensitivity to the existence of unspoken rules, no respect for them or their existence, and no sense of the shared enterprise, or presumably considers it mostly corrupt. (Anonymous xia)

When I asked this committee chair why the overtalker's ideas were met with silence rather than articulated opposition or discussion, the chair wrote,

> I suspect [the overtalker] meets silence because anyone who talks to her knows that there's no point in trying to exchange views if the two of you are opposed. Sometimes things meet silence or a quick brush off because they are so appallingly ignorant: "Why shouldn't we just hire our own PhDs who don't get jobs?" (Anonymous xib)

The chair continues to rationalize the silence she uses by invoking Kurt Vonnegut's idea that "in America, ideas are badges of friendship, and to oppose someone's ideas is to declare yourself an enemy." Interestingly, even the most "appallingly ignorant" statements are met with silence rather than discussion.

Another committee chair shared with me her uses of silence in a similar situation:

> I can recount experiences of using silence as a reprimand. . . . I did that at the [search committee] meeting with [X], [Y], and [Z]. While they said their idiotic things, I sat stonily in silence. I think all I said was something like, "Well, we'll have to discuss that." Of course, I wasn't there observing myself, but I think I was stony—for me. (Anonymous v)

Mostly, then, committee chairs and other members sit stony-faced, employing silence as direct and shared disapproval of the prate. Their silence is understood by everyone else, including the overtalker, who suspects something is not right. So he or she may talk even more or push even harder in an attempt to get the favored item on the agenda. The others leave the meeting, relieved that they had not said anything they will later regret, but wonder if their silence had communicated anything other than agreement.

When I ask various committee members what group-dynamic options they envisioned for themselves, they all came up blank. They did, however, think of their reactions and behavior in these situations in what I would call gendered terms. Some of the white women wondered if they had settled for giving off disapproving "looks" and remained silent because of their sex, while one white man wondered if he had remained nonconfrontational (i.e., silent) because of his secure place in the company hierarchy and his designated role as leader. A black man, also high in the organization, had spoken up in such a situation, but only in response to the white overtalker's complaints rather than as a way to forward the agenda. One black woman, the newest member of a similar group, remained silent for "all sorts of reasons," she said (Anonymous iii).

From bottom to top. Adults are not the only ones to use silence as a way to control their situation and others. Children and adolescents do, too. In chapter 1, I alluded briefly to Perry Gilmore's research on classroom silence and sulking that she conducted in a "predominantly low-income, black urban community and elementary school" (139). I want to expand upon my initial comments because her work relates so well to the gendered nature of silence and silencing. When she discusses the "good attitude" that these young black children are expected to demonstrate for their ongoing success (to ensure their access to the Academics Plus Program or for honors or special academic preferences), she is describing a kind of self-silencing that translates into obedience, academic concentration, and respect for authority. These children are habituating the bodily practices of those high-achieving young females described by Carol Gilligan: they work hard, they are silent; when they speak, they speak in "a different voice," a voice different from that of power. All bodily signals, facial expressions, and nonverbal postures, then, align with this concept of "good attitude."

But not all silences are created equal, as Gilmore's students make clear. There is the silence of what she calls the submissive subordinate and that of the nonsubmissive subordinate. To wit, although every bit as silent as the first group, a second group was considered to share a "bad attitude," an attitude revealed by their nonverbal behaviors, for not a word was uttered. Erving Goffman defines such a package of bodily signals as "ritual display," readily readable expressions of intent (69), and parents, teachers, and other students alike interpreted those signals as aligning with "bad," as intentionally negative. Gilmore refers to this ritual display as stylized sulking, a phrase that handily transfers to a range of adolescent behaviors, slightly different for boys and girls:

> Girls will frequently pose with their chins up, closing their eyelids for elongated periods and casting downward side glances, and often markedly turning their heads sidewards a well as upwards. Girls also will rest their chins on their hand with elbow support on their desks. Striking or getting into the pose is usually with an abrupt movement that will sometimes be marked with a sound like the elbow striking the desk or a verbal marker like "humpf." . . . It is necessary to draw some attention to the silence, and with the girls it seems to be primarily with a flourish of getting into the pose.
>
> Boys usually display somewhat differently. Their "stylized sulking" is usually characterized by head downward, arms crossed at the chest, legs spread wide and usually desk pushed away. Often they will mark the silence by knocking over a chair or pushing loudly on their desk, assuring that others hear and see the performance. Another noticeable characteristic of the boys' performance is that they sit down, deeply slumped in their chairs. This is a clear violation of the constant reminder in classrooms to "sit up" and "sit up tall." . . . The silence displays go against all the body idiom rules of the classroom. (149)

The most relevant features of Gilmore's work for my study is that these stylized sulks and silences are directed at and affect the teacher; they move from the bottom up. The other students notice these silences but can do nothing to melt them; they can only show their support by seeming to try to. Only the teacher, to whom the silence is directed, can melt the sulk—but not by exerting institutional authority or power. The only means of melting the sulk are positive: joking, affection, or changing the performance frame. These stylized silences, delivered by young students, successfully get and sustain the teacher's attention. Whenever the student—not the teacher—is the center of attention, classroom power and control have been redistributed.

But the classroom is not the only place that stylized sulking and silence "work" for those in subordinate positions. Any of us who have lived with a teenager have been held hostage by their stylistic sulking. Whether their silence is a response to our tempers, our edicts, our threats, our commands, our wheedling, or our righteousness, we do not like to confront it, see it, deal with it. Adolescent silences are particularly effective after the adults have cooled off and want to start up negotiations. No matter how much their silences trouble us and make us want nothing more than to reconnect with our children, these displays are necessary for the teenage performers. Stylized silence can function as a face-saving device, a way to maintain one's dignity and individual authority in the face of authority and power. After experiencing any measure of shame, stylized sulking is a way to (re)align with one's own peer group and to sustain distance and separation from the shamer. It is also a simultaneously subtle yet obvious way to punish the shamer. Only the most unaware of adolescents would not realize the power of stylistic sulking and silence.

EXPERIENCING SILENCE

But when we are silent we are still afraid.
                    —Audre Lorde, "Litany for Survival"

"One can distinguish primarily two types of silence," writes Dennis Kurzon, "(i) psychological, and (ii) intentional" (3). Kurzon is correct, and his rubrics are fairly stable, when applied only to legal situations. In that case, he is right to continue that

> The first type is unintentional, and stems from various temporary or permanent inhibitions present in the person being questioned. Under the temporary inhibitions we may include embarrassment due perhaps to the topic under discussion, while among more permanent inhibitions figure shyness and various neuroses. Intentional silence, on the other hand, seems to indicate, to put it mildly, a lack of cooperation. (3)

But when silence is experienced outside a legal situation, the rubrics ebb and flow in richly compelling ways.

When willfully employed, as I have demonstrated at length above, silence as a mode of communication can be powerful, harmful, punishing, especially when the profound human need to communicate with words is not met (as with the men on the elevator). In such instances, language-as-power becomes a moot issue.

The power of language itself, however, can yield silence in cases where words and actions are used to impose silence on someone else or to suggest silence as the best tact for someone else. Thus, those who embrace silence in these situations do so for psychological and intentional purposes. That person must remain silent or be hurt in some way, some emotional, intellectual, physical, or professional way. The silencer dominates the silenced, once again gendering the conditions of speaking and silence.

"You have the right to remain silent. Anything you say can and will be used against you in a court of law." As a result of the 1966 Miranda case, police are now required to read this "warning" to suspects, offering them the option of remaining silent rather than talking to the police. For suspects, the warning is an opportunity. People who feel or are silenced, however, interpret this warning as a threat: anything they say might be used against them—at work, at school, at home, and in social situations. They realize full well that the powerful are rarely silenced but that subordinates, like themselves, often are. And those who feel silenced fear that if they tell, if they speak, if they so much as discuss a bad situation, they will be harmed in some way—if not immediately, then eventually.

In "I'm Telling," Robin Becker writes about her family contract: honor the family secrets and keep your family support; tell these secrets and lose your emotional and material support. No warning needed here; like many families, hers had secrets that were not to be spoken of outside the family. So Becker tried to keep silent on her mother's first marriage, the family's nose jobs, her own lesbianism, her sister's epilepsy—all subjects of shame, Becker figured, if they had to be kept silent.

> Epilepsy is not, like sickle-cell anemia or Tay-Sachs disease, associated with a particular population. Faced with my sister Jill's neurological disorder that bewildered and frightened them in 1957, my parents coped the best they could. Like certain other neurological disorders, epilepsy takes a visible form, subjecting the epileptic (and her family) to the reactions of those around her. What motivated me to study the text accompanying my sister's medication was a talk I had with my mother. "You are to discuss your sister's problem with no one. We're taking care of it, and it is a family matter." (217)

But the silence and the sneaking became too much for Becker, steeped as it was in shame: "secrecy and shame hold hands in the night" (210). So, one by one, she told her family's secrets even as she withheld her own secrets from them:

> I do not know if my mother actually thought I could "keep" such a secret, but in truth I could (or would?) not. Class clown, bossy schoolyard tomboy, I told friends at school and on the street that my sister had epilepsy. Writing these sentences today, forty years after they were spoken, I feel the guilty shame of the "betrayer." (217)

She told, despite the punishments she knew her father would dole out:

> In the household of my childhood, only my father was permitted to express opinions. I thwarted his design by speaking my mind, holding contradictory perspectives. From an early age, I was his combatant. Once, after an argument

with my father, I ran into my room and locked the door behind me. I must have been thirteen or so. I remember the sound of his footsteps, as he came after me, and the sight of the splintering wood as he kicked a hole in my bedroom door. "To show you that you can't keep any secret in this house!" he shouted. Familiar images of revenge swam through my mind: my father stricken by a heart attack; my father tied to a chair as I screamed my hatred into his ears; my father humiliated by a mock trial, in which the judge decrees he is a cowardly bully and must atone for his sins against me.

My parents never repaired the hole in the door. Year in and year out, it remained, a symbol, my father believed, of his ongoing efforts to suppress my secrecy. As in any dictatorship, the despotic power he exercised engendered reactions he could not control. While he wished to subdue me, I eluded him. When he prohibited particular activities, I lied and did whatever I'd planned. Whatever secrets he desired to keep within the household, I carried outside. (220)

Despite Becker's refusals and resistance, she was profoundly affected by the attitude of her family, particularly of her aging parents: "Sometimes, I try to talk to my family or friends about the unspoken inarticulate sadness that fills me when I spend time with my parents" (219). Her relationship with her parents seems solid now, with her sister's suicide nearly fifteen years behind them all. But like every child of secrets and silences, Becker wonders if her telling, her speaking out, her contempt of the family court, contributed to or saved her from the family tragedy.

How It Feels to Be Silenced Me

Whenever I ask a question in public, at faculty senate or at a national meeting, I am nervous. My voice quavers, my heart beats fast, my entire body shakes.

As an undergraduate, I would sit in classes, whether large or small, and when the teacher asked a question I would think of the answer but then go on to think, "Oh, that can't be right." When someone else would say what I was thinking—or something worse—I would always think somehow that it was just an accident that I'd thought the same thing. I spoke little if anything during all my undergrad classes, even my English classes. (Anonymous v)

These instances, recounted by a white female, belie her status as a distinguished professor. Even the successful and allegedly empowered, even those with access to the dominant discourse (of language, behaviors, bodily movement, gestures), feel silenced by the knowledge that speech makes one vulnerable: whatever she says at faculty senate, a professional meeting, or in class can and will be used against her—or so she still fears.

Not surprisingly, traditionally subordinated people live with this fear on a daily basis, whether at work or at school:

> When I was an undergraduate at Cleveland State, I had a course in 18th-century British Literature. I don't remember the exact question I asked, but the professor was lecturing, and I raised my hand and asked something. He looked at me with that look that says, "Why do they let you stupid niggers in here?" And then he almost literally said it: "You have asked a non-question. If you could read and use the dictionary, you wouldn't have to ask such a question."
>
> From that day forward, I never asked another question in his class. I never said anything to anyone. I was the only person of African descent in the class and that made me unsure of myself. The thing that I used to get me through that class and all the others was this: "I know I ain't stupid. These white folks ain't no better than me. I know I can read and write." As for that class, I struggled to get a C and was glad to get it—and get out. (Anonymous VI)

Written by a young black female professional, this letter demonstrates how being silenced can make one feel: embarrassed, unsure, and afraid to speak. Fortunately, she had a determination that fueled her undergraduate and then her graduate career. Most silenced people do not fare so well, but some do, some continue to strive, despite the pressures of silencing or containment.

> I feel compelled to provide a specific, traumatic event with much at stake materially, academically, or emotionally. But since frequent and quite vulgar attempts to silence me occur on a regular basis, I cannot draw on one specific incident. I am a Black male, and silencing, like police harassment, comes with the territory; besides, to draw on one incident might neutralize the gravity of the phenomenon.
>
> My psychological, spiritual, and cultural health and survival depend, in part, on my ability to deflect the transgressions of singular instances of silencing, overcome them, when possible, and ultimately ignore or blunt the emotional and psychological sharpness of their effects—therein lies the rub. Escaping the shadow of a dominant discourse which allows others to consistently control or contain what Blackness and Black maleness means inside or outside the classroom seems to be a tasks of Sisyphean proportions. Of course, I intervene; of course, I interrogate; of course, I resist—but much too often, the final word, the final definition is left in the mouths of others. (Anonymous VII)

The relationship of language—and silence—to deprivation is profound. What happens when one needs to—or should—speak and is cut off from the possibility of speaking? What kind of deprivations does the silenced body experience?

To speak of this silencing is too often to risk being accused of a sort of racial paranoia; to complain about a shadow is to construct myself into a low intensity insanity in the eyes of others. Silencing's very nonspecificness, its insentientness, makes speaking of it dangerous, dangerous because the very speaking of it admits to vulnerability.

To speak of it (my shadow, my containment) now feels emancipatory, but only temporally, because tomorrow I will be contained again. And the residue of my temporary emancipation in this moment will linger with me, offering me further hope along with further frustration. (Anonymous VII)

This writer does not describe the profound language deprivation that accompanies systematic neglect, abuse, or wildness. He does not claim to be a Genie, a Victor, a Kamala, or Amala, not a wild boy, a gazelle-boy, a wolf child, or a bear child.[10] His deprivation is much more subtle and yet much more conscious. He has not been deprived of language or speech altogether; rather he continues to be deprived of the right to speak as the man he is, whenever he deems it appropriate. He wants language use on his terms, not at the expense of anyone else, but not always/already at his own expense.

Such sickening silencings are not restricted to black scholars; white scholars, too, are disciplined into silence. A white associate professor at a private northern university writes that her "most traumatic silencing" occurred when she was an "assistant professor [at another university] confronted with a chair who did not like [her] field (rhetoric and composition) or [her] theoretical orientation (materialist feminism)" (Anonymous XII). She continues by saying that her chair

functioned within Lacanian theory as if it were a closed cult that totally explained and predicted the world. I definitely felt silenced.

With [the chair], either I had to play within the Lacanian universe (a game I couldn't win) or I had to be positioned as the "nice but not too smart" outsider (if it had been a medieval play, my name would have been Poor [xxx] the Nice; if it had been a modernist novel, I would have been [Virginia] Woolf's angel in the house, the good girl who tried to get by by getting along, without much success). . . .

I finally realized something was really wrong when I finally broke down at a Conference on College Composition and Communication and told [two friends] all about this and realized, once [one friend] pointed it out, that I was actually whispering. (Anonymous XII)

As Lorde had warned her, her silence did not protect her. Instead, her silence harmed her in a number of ways, all of which she easily enumerates:

The professional fallout of all this was: (1) I didn't publish for a while because I developed a writing block, which a therapist helped me get over; and (2) I was relatively silent in department meetings, much more than I am now [at a different university].

The personal fallout of all this was: (1) I lost a sense of self-confidence and self-worth; (2) my bulimic impulses from college years reared their ugly head.

"To be honest," she continues, "it was the latter that made me decide to go to the therapist."

Her therapist helped her devise a stance that she could take toward her department chair and her bulimia: "I had a choice (not an easy one, not an immediate one): I could work and get the credentials to get myself out of there." "By 'writing to get out,'" she found a purpose, an audience, and her "voice on the page." Later, her "speaking voice followed."

How does it feel to be silenced me?

For many of these people, being silenced felt like being disciplined, not the sort of self-discipline so highly touted in advanced societies, but a discipline from without, a discipline imposed on a person as a necessary measure for ensuring the circulation of cultural capital (whether white, male, or Lacanian) and ever-dominant discourse. In *Discipline and Punish,* Michel Foucault defines the chief function of the disciplinary power as "to train." He writes that

> Discipline "makes" individuals; it is the specific technique of a power that regards individuals both as objects and as instruments of its exercise. It is not a triumphant power, which because of its own excess can pride itself on its omnipotence; it is a modest, suspicious power, which functions as a calculated, but permanent economy. (170)

Some of the testimonies in this section align with the disciplinary facet of silence, particularly when the need is *to* discipline rather than *for* discipline.

As I said earlier in this chapter, silence can, indeed, feel like torture, prolonged yet intermittent. Silence as torture is painful at the moment, to be sure, but also during the long period of anticipation and extended as memory. For Foucault, torture makes the body of the condemned "the anchoring point for the manifestation of power, an opportunity of affirming the dissymmetry of forces" (*Discipline* 55). In the case of silencing, the body can be condemned solely on the basis of its cultural capital, as many of the previous personal accounts attest. They remember the silence and the silencing long after the torture was suspended.

Although Foucault speaks of the "condemned" and the forces applied to the condemned body, I want to speak of the "accused" or the "suspected," or even the "scapegoated." As the preceding series of personal accounts corroborates, the forces of silence besiege their bodies as well, for as punishment, silence enacts the power relation at the "heart of all mechanisms of punishment" (55). The aim of silence-as-punishment is "to make an example, not only by making people aware that the slightest offence [is] likely to be punished, but by arousing feelings of terror by the spectacle of power letting its anger fall upon the [allegedly] guilty person" (58). What is important, then, on the part of the sovereign power, is not only that other people know about the punishment, but that they witness it, too. Silence is the perfect tool in its subtlety, for it can spread fear and hesitation widely throughout the social body.

How does it feel to be silenced me? It feels like discipline, like torture, like punishment. It feels frustrating, humiliating, maddening. Thus it successfully fulfills its intended purpose. In "Against Silence," Becker writes,

That silence on your end will cost us:
It's a meadow, guileless, gesturing with indigenous
Grasses and wildflowers. Walk into it and the bees rise.
Silence is the thousand-leaved woods in rain.
New England turned jungly, fungal, a grid of humidity.
Insect farms seethe waist-level, crown my martyred head.

Silence is a game of dodgeball at dusk—
A matter of time 'til someone knocks you out
Of the circle of bodies. I used to sway alone, slow
Motion, the ball floating past my chest. Eyes in my hands,
Eyes in the small of my back, I could anticipate the blow
And dodge it, schooled in the feint, the simulation.

Silence is the Old City of partition and quarter,
Where a colonial fog blots the sun.
And all the charm of the regime
Hurried away, into museums: see the gold ear plugs?
The short musket with the flaring muzzle?
I don't want to waste our time haggling in the souk,

I want your blessings, ok? I want to hear the circular saw
Rotating at high speed, excoriation, whine, orchestration
Of birds. Describe the sexual practices of several
Peruvian cultures. Harpsichord me. Entail me. Dispose me.

> The dangerous meadow shuts down at night.
> The moon, rabbinical, mutters a prayer.
>
> (79)

Silence as a dangerous meadow filled with bees, a jungle, a game of dodgeball, the Old City—these negative images of mistrust, disappointment, and futility reveal how silence feels.

Perhaps the first anonymous testimony in this chapter best reflects the frustrations of silence: "I found myself confronting what was, by closest analogy, a kind of existential void. . . . I filled the gaps with hallucinatory images of myself with shorn hair, in some kind of total non-speaking state for the rest of my life in the institution." But Louise Erdrich captures the terror of silence as well, when she describes the fighting of an old Indian couple: when they fought, "stinging flames of words blistered their tongues," but—

> Silence was worse. Beneath its slow-burning weight, their black looks singed. After a few days their minds shrivelled into dead coals. Some speechless nights, they lay together like logs turned completely to ash. They were almost afraid to move, lest they sift into flakes and disintegrate. (74)

3
Witnessing Silence

> What is the source of our first suffering? It lies in the fact that we hesitated to speak. It was born in the moment when we accumulated silent things within us.
> —Gaston Bachelard, *Water and Dreams*

Some of the most important, powerful, and influential men and women in the free world work in Washington, D.C., inside the beltway. Given their easy access to the dominant discourse, their lives circulating as cultural capital, and their professional excellence and superiority, one might think these Old City Americans could have outdistanced their need for silence and silencing as gendered disciplines of control and punishment. But they have not. In order to maintain a practical sense of power, the powerful must maintain their distance from their inferiors, just as they must have a coherent entity of subordinates. Every cultural group seems to need to dominate an identified entity.

In this chapter, I will draw on two key rhetorical moments: the testimony of Anita Hill during the Clarence Thomas hearings and the "nonhearings" of Lani Guinier. Within these moments, I will explore the rhetorical dimension of silence and silencing, particularly as it intersects with sociopolitical power, domination, and subordination. To help explain the cultural need for domination and the reciprocal acquiescence to subordination, I will extend the gender theories I developed in the previous chapter into the realm of rhetorical and critical race theories.

A Rhetorical Rationale for Domination

Kenneth Burke's rhetorical theories of consubstantiation and scapegoating help to explain the social movements of coming together to form a group, no matter how big or small, as well as necessary process for galvanizing a coherent group in terms of a catalytic Other, the scapegoat. For consubstantiation to occur, one's inner substance (or essence) and external substance (or the beliefs on which one stands) must overlap with the substance of another, rendering the two parties consubstantial (*Grammar* 23; *Rhetoric* 21):

A is not identical with his colleague, B. But insofar as their interests are joined, A is identified with B. Or he may *identify himself* with B even when their interests are not joined, if he assumes that they are, or is persuaded to believe so.

Here are ambiguities of substance. In being identified with B, A is "substantially one" with a person other than himself. Yet at the same time he remains unique, an individual locus of motives. Thus he is both joined and separate, at once a distinct substance and consubstantial with another. . . .

. . . To identify A with B is to make A "consubstantial" with B. . . . A doctrine of *consubstantiality*, either explicit or implicit, may be necessary to any way of life. For substance, in the old philosophies, was an *act*; and a way of life is an *acting-together*; and in acting together, men have common sensations, concepts, images, ideas, attitudes that make them *consubstantial*. (*Rhetoric* 20–21)

To put it another way, when the first person identifies his or her cause with the other person's interests, then they share identification, a crucial property of rhetorical persuasion.[1] Both consubstantiation and identification help contain and cohere a group.

But every bit as important to Burke's notions of coming together, of cohering, is the psychic and emotional importance of leaving some one, or some coherent group, *out*: the scapegoat. Nothing brings people together, helps them identify, makes them consubstantial faster than a common enemy on whom they can transfer all their frustrations, disappointments, guilts, and grudges. Burke helps clarify the process of scapegoating:

The scapegoat is "charismatic," a vicar. As such, it is profoundly consubstantial with those who, looking upon it as a chosen vessel, would ritualistically cleanse themselves by loading the burden of their own iniquities upon it. Thus the scapegoat represents the principle of division in that its persecutors would alienate from themselves to it their own uncleanlinesses. For one must remember that a scapegoat cannot be "curative" except insofar as it represents the iniquities of those who would be cured by attacking it. In representing *their* iniquities, it performs the role of vicarious atonement (that is, unification, or merger, granted to those who have alienated their iniquities upon it, and so may be purified through its suffering). (*Grammar* 406)

Burke's sociological analysis casts a rhetorical light on Toni Morrison's equally insightful cultural criticism, and both of their analyses underpin the rhetorical one that follows. Silence and silencing circulated broadly within the Hill and Guinier public dramas, maintaining gendered and raced power differentials in both situations. At the same time, any rhetorical listening made possible through silence circulated markedly unevenly.

A Critical Race Explanation of Domination

In *Playing in the Dark,* Toni Morrison demonstrates this need for and process of one group to come together at the expense of an Other when she describes what can only be defined as the gendered roles blacks and whites have played in the production of "American" literature.

According to Morrison, a two-part, "tacit agreement among literary scholars" is that (1) American literature has been the province of white male views and genius, an assertion she does not deny; and that (2) the white literary productivity has gone without any relationship with or need for a black presence, an assertion she handily refutes, arguing that

> The major and championed characteristics of our national literature—individualism, masculinity, social engagement versus historical isolation; acute and ambiguous moral problematics; the thematics of innocence coupled with an obsession with figurations of death and hell—are . . . in fact responses to a dark, abiding, signing Africanist presence. (5)

This literary response to a "dark, abiding, signing Africanist presence" constitutes the necessity of whites to dominate a "real or fabricated Africanist presence" (6). And it is this domination that continues to be "crucial" to such a gendered (and raced) rendering of Americanness.

Just as Morrison's American literary establishment needs an Africanist presence by which to constitute itself as a coherent entity, all powerful (i.e., masculine) groups, regardless of their affiliation, need an opposing, weaker ("feminine") presence. Hence, with a common Other, whether it be an Africanist presence, a sexualized female presence, or whatever, a social group works to maintain its power, which brings me back to the beltway and to an ever-expanding list of (Burkean) scapegoats, starting with Hill and Guinier.

> Silence is the Old City of partition and quarter,
> where a colonial fog blots the sun.
> —Robin Becker, "Against Silence"

The U.S. political scene continually demonstrates how the processes of identification and scapegoating as well as the processes of silence and silencing work, in terms of power and punishment. Our country has stood witness to the silence and silencing that has kept some people in power and others outside the reach of it. As I said earlier, the experiences of Anita Hill and Lani Guinier are the focus of this chapter. In the chapter that follows this one, I will be extending that same analysis, concentrating on a group of women, ranging from Gennifer Flowers to Monica Lewinsky, that has been wryly referred to as "all the president's women." Hillary Rodham Clinton played a strong supporting role in this second group, but, since then, she has taken her voice on the road: first stop, senator of New York.

I Could Not Keep Silent

> I was going to die, if not sooner then later, whether or not I had ever spoken myself. My silences had not protected me. Your silence will not protect you.
>
> —Audre Lorde, "The Transformation of Silence into Language and Action"

In chapter 1, I briefly discussed Hill's use of silence as a choice and recounted her ability to seize the national consciousness when she transformed her silence into language and action. In this chapter, I will outline some possible reasons for Hill's silence and for breaking of her silence, and then I will outline the public reactions to both rhetorical stances (silence and speech). As Hill's experience demonstrates, silence can be a rhetorical imposition of subordination, or it can be inhabited as a rhetorical position of often undisputed power.

In 1991, Hill testified with

> It would have been more comfortable to remain silent. I took no initiative to inform anyone. But when I was asked by a representative of this committee to report any experience [with Supreme Court nominee Clarence Thomas], I felt I had to tell the truth. I could not keep silent. (qtd. in Morrison, *Race-ing* vii)

Very quickly, Hill—and all her watching and listening audience—would see that her silence would not protect her. But until that moment, her silence had worked to protect her from becoming the focus of a public spectacle.

No one had explicitly silenced her, but Hill inhabited a regulatory norm that implicitly kept her disciplined and silenced. In her statement to the Senate Judiciary Committee, she writes that Thomas had told her that if she "ever told anyone of his behavior that it would ruin his career" (22). She also went on to write, "I was aware . . . that telling at any point in my career could adversely affect my future career" (23). Little wonder that it had been "more comfortable" for her to remain silent. Hill's silence did nothing to rock party politics or draw negative personal or professional attention to herself. Thus it was that Anita Hill first chose the rhetorical art of silence (and seeming subordination)—perhaps out of self-protection, perhaps out of professional protection. But eventually, upon subpoena, she chose to speak out (perhaps for the same reasons): "This is the oppressor's language yet I need to talk to you" (Rich, "Burning" 117).

Except for confiding in three very close friends over the course of a decade, Hill had remained silent about her systematic submission to sexualized conversation by her superior at the Department of Education and the Equal Employment Opportunity Commission, Clarence Thomas. But remaining publicly silent for whatever reason does not necessarily equate with remaining passive or subordinate. Judith Butler teaches us that through the reiteration of regulatory norms, something like "remaining silent" occurs. "And yet," she goes on to say,

> it is also by virtue of this reiteration that gaps and fissures are opened up as the constitutive instabilities in such constructions, as that which escapes or exceeds the norm, as that which cannot be wholly defined or fixed by the repetitive labor of that norm. (*Bodies* 10)

Thus, even at her most regulated silence, Hill was confiding in close friends. Besides, as Butler argues, Hill's speech act of silence might not have meant what it appeared to mean: "That speech is a kind of act does not necessarily mean that it does what it says; it can mean that it displays or enacts what it says at the same time that it says it or, indeed, rather than saying it at all" (*Excitable* 102). Thus it comes as no surprise that Hill would admit her ongoing nonsilence in her initial public statement: "It is only after a great deal of agonizing consideration that I am able to talk of these unpleasant matters to anyone except my closest friends" (23). In Hill's case, her silence and nonsilence could well indicate something entirely different from passivity or obedience; these rhetorical positions could mean that she was coming to understanding, what Ratcliffe cogently defines as "rhetorical listening."[2]

After all, Hill's testimony made clear that, during her silence, she had been listening carefully to the politicocultural logics of appointing Clarence Thomas (whom President George Bush called the "best-qualified" jurist for the job) to the Supreme Court. Conservatives and liberals predicted the permanent effect that the conservative Thomas could have on the Supreme Court. He could help dismantle the civil rights edifice so carefully constructed by William J. Brennan Jr., William O. Douglas, Thurgood Marshall, and Earl Warren. In nominating Thomas, Bush was responding to the imminent retirement of the only black— and the most liberal—Supreme Court justice, Marshall.[3]

Therefore, in terms of political maneuvering, Bush's choice was brilliant: Thomas

> was a black and a jurist, but he was also a conservative with a long record of opposition to existing civil rights legislation and affirmative action programs.

Thomas, a graduate of Yale Law School, had also publicly upbraided Thurgood Marshall and civil rights leaders. (Chrisman and Allen xvii)

In short, Thomas provided the perfect "necessary Africanist presence" for the U.S. Supreme Court. What liberal, what NAACP member, what civil rights leader, could vote against black representation, however conservative, on the Supreme Court?[4] What black woman would want to go up against his appointment? Although broad, Thomas's support remained mostly unenthusiastic—and unalterable.[5]

Hill had never wanted her complaints translated into a charge of sexual harassment, let alone made public. Although she had been speaking privately about Thomas, until then, she had remained publicly silent, rhetorical decisions that grew out of her personal and professional ones. In the film *Sex and Justice,* narrator Gloria Steinem tells us: "In fact, [Hill] hadn't approached the committee; it was a Yale law school classmate of hers . . . who [had done so]." *Only* in response to a federal subpoena did Hill appear in Washington.

When Hill finally spoke out to the Senate Judiciary Committee, she calmly recounted, in credible detail, a sparse narrative of "words, dates, and details shorn of any embellishment or conceptualization," never using the words "racism," "sexism," or "sexual harassment" (Lacour 132):

> After approximately three months of working there, he asked me to go out socially with him. . . . I declined the invitation. . . . I thought it would jeopardize what at the time I considered to be a very good working relationship. . . . [However,] my working relationship became even more strained when Judge Thomas began to use work situations to discuss sex. . . . His conversations were very vivid. . . . On several occasions, Thomas told me graphically about his own sexual prowess. . . . I told him that I did not want to talk about these subjects. ("Statement" 20–21)[6]

Conceptually, her narrative can only be read as one of sexual harassment, despite the fact that complaints such as hers were almost unheard of in 1981, that the Supreme Court did not recognize sexual harassment as employment discrimination until 1986, and that current guidelines for sexual harassment were not codified until 1988.[7] Rhetorically, however, her narrative and the events that followed can be read in a number of ways, as the following analysis will demonstrate.

A Hearing Without Listeners

> I speak but I cannot be heard. Worse, I am heard but am not believed. Worse yet, I speak but I am not deemed believable.
> —Jacqueline Jones Royster, "When the First Voice You Hear Is Not Your Own"

As Hill recited instances of Thomas's inappropriate office behavior (exaggerated masculine behavior out of the realm of racist mythology), she testified herself into what Kathleen Hall Jamieson describes as the "double bind," "a [rhetorical] strategy perennially used by those with power against those without" (5).[8] The Senate Judiciary Committee had power and an already-established public voice; Hill had neither. So the committee and the nation looked on while Hill spoke and wrote herself into that double bind: "to establish she was virtuous, she would have to engage in public behavior that confirmed she lacked virtue" (Jamieson 78).[9] "The implication is that if Hill was a victim, she was not an honorable woman" (Darwin 199).

Hill's written account bound her as doubly dishonorable: not only was she suspected of lying, but her statement was initially declared irrelevant to both the FBI's and the Committee's ongoing investigation into Thomas's nomination. An excerpt from her statement follows:

> He would call me into his office for reports on education issues and projects, or he might suggest that because of the time pressures of his schedule we go to lunch to a government cafeteria.
>
> After a brief discussion of work, he would turn the conversation to a discussion of sexual matters. . . . He spoke about acts that he had seen in pornographic films involving such matters as women having sex with animals and films showing group sex or rape scenes. He talked about pornographic materials depicting individuals with large penises or large breasts involving various sex acts. On several occasions, Thomas told me graphically of his own sexual prowess.
>
> . . . I was extremely uncomfortable talking about sex with him at all, and particularly in such a graphic way. . . . My efforts to change the subject were rarely successful. ("Statement" 20–21)

Interestingly, when Anita Hill used public silence, she also held power. Neither the white men on the committee nor the president of the United States knew what she knew. Neither those men nor Thomas knew what she might say under oath. And when she held to her position of silence by refusing to testify, she held power for those same reasons.

But as soon as she spoke the preceding, described the series of incidents that now would be considered a textbook case of workplace sexual harassment, the white male senators sat silently, judging her to be a liar, if not a "scorned, vengeful, psychotic woman" (Higginbotham 32). Quickly, they exerted their sociopolitical power (and regulatory norms) over the nonvoluntary testimony of the nonwhite woman whom they had subpoenaed to speak. As they scapegoated her, they also rendered her a sexualized female presence, barely bothering to conceal their privilege of race and gender.[10] They spoke their rhetorical power, reminding Hill and the rest of the viewing nation that she should have remained silent, subpoena notwithstanding.

Yet her testimony afforded their nominee an opportunity to pronounce the entire hearing nothing but "a national disgrace":

> And from my standpoint, as a black American, it is a high-tech lynching for uppity blacks who in any way deign to think for themselves, to do for themselves, to have different ideas, and it is a message that unless you kowtow to an old order, this is what will happen to you. You will be lynched, destroyed, caricatured by a committee of the U.S. Senate rather than hung from a tree. ("Second")

As far as destruction and caricaturization went, Hill suffered every bit as much as Thomas did, maybe for the very same reasons he enumerated.

A lesson in high-tech harassment. For speaking out and thereby resisting the institutional discipline that required her silence, Hill was attacked. Many observers compared the negative response to "high-tech" sexual harassment.[11] Instead of letting Clarence Thomas's credentials—let alone future Supreme Court decisions—speak for themselves, the entire nation (especially the Senate) was suddenly riveted by the spectacle of racialized gender politics.[12]

The Senate Judiciary Committee was riveted, but it was not listening, not rhetorically, anyway, for "what is at stake in any 'listening,' in any striving for comprehension, is that which our own structures of thought have made impossible to think: the unthinkable, the unhearable" (Ballif, Davis, Mountford 587). Several of the senators—Arlen Specter, Orrin Hatch, and Joseph Biden, in particular—had not listened, let alone tried to comprehend the situation. Instead, they spoke with a sense of entitlement, knowing that they could say or ask anything that came to mind: "Is 'Long Dong Silver' a stereotype?" "What was the most embarrassing of all the incidents that you have alleged?" "Tell the committee again about the [pubic hair on the] Coke can."

A. Leon Higginbotham Jr. decried the racist, sexist performance of the Judiciary Committee: "Professor Anita Hill was questioned, berated, and abused by many members of an all-white and all-male Senate committee" (32).[13] Referring to the "televised gang-rape of Anita Hill," Calvin Hernton recalls such racialized gender politics as one and the same, "vulgar": "Race is sexualized and sex is racialized, but race is ranked higher than sex, which means that racial equality between white and black men is more important than the 'lesser question' of sex equality" (87).

In hindsight, it comes as no surprise that the dissenting opinion on and the collective guilt about Thomas's appointment would be thrust upon Hill. As both

Burke and Morrison could have predicted, she became a sort of national scape-goat, as though she alone were the deciding factor in Thomas's confirmation.[14] June Jordan describes the cost of Hill's speaking out when she writes,

> Anita Hill was tricked. She was set up. She had been minding her business at the University of Oklahoma Law School when the Senators asked her to describe her relationship with Clarence Thomas. . . . Clarence Thomas was supposed to be on trial but he was not: He is more powerful than Anita Hill. And his bedfellows . . .—way more powerful than Clarence Thomas and Anita Hill combined.
>
> And so, at the last, it was she, Anita Hill, who stood alone, trying to tell the truth in an arena of snakes and hyenas and dinosaurs and power-mad dogs. And with this televised victimization of Anita Hill, the American war of violence against women moved from the streets, moved from hip hop, moved from multimillion-dollar movies into the highest chambers of the U.S. Government. (123–24)

Rich captures the dynamic when an Other speaks truth to power: "If we have learned anything in our coming out of silence, it is that what has been unspoken, therefore *unspeakable* in us, is what is most threatening to the patriarchal order in which some men control, first women, then all who can be defined and exploited as 'other'" ("It Is the Lesbian" 199).

If Hill's spoken and written allegations had been listened to rhetorically (which is *not* the same as whether Hill was believed), Thomas would not have been confirmed, nor would male dominance have been confirmed, whether inside or outside the beltway. A black woman can speak—to be sure. But Hill's public speaking demonstrated that no one in power will actually listen to her. And she will be punished, however obliquely.

High-tech punishment. For breaking her silence, Hill would have to be punished: by blacks, for undermining the appointment of a black judge, by calling attention to the power differentials harbored within the black community (and in front of a white audience, no less); by blacks and whites, for playing the victim when she was, after all, "'uppity' by class position, education, job, presumed equality in a world of men" (Hernton 89); by women, who knew if they sided with Hill, they too would be punished; by men, for claiming that *her* sex and humanity (and thereby the sex and humanity of *all* women) were equal to that of every man and every race; and by much of the viewing audience, for allegedly being an instrument of a left-wing (read "feminist") conspiracy.

Conservative Harvard professor Orlando Patterson, one of Thomas's staunch-est supporters, argues that even if Thomas did resort to a "down-home style of courting," "there is no evidence that [Hill] suffered any emotional or career damage, and the punishment she belatedly sought was in no way commensurate with the offense" (163, 161–62). And Beverly Guy-Sheftal writes, "The overwhelming reaction among blacks . . . , despite what the polls may have revealed, seems to have been that even if the allegations were true, she should have remained silent" (73). Gender plays a strong role in terms of who gets to speak out and be listened to—and who should remain silent. For many, then, Hill should not have betrayed her race for the benefit of her sex. She should have remained silent, though how she was to do so in the face of a subpoena has never been made clear.

High-tech support. In the face of these sentiments, only feminists and womanists listened to Hill. Barbara Mikulski of Maryland, one of only two women then in the Senate, addressed the issue of Hill's taking the stand, "To anybody out there who wants to be a whistle blower, the message is, 'Don't blow that whistle because you will be left out there by yourself'" (qtd. in *Congressional Record* 14508). The African American Women in Defense of Ourselves group extended Mikulski's incrimination of the nonlisteners and responded to Hill, Thomas, the Senate, and all of America when they placed a full-page advertisement in the *New York Times,* stating that they were

> particularly outraged by the racist and sexist treatment of Professor Anita Hill, an African-American woman who was maligned and castigated for daring to speak publicly of her own experience of sexual abuse. The malicious defamation of Professor Hill insulted all women of African descent and sent a dangerous message to any woman who might contemplate a sexual-harassment complaint.
>
> . . . We cannot tolerate this type of dismissal of any one Black woman's experience or this attack on our collective character without protest, outrage, and resistance.
>
> We pledge ourselves to continue to speak out in defense of one another, in defense of the African-American community and against those who are hostile to social justice, no matter what color they are. No one will speak for us but ourselves. (Chrisman and Allen 291–92)

All of these women recognized immediately how gendered power differentials continue to determine who gets to speak out, who should remain silent, who gets to decide—and when. As Linda Martin Alcoff puts it, "Who is speaking to whom turns out to be as important for meaning and truth as what is said; in fact, what is said turns out to change according to who is speaking and who is listening" (235).

After the hearings and the testimony, after Thomas had been confirmed 52–48 (the closest confirmation vote since 1888), after the entire country bore witness to Hill's breaking her silence, the question lingered, even among her supporters: why had she remained silent for so long? Was silence the only appropriate course of action for Hill at the time?

A Timely Response

> I have come to believe over and over again that what is most important to me must be spoken, made verbal and shared, even at the risk of having it bruised or misunderstood.
>
> —Audre Lorde, "The Transformation of Silence into Language and Action"

By all media, governmental, and personal accounts, Hill was a reluctant witness to Thomas's character. Again and again, she claimed that she had "no personal vendetta" against him. But since reluctance and silence are not inextricably linked, the question remains: why had Hill remained silent for so long? If, as I mentioned in chapter 2, a 1.7-second conversational gap can create suspicion, it is understandable that Hill's ten-year silence would create suspicion if not fiery controversy.

Why had Hill remained silent?

If it was true that she had "no personal vendetta" against the nominee, if it was true that she had indeed followed him from the Department of Education to the Equal Employment Opportunity Commission, if it was true that she had remained on a relatively friendly basis with him after her departure (she had placed 1.5 calls a year to his office), if it was true that she had filed no grievance against her superior during her employment, and if it was true that she had not been harmed professionally, why come forward now? Was silence the only appropriate course of action for Hill at the time?

In rhetorical terms, the answer is a definite "maybe." Kairos depends on the rhetorical situation, in this case one constructed by powerful political (mostly white) males, a nonwhite female, and a prevalent belief that any harassed woman is somehow responsible for the behavior. All together, these lines of reasoning fasten the double bind that I explained earlier: keep silent, or speak and be shamed. Put another way, as soon as Hill spoke, she confronted that double bind constructed to ensure that she was, indeed, "guilty until proven guilty" (Jamieson 3). As Hill admits:

> I had kept my secret for all those years . . . and had been fully prepared to go on keeping the secret. Now I would do so no longer. I was not happy about what I felt I had to do ten years before—keep quiet—nor was I happy about what I must do now—speak out. . . . The shame I felt should never have been mine, but I had taken it on by my own silence. (*Speaking* 110)

Not even Hill herself can determine a single reason for her silence, only that she employed it—for a number of reasons, which she tried to articulate during the hearings. Among Johannesen's twenty functions of silence (which I enumerated in chapter 1), four might apply here: Hill might have been silent because she was "carefully pondering exactly what to say next," because she was "avoiding discussion of a controversial or sensitive issue out of fear," because she was "emotionally overcome," or because she felt "inarticulate despite a desire to communicate" (29).

Whatever the underlying reasons for her silence, when Specter asked her what went through her mind—"if anything"—on whether she "ought to come forward," she replied:

> I can only say that when I made the decision just to withdraw from the situation, and not press a claim or charge against him that I may have shirked a duty, a responsibility that I had. And to that extent, I confess that I am very sorry that I did not do something or say something. But at the time that was my best judgment. Maybe it was a poor judgment, but it wasn't a dishonest one, and it wasn't a completely unreasonable choice that I made. (*Sex and Justice*)

When Senator Patrick Leahy followed up with, "Had you not been contacted, would you have come forward at this time," she answered, "I cannot say that I would have" (*Sex and Justice*). She might have continued to remain silent.

The comfort and stress of silence. As I explained in chapter 1, Kahn details purposeful silence in terms of an active "nonengagement"; such silence offers people like Hill the possibility of choosing what to do first or next, enclosing or distancing themselves from various events or other people, and making themselves known or not (204). Hill's descriptions of disbelief, rationalization, self-doubt, strategization—and specifically silence—attest to the most common responses and attempts to undo what a person fears might be sexual harassment by a superior. In *Speaking Truth to Power,* Hill recounts how she and her close friend Ellen "talked as though I had control over the behavior though we both knew that I did not" (71). Of the friends she told, "not one" suggested that Hill speak out, let alone "bring a charge of sexual harassment against Clarence Thomas," or "file a complaint with the EEOC" (71).

Regardless of position, profession, or race, silence is the most common response to sexual harassment—despite the stress of remaining silent. Susan Ehrlich Martin tells us that harassment is never totally absent in any position and that it increases for those women whose impressive occupations appear to be direct challenges to patriarchal authority. Although many working-class women silently endure sexual harassment because they need their jobs, professional women endure for exactly the same reason; sexual harassment predicated on professional sabotage is a particularly insidious kind of victimization.[15] As Naomi Wolf tells it:

> It is those professional women on the "inside"—with the most to lose—who express the greatest fear of what they describe as the professional suicide of speaking up for one's own rights or beliefs as a woman. This silence is neither apathy nor selfishness nor cowardice. It is silencing by economic pressure in a male-dominated workplace during a worldwide recession.

In a culture where we have all been led to believe that achievement, education, mobility, and a good job will protect and insulate us, professional women may not want to be a disappointment to themselves, their families, their communities. Therefore, harassed women, whatever their status, experience considerable emotional stress, often leave or get fired, and yet they all claim that silence is their most reliable and advantageous strategy (Kemp 310). Silence is their modus operandi.

In "Hill's Accusations Ring True," legal trailblazer Catharine MacKinnon tells us that Hill's long silence is representative of women's tendency to personalize the experience, thinking that it is up to them to understand, change, take control. This individualization leads to feelings of isolation and uniqueness; therefore, they do not report such incidents. This individualization also leads to stress. In her official statement, Hill submitted that she "began to feel severe stress on the job. . . . I was hospitalized for five days on an emergency basis for acute stomach pains, which I attributed to stress on the job" ("Statement"). Besides, if and when women speak up, they are admitting publicly that they have sustained damage, and they are also admitting their willingness to move into the even more public (i.e., vulnerable) status of "victim," however that term might be defined. Little wonder, then that mental health professionals who study experiences such as Hill's say that the "emotional, physical, and financial risks that come with reporting sexual exploitation are so devastating [that the professionals] increasingly advise women against going public or making a formal complaint" (Leonard 31).

Despite silence's being a common response to harassment, Hill's decision to maintain it was roundly ridiculed, even by other women in high-profile positions. Katherine Boo of the *Washington Monthly* wrote that "it's important for women to acknowledge, no matter how caught up we are in the quest for professional equality, that . . . women can choose principle over professional status; they can decide that integrity matters more than a rung up on the corporate ladder. Anita Hill didn't" (45–46). What Boo does not take into full consideration is Martin's finding that women like Hill, who inhabit prestigious (and therefore untraditional) occupations are often more resented than women in traditional positions. Thus, what critics saw as "compromising personal principle to promote immediate self-interest," sympathizers understood as a "forgivable, human response to an extremely stressful situation" (Boo 46). Trying to explain Hill's silent behavior to her fellow senators, Mikulski said, "If you talk to the victims of abuse the way I have, they will tell you they are often doubly victimized by both the event in which they are abused and then subsequently by the way the system treats them" (*Congressional Record* 14508). And Mikulski emphasized her point when she accused the Judiciary Committee of "taking a walk on this one."

Employing silence. Anita Hill did, indeed, remain silent, whether for the preceding reasons I have sketched out—or for reasons no one may every fully understand. Nor may anyone ever know if she would have come forward without the insistence of media and government representatives. Not even Hill herself can determine the reason for her silence, only that she was silent—and for a number of unarticulated reasons. Maybe she was employing a silence of loyalty—to her race, her workplace, or herself; after all, she did not have another job at the time of the alleged offenses.[16] She might have been employing the silence of incubation that permitted her to make sense out of events (after all, most women subordinated by harassment try to make sense out of it). Hill writes that she and Ellen "struggled to discover a way" for Hill to keep her job but "avoid the behavior," even going so far as to decide that Hill should change her perfume. Pat Belanoff has recently argued for silence as reflection, meditation, contemplation, three activities that can be attached to thinking through or thoughtful uncertainty, surely a resource for Hill in this situation (413, 418). Anne Ruggles Gere writes of the ethical and political resources of strategic silence, differentiating that "good" silence (that of Hill's thoughtful silence) from the "corrosive effects of ('bad') inarticulate silence," which could be attached to the nonlistening senators (219). So, perhaps, Hill was employing silence in the interest of working out her own timeline, agenda, context, and speaking moment—premeditation being one thing that Hill was not accused of.[17]

It is also possible that Hill remained silent for so long because she predicted the line of humiliating questioning that she would eventually face and endure. When she moved into the public sphere and testified, she refused the status of victim as well as the sociopolitical discipline that had made silence "more comfortable" in the first place and instead sustained repeated demands to speak of "pubic hair, large breasts, and long dongs," while Thomas was guided to speak of "boot straps, hard work, and rugged individualism" (Travis and Barlowe 38). Maybe she remained silent for so long because she predicted just the kind of capricious reprisals and public dismissals that her publicized, politicized, and ambitious sisters Professor Lani Guinier, Surgeon General Joycelyn Elders, and Hillary Rodham Clinton would eventually face and endure.

The Last Word

> The Hill-Thomas hearing . . . was about finding our voices and
> breaking the silence forever.
>
> —Anita Hill, *Speaking Truth to Power*

Hill's coming to voice out of silence galvanized the attention of the U.S. public—but at whose expense? (Hers, temporarily.) And to whose advantage? (The American public's—for a long time.) The answers to those questions may be arguable, but one thing is not: when Hill raised her voice to those fourteen white men on the Senate Judiciary Committee in October 1991, she alerted Americans to the pervasiveness and difficulty of sexual harassment.

Indeed, the aftermath of the Thomas-Hill hearings brought some positive response. Just one week after Thomas's confirmation, President Bush signed the Civil Rights Act of 1991, a different version of which he had vetoed the previous year. For the first time, victims of sexual harassment could sue for and be awarded monetary damages "in amounts up to $300,000 per complainant, depending on the size of the employer" (Ross 229). And, expanding on what I mentioned in chapter 1, in the nine months following Hill's testimony to the Senate Judiciary Committee, "inquiries about sexual harassment to the Equal Employment Opportunity Commission . . . increased by 150 percent, and a record-breaking number of charges (7,407) were filed, a 50 percent increase over the same period a year earlier" (Bystrom 267–68). More than 12,000 complaints were filed with the EEOC in 1993 (268).

Within two years of the hearings, the U.S. Supreme Court strengthened and clarified the law, broadening the definition of "hostile environment" beyond the former "quid pro quo" harassment situation. No longer would victims of sexual harassment "have to prove that they became mental basket cases or stopped being productive employees [or students] in order to prevail, although evidence of either effect would obviously be relevant to their case" (Ross 232). According to this unanimous Supreme Court ruling, sexual harassment is intolerable—not to be sanctioned—no matter where.

Reflecting on her experience, Hill writes,

> It is as important today as it was in 1991 that I feel free to speak. If I let my fears silence me now, I will have betrayed all those who supported me . . . and those who have come forward since. More than anything else, the Hill-Thomas hearing of October 1991 was about finding our voices and breaking the silence forever. (*Speaking* 7)

A Quick Next Word

> The liberatory voice . . . is characterized by opposition, by
> resistance. It demands that paradigms shift—that we learn to
> talk—to listen—to hear in a new way.
>
> —bell hooks, *Talking Back*

I am not as sanguine as Hill that her coming to voice helped the rest of us find
our voices and break the silence—not always and not forever, anyway. Instead, I
think of all the powerful men and women inside the beltway who have yet to
outdistance their need for purposeful silence and silencing as gendered disciplines
of (self-)control, punishment, surveillance, and judgment. Whether to protect
their power base or their reputations, people from Guinier, both Bill and Hillary
Rodham Clinton, and Joycelyn Elders to Monica Lewinsky, Gary Condit, and
the tragically silent Chaundra Levy have systematically refused calls to speak out
and disturb their practical sense of sociopolitical power and discipline.

> Negotiating Silence/ing
> What I must engage . . .
> is meant to break my heart and reduce me to
> silence.
>
> —Adrienne Rich, "North American Time"

Two years after the Hill-Thomas hearings, Lani Guinier followed Hill onto the
public, political, politicized stage. On 29 April 1993, President Bill Clinton nominated Guinier to head the Justice Department's Civil Rights Division, as Assistant Attorney General under Janet Reno. Brilliantly educated, a highly respected
professor and experienced civil rights litigator, Guinier was hailed by U.S. Attorney General Janet Reno as "the best possible choice" for the position (West
38).[18] She was also perhaps the best qualified for the position, given her Radcliffe
and Yale educations and her experience: she had served a clerkship with the Chief
Judge of the United States District Court in Michigan before being enticed away
from Detroit to D.C., where she worked as special assistant to the Assistant Attorney General for Civil Rights, under President Jimmy Carter. After leaving that
post, she spent seven successful years as a litigator with the NAACP Legal Defense and Education Fund, during which she had filed an effective suit against
then–Arkansas governor Bill Clinton for voting rights violations.

At the time of her nomination, she was a respected, energetic, and popular
professor at the University of Pennsylvania Law School. As the *New Yorker* put
it, "no nominee for the post has ever been better prepared than Lani Guinier"
("Idea Woman" 4). It would follow, then, that Guinier's nomination was "sup-

ported by a letter signed by more than 400 law professors, including the deans of twelve major law schools" (Garrow 28)—a fact resolutely ignored by the press.

Once again, the nation focused on a nomination process, zooming in on the words and body of a nonwhite woman, doubly gendered (in terms of power) by her race and sex. Once again, a nonwhite woman would be rendered highly visible yet apparently powerless, which suggests (as I tried to demonstrate with the example of Hill) that only *a*political middle-class nonwhite women garner any measure of public reward. Hill's testimony had counted for little, but, at least, she had been permitted to speak publicly. Guinier, on the other hand, was gendered feminine in yet a third manner: this high-powered scholar and attorney would be silenced by someone else.

Why Silence?

> Everything we write
> will be used against us
> or against those we love.
> These are the terms,
> take them or leave them.
>
> —Adrienne Rich, "North American Time"

Lani Guinier had not charged any one (let alone a nonwhite man) with anything; she simply (or not so simply) was well known and in legal circles highly respected for her thinking on the fairness of voting procedures. Her scholarship assessing the Voting Rights Act rests on this critical question: "Is majority rule a reliable instrument of democracy in a racially divided society?" Her answer is "no," and her scholarly project, long centered on collective decision making and power sharing, maps out possible ways for voting to be ultimately and truly "democratic." In other words, "although the mere ability to vote counts for a great deal, the power that voting brings matters as much or more—at least to people who have long been denied their chance at self-governance" (Carter xiv). According to Guinier, majority rule does not automatically equal or ensure democracy, for the issue is "not that blacks can't register and vote—they can—it's that they can register and vote without success in electing people who will be responsive to their needs" (Garrow 31).[19]

By thoughtfully engaging civil rights legislation with voting practices, Guinier had discovered how easily a nonwhite—or white—candidate could be elected by a majority (even by a majority of a minority population) without ever being responsive to the needs of that minority population. But by the time this footnote (or an interpretation thereof) from her scholarly writing gained circulation in the popular press, it had morphed into a *New York Times* editorial newsbite: Guinier "questions whether [Douglas Wilder of Virginia] is an 'authentic' figure for blacks—because he owes his job to white voters as well" (qtd. in Gigot). This interpretation of her opinions did not reflect what she had ever said, let alone written.[20]

Guinier soon faced the burden of even more public criticism. Some conservatives launched a powerfully effective smear campaign against her. Libertarian Clint Bolick addressed NPR's "Morning Edition" audience with such distortions of her politics as "Lani Guinier's writings are profoundly anti-democratic" and "in my view, they amount to a racial apartheid system" (qtd. in Carter ix). Senate minority leader Bob Dole was quoted as saying that she was "a consistent supporter not only of quotas but of vote-rigging schemes that make quotas look mild" (N. Lewis, "Clinton Selection"). Mary Ann Glendon writes that the roots of Guinier's difficulties lie in her "growing disdain of the practical aspects of law, a zany passion for novelty, a confusion of advocacy with scholarship, and a mistrust of majoritarian institutions." But it would be Bolick's *Wall Street Journal* column, appearing under the headline "Clinton's Quota Queens," that would soon successfully exile Guinier to the realm of imposed silence.

So it was not Guinier's politics that got her silenced; rather, it was an uninformed reaction to her politics that got her silenced. More to the point, it was a deliberately ignorant and manipulative reaction to her politics that got her silenced. As she herself says, it was not "a question of being lost in the translation; it [was] a question of really being a fabrication" (Garrow 32). And she was a fabrication—a silenced, suddenly silent one. Even her own mother called her to say, "Lani, someone is using your name. I see your picture in the paper, but I do not recognize you" (qtd. in Guinier, *Lift* 57). The bigger her silenced image became, the more it served as a blank screen for projected threats, insecurities, and frustrations.

The Blank Screen

> It doesn't matter what you think
> Words are found responsible
> all you can do is choose them
> or choose
> to remain silent.
>
> —Adrienne Rich, "North American Time"

Guinier was, like Hill, a visible Nonwhite Lady Overachiever—suspect and strange (at least to some). Daniel Moynihan described Guinier as the "black lady, the one whose disproportionate overachievement stands for black cultural strangeness" (qtd. in Rainwater and Yancey 75). Hill's cultural strangeness (as an overachieving nonwhite female) had reduced her to a "lunatic," "lesbian," and "liar"; whereas, Guinier was suddenly reduced to the "Quota Queen," a racialized sobriquet resonating with all the disapproval and disgust thrust on women from all the nonwhite "Welfare Queens" to "Condom Queen" Joycelyn Elders (otherwise known as the U.S. Surgeon General) to "Hotel Queen" Leona Helmsley.[21] Thus, Guinier's complex and carefully nuanced legal writing about the U.S. system of voting had been reductively if not purposefully dismissed as a "quota" system, with her the reigning Quota Queen.[22]

The vilification of Guinier's body of legal politext was one thing, part of the game politicians and the media play so well; after all, Americans have become nearly desensitized to the mean-spiritedness, untrustworthiness, and sleaze of politics, particularly when spun by the media.[23] With the hope of being "her worst nightmare," Bolick characterized Guinier as demanding "equal legislative outcomes, requiring abandonment not only of the 'one person, one vote' principle, but majority rule itself" ("Clinton's"). In another piece, he situates her "at the cutting edge of 'critical race theory,'" proponents of which "agitate for regulation of 'hate speech' and racial quotas for law school faculties" ("Legal"). He goes on to say, "[Guinier's] confirmation would reignite the smoldering embers of racial division, while imperiling some of the very democratic institutions on which our nation's moral claim is staked" ("Legal"). Soon after, Guinier faced the burden of even more public criticism—an effective smear campaign against her.[24]

The deliberate misreading of Guinier's politics was one part of the campaign, but the vilification of Guinier's physical body as a kind of cultural biotext went beyond the pale. A third-generation lawyer, daughter of a black West Indian father and a white, Jewish mother, Guinier incited nationwide skepticism focused on her "race." Was she black or white? Why was her hair so wild? What gives with her "Madisonian majority" politics?[25] The audacity of the media to fuse her politics with her physical characteristics with such broad, crude strokes was shocking. Several magazines featured raw caricatures of Guinier, with electrified hair and a prominent nose. In what Patricia Williams described as a "fit of exoticizing, xenophobic preschoolishness," Linda Chavez opined on the *MacNeil/Lehrer Newshour* that "You can't even pronounce her name" (qtd. in Williams, *Rooster's* 141). *U.S. News and World Report* launched countless repetitions and permutations: "Strange name, strange hair, strange writing—she's history" (Leo).

Like Hill, she was rendered publicly powerless, whether she chose to speak (no one was listening), chose to remain silent, or obeyed the silencing that was soon to come down on her. Meanwhile President Clinton would soon choose strategic silence, where he could resist sociopolitical disciplines of equal rights and civil rights.

A Silent, Well-Mannered Other

> I have been compelled on too many occasions to count to sit as a
> well-mannered Other, silently, . . . while colleagues who occupy a

place of entitlement . . . have comfortably claimed the authority to
engage in the construction of knowledge and meaning about me.
—Jacqueline Jones Royster, "When the
First Voice You Hear Is Not Your Own"

Guinier had accepted the nomination with enthusiasm. After her first meeting
with newly appointed Attorney General Janet Reno, she "desperately wanted the
job" (*Lift* 31). She imagined herself fulfilling a life's dream and a dual mission:
not only did she want to enforce existing civil rights legislation, but she wanted
to change direction in the fight for civil rights, moving beyond what she felt was
an outdated 1960s vision of formal equality (34). Most of all she wanted to "start
a genuine dialogue to bridge the different world views on race." She writes, "I
had hoped to begin that conversation, using the first public announcement to
signal a new civil rights commitment and mission. I wanted to use the job to
create a space for people to begin to speak for themselves" (35). But there would
be no dialogue, no conversation, no speaking, no hearing—not yet.

Following White House protocol not to speak to the press pending Senate
confirmation hearings, Guinier remained silent. This protocol, which mightily
resembles censorship (an ironic situation for a civil rights attorney) was predicated on a future hearing, which Guinier fully expected. After all, Vernon Jordan, Clinton's right-hand man, had assured her not to worry: "The president . . .
won't abandon you"; and "I'll help you, when the time comes" (qtd. in Guinier,
Lift 134).

So it was that despite ridiculous, racist, and sexist attacks, Guinier was not
allowed a public hearing to respond to her critics or even to summarize the views
for which she was taken to task in the media. Although writing within the ongoing scholarly conversation about voting rights and democracy, continuing at
least since the 1965 Voting Rights Act had been passed, although questioning
various definitions of "democracy," so that it "promises a fair discussion among
self-defined equals about how to achieve . . . common aspirations," although
devoting her legal career to issues of collective decision making and power sharing, Guinier was deemed unready for public conversation (*Tyranny* 6).

Guinier yearned for the same opportunity that Clarence Thomas had enjoyed
two years before—to speak publicly. She was denied the experience, by what was
described as a "combination of editorial racism, Senatorial cowardice, and White
House incompetence" (qtd. in Guinier, *Lift* 23). There would be no speaking—
let alone listening—to anyone.

Guinier was effectively shut out of any rhetorical situation: she could not
speak; she had no audience; she had no opportunity to tell her story, the all-
important device that would allow the American public to organize, recall, and

make sense of the swirl of evaluations and opinions they were encountering about her and her nomination (Cappella and Jamieson 86). Patricia Hill Collins tells us that after being "forbidden for weeks to speak on her own behalf," Guinier

> pleaded on nationwide television for the opportunity to explain and defend her ideas in the open forum of a confirmation hearing. Guinier never got her public hearing. Unlike that of Hill, Guinier's treatment demonstrated that Black women in the public eye could be destroyed at will, with no opportunity for redress to speak on her own behalf. (41)

Her credibility had been sorely compromised by her inability to speak or speak back to the press or to the Senate Judiciary Committee in a formal hearing. Yet, as Butler teaches us, Guinier's regulated silencing naturally contained gaps and fissures, which would eventually appear. But at the time of her silence, it appeared that she had to remain silent and that no one wanted to hear what she had to say about herself or her legal writings, anyway: no one was asking her questions; no one was listening to her. The White House was saying very little, thereby exerting its masculinist power through silence. Resisting her professional training as a speaker, writer, and arguer, Lani Guinier was saying nothing, thereby inhabiting a traditionally feminine im/position of silence. Clinton, on the other hand, used his silence to deliver his power.

The All-Powerful Silent Center

> It is not the case that a man who is silent says nothing.
>
> —Anonymous

In response, in defense of his nominee, the most powerful person in the free world, and also her sponsor, enjoyed the presidential prerogative of shifting strategically from speech to silence. Even if Clinton felt that remaining silent was wiser than speaking out, he was still communicating his power. After all, "one of the widely held assumptions of human communication theory at present is that a person cannot *not* communicate" (Johannesen 25). Especially as president. Clinton's silence would communicate "because listeners and observers . . . attach meaning to silence whether the sender wishes so or not" (Johannesen 25)

Shifting from speech to silence can be particularly communicative and thus rhetorically effective. In his 11 May remarks to the Leadership Conference on Civil Rights, Clinton reminded the crowd that his nominee had once been his legal adversary, invoking her law suit against the governor of Arkansas: "not only that, she didn't lose. And I nominated her anyway, so the Senate ought to be able to put up with a little controversy in the cause of civil rights and go on and confirm her" (qtd. in Apple A8). A few days later (14 May), he said that he nominated her because "there had never been a full-time practicing civil rights lawyer with a career in civil rights law heading the civil rights division"; and "I would never have appointed anybody to public office if they had to agree with everything I believe in" (qtd. in Apple A8). Then on 2 June, he announced that he "was concerned" that she did not believe in one person/one vote but that he was basically behind her nomination because, after all, "no real civil rights lawyer has ever held that position before" (qtd. in Apple A8).[26] By this time in the process, Clinton was already beginning his famous back-pedaling: "I think that a lot of what has been said [about her] is not accurate. On the other hand, I have to take into account where the Senate is" (qtd. in Apple A8). At another press conference (2 June), he apologized for all the controversy over his nominee, from whom he was obviously trying to distance himself: "I never have associated myself with all of her writings" (qtd. in Apple A8). Then he stopped addressing the issue of her nomination altogether.

To and about her he was silent.

Again, Johannesen's functions of silence include several that can be applied to Clinton, ranging from "the person feels no sense of urgency about talking" and "the person is doubtful or indecisive" to "the person's silence is a means of punishing others, or annihilating others symbolically by excluding them from verbal communication" (29–30). So it was that after listening to Clinton's often ill-conceived comments and then his silence, after realizing that the White House press presence was doing nothing to rectify the negative situation she was forced to endure, Guinier immediately went to work.

Guinier asked Clinton assistant Ricki Seidman to inform the president on three pressing issues, to wit, that she did, indeed, believe in one person/one vote, that she would like the opportunity to supply information for her defense, and that, just as important, she needed the president to draft a compelling statement supporting her nomination.[27] Her requests were met with resolute silence—by the White House communications office as well as the president himself. He remained noncommittal—silent, in fact—with regard to her nomination, instructing her to remain silent, too—until her hearing.

The One Night Stand

> Silence is a game of dodgeball at dusk—
> A matter of time 'til someone knocks you out
> Of the circle of bodies.
>
> —Robin Becker, "Against Silence"

Guinier's silence was lifted for one night, just hours before her nomination was finally withdrawn. She was permitted to appear on Ted Koppel's *Nightline*, where she tried valiantly to express her legal views, which had been so brutally misrepresented, and save her nomination:

> I perhaps have not been as clear as I should have, but I was writing to an academic audience and in the context of the expectations of academic scholars. One has to appreciate the various nuances and complexities and you write in a way that's dense and ponderous and often misunderstood, particularly when it's reduced to a sound bite. (qtd. in Carter xiv)

Like the victim of abuse she truly was, Guinier implies that she alone is responsible for the mess her reputation was in, as though if she had just been better, clearer, her words would never have been used against her.

After her appearance, the White House again reimposed her silence, for fear, administrative spokespeople cautioned, that "any further statements would whip up public sentiment in her favor, forcing a hearing that would result in a 'divisive' public discussion of race" (qtd. in Williams, *Rooster's* 141). In this case, neither Guinier's words or silence seemed to help anything—except to make it easier for President Clinton to withdraw her nomination and finally advise her to co-ordinate a press statement.[28]

The Dis-Appointment

> Silence and obedience to authority were not rewarded.
>
> —bell hooks, *Teaching to Transgress*

The next morning, Clinton called Guinier, saying that he had decided to withdraw her nomination, that she had done nothing wrong, that he would spend the rest of his life making it up to her. In light of her *Nightline* appearance, he said that she had made the best case imaginable, but that it did not change his mind.

At the press conference, Clinton claimed that he had never actually read Guinier's legal writing, a claim impossible to fathom, given Clinton's well-known voracity as a reader, his amazing capacity to scan and yet digest vast amounts of information, and his ability to work on just a few hours of sleep a night. Suddenly, or so he claimed, he realized that her writings "clearly lend themselves to interpretations" that do not express the views that he expressed "on civil rights during the campaign" (Guinier, "Who's Afraid" 44). He went on to pronounce Guinier's views to be "antidemocratic" (a term that humiliated her) and "difficult to defend." Then he said that he could not ask for confirmation of a nominee with whom he disagreed, after all, "I really don't think what's in her articles matches what I stand for" (qtd. in Apple A1).[29]

As he continued his rationale for her dis-appointment, Clinton implemented his skill at disassociating private from public behavior, for which he has come to be so well known. He dismissed his demeaning remarks about her legal writing and her mistake-of-a-nomination all the while protesting his personal fondness for her: "I love her. I think she's wonderful. If she called me and told me she needed $5,000, I'd take it from my account and send it to her, no questions asked. It was the hardest decision I've had to make since I became President but you can't fight on and on when you don't believe in it" (qtd. in Apple A1).[30] And in one of his most litotes-drenched statements, he proceeded with, "I regret the pain that has been caused to Ms. Guinier, who bears none of the responsibility for the situation in which we find ourselves" (qtd. in Guinier, *Lift* 127). Finally, he made his most outrageous claim: "It is not the fear of defeat that prompted this decision" to withdraw Guinier's nomination (qtd. in Williams, *Rooster's* 142).

The Non-Hearing

> When you are silent, it speaks;
> When you speak, it is silent.
>
> —Tseu

Lani Guinier never enjoyed a hearing before the Senate Judiciary Committee. As Collins sees it, the problem was not the wildness of Guinier's ideas but the actuality that they could, indeed, be implemented and thereby provide a truly democratic voting system.[31] Her civil rights ideas were easily applicable, and she had had the backing to prove it. Members of the NAACP Legal Defense Fund were mobilizing a national press strategy emphasizing her widespread support. In one of their many faxes, they argued that

> Beyond defending Lani's writings, it was critical that we relay the message that she has wide support and that she is not the Bork of the Clinton Administration as she is being portrayed by her right-wing opponents. Even the stories that have been favorable have not been helpful in galvanizing support, building momentum or effectively responding to the negative attacks that distort her writing. (qtd. in Guinier, *Lift* 39–40)

But Guinier had not been permitted to break her silence, let alone leverage support or influence on behalf of her nomination.

Suddenly, the "best qualified" person for the job was unqualified, an ironic twist since the most common complaint about affirmative-action hirings is the difficulty of finding qualified hires. Guinier's experience and qualifications were coming to mean nothing—except that she might be qualified to hold a learned opinion meriting consideration. Lani Guinier was never to be Assistant Attorney General of Civil Rights. No nonwhite female, no Black Lady, would have the opportunity to challenge—or even begin to unsettle—the age-old structure of white male dominance, or what Karla Holloway refers to as "the cultural biotext of legislative racism" (46).

The Last Word

> The media were describing someone who may have been using my name but hadn't written my articles and certainly had not lived my life.
>
> —Lani Guinier, *Lift Every Voice*

After her nomination had been withdrawn, Guinier broke her silence, appearing before the press with her husband and young son, to say that she was disappointed that she did not have a chance to argue her views before the Senate:

> Had I been allowed to testify in a public forum before the U.S. Senate, I believe that the Senate would also have agreed that I am the right person for this job, a job some people have said I trained for all my life. I deeply regret that I shall not have the opportunity for public service in the civil rights division. (qtd. in N. Lewis, "Clinton Tries")

Clearly, she understand how an inept White House, which had not lifted a finger to support her, together with a calculated media blitz (invigorated by conservatism activism) worked together to undermine her nomination.

In direct response to "the" Lani Guinier and the so-called Guinier agenda that had been constructed by the media, she immediately initiated her goal of recovering her self: "I have always believed in democracy and nothing I have ever written is inconsistent with that. I have always believed in one person, one vote, and nothing I have ever written is inconsistent with that" (N. Lewis, "Clinton Tries"). She was not the "imperious black woman who did not know her place" that the media had created, nor would she "do to whites what centuries of whites had done to blacks" (*Lift* 37).[32] She was, she assured the audience, a "democratic idealist who believes that politics need not be forever seen as I win, you lose, a dynamic in which some people are permanent monopoly winners and others are permanent excluded losers" (N. Lewis, "Clinton Tries").

After months of negotiating her own silence and silencing, Guinier stressed the need for public conversation:

> I hope that what has happened to my own nomination does not mean that future nominees will not be allowed to explain their views as soon as any controversy arises. I hope that we are not witnessing that dawning of a new intellectual orthodoxy in which thoughtful people can no longer debate pro-

vocative ideas without denying the country their talents as public servants. (N. Lewis, "Clinton Tries")[33]

Thus, her opening salvos, after several months of retreat, were just the beginning. Although the "Quota Queen," threat to democracy, had been gendered silent and rendered powerless, the situation was to be temporary. She would rupture the regulatory norm.

FROM SILENCE TO SPEECH: A RHETORIC

> Moving from silence into speech is for the oppressed, the
> colonized, the exploited, and those who stand and struggle side
> by side, a gesture of defiance that heals, that makes new life and
> new growth possible.
>
> —bell hooks, *Talking Back*

Both Anita Hill and Lani Guinier sought redemption, available for neither of them in Washington, D.C. Both women left D.C. to renew themselves among friends and family and to reinvigorate their faith and sense of purpose. Both women began publishing and speaking widely to stimulate national public dialogues on important issues of sexual harassment and participatory democracy. Their transformation of silence into language and action effected their rebirth, which Burke describes as an initial state of tension, catharsis, and redemption— in which a new identity (physical, psychological, or spiritual) is achieved.[34]

From Silence to Speech

Among their many redemptive writing projects, Hill wrote *Speaking Truth to Power*,[35] and Guinier wrote *Lift Every Voice*,[36] anthem-like books that created open-ended conversations, opportunities for speaking, listening, and productive silence—not dysfunctional silence or silencing.

For Guinier, lifting her voice, addressing laws, and transforming them into effective mandates, according to the energetic spirit of Dr. Martin Luther King Jr., meant that she had to reconceptualize her audience, which was no longer Washington, D.C., insiders. "Who are you speaking to?" asked her mother. "If you think you are speaking to Bill Clinton, you are wasting your breath. He isn't listening" (qtd. in Guinier, *Lift* 281). Open-ended conversations have been possible, however, with cabdrivers, hotel cooks and waiters, YMCA members, dairy farmers, and other real people who are willing to talk and listen. It was their willingness that filled Guinier with the possibilities for public conversations of race that easily link to issues of "fairness, justice, and the distribution of scarce resources in a democracy" (*Lift* 273). "Ideas matter," she writes. "They're not sound bites, nor are they a monologue. . . . I can use my ideas . . . to expand the conversation. I hope to participate in that conversation as a voice of conscience" ("Who's Afraid" 66). Of course, these conversations have become opportunities for further misunderstanding, but Guinier often tells her mixed audiences, "We've got to learn to talk to each other even when we don't understand each other" (qtd. in Mansnerus). Guinier's commitment to participatory democracy, racial justice, and inclusivity entails listening—and talking—"not silencing" (*Lift* 273). Indeed, both Hill and Guinier have moved far beyond their silence/ing—further, perhaps, than they would have had they permitted to speak—and been listened to—all along. Their silence/ing provided them greater reasons—and according to Butler, built-in opportunities, to resist—and speak out.[37]

From Silence to Rhetoric

> Let a woman learn in silence with all submissiveness. I permit
> no woman to teach or to have authority over men; she is to
> keep silent.
>
> —1 Tim. 2:11–12

Given that silence is still most often perceived as emptiness, it may be difficult for some readers to imagine a rhetoric of silence, let alone silence as resistant rhetoric. As the examples of Anita Hill, Lani Guinier, and Bill Clinton have demonstrated, silence and silencing can be sites of disciplinary resistance—resistance to pigeonholing that comes with being a nonwhite overachieving female or with being a liberal president. Silence and silencing can also work to resist the regulatory training of sociopolitical culture. In these cases, the attorneys were all expected to speak out, to speak their minds, to persuade, control, dominate. Only Clinton, the only male, the only white person, was able to use his silence to his advantage—and use it he did. He resisted a disciplinary training that prepared him to take the verbal offensive and, instead, remained silent, more powerful than if he had spoken.

As I said in the opening chapter, not all silences are positive, feminist, rhetorical, or successful. Silence can deploy power—as in the case of Bill Clinton, whose use of silence was the most successful, at least in the short run: he found a way to dis-appoint Guinier. And to some extent and for a while, Anita Hill also deployed the rhetorical power of silence. But silence can also defer to power—as in the case of Lani Guinier, and, to some extent, Hill. It all depends. In the long run, the silences and silencings of Hill and Guinier seem to have carried with them far more resistance and a tranformative potential than the short-lived silence of Clinton. Both of these women were indeed silenced. But when nonwhite overachieving women come out of their silence, they can deploy their resistance to greater influence than they might ever have if they had spoken and been heard at the time. And such resistance can be used to confront, resist, and transform—even the discipline of rhetoric.

4
Attesting Silence

It is important to remember that in the nineteenth century,
women—all women, were forbidden by law to speak in public
meetings. Society depended on their muteness.
                    —Adrienne Rich, "Invisibility in Academe"

SILENCE: AN ACCEPTED STATE OF OLD CITY AFFAIRS

As William Jefferson Clinton's two-term presidency came to a close, the news-
papers were filled with speculations about his legacy. Would he go down in history as one of the finest American presidents, in the company of Franklin Delano
Roosevelt? Would he make the second tier, with Harry Truman, Theodore
Roosevelt, Andrew Jackson, and Ronald Reagan? Would he be remembered for
the balanced budget, reduced inflation and unemployment, a record Dow, mi-
nuscule interest rates, and then record-low oil? Would his legacy be one of me-
diocrity, in a category with Calvin Coolidge, Grover Cleveland, and William
Howard Taft? Or could his legacy be worse?

Bill Clinton would be the third president in history to face impeachment
proceedings, following the footsteps of Andrew Johnson and Richard M. Nixon.[1]
Clinton was suspended from the Arkansas bar for five years and fined $25,000;
he was also suspended from the Supreme Court bar. Indeed, his legacy could be
even worse. As Jacob Weisberg writes, "Clinton is now and probably forever our
priapic President, who takes his place alongside our drunken President, Ulysses
S. Grant, our napping President, Calvin Coolidge, and our treacherous President,
Richard Nixon" (35). For certain, the history books will include references to his
sexual escapades, the ones he has admitted to as well as the ones to those still
silenced and silent. Old City society depends on women's muteness in such
matters of the heart and flesh, but such silence is, after all, "a game of dodgeball
at dusk— / a matter of time 'til someone knocks you out of the circle" (Becker,
"Against" 79).

Despite "the desperate attempts at recontainment of the narratives," spoken
silences knocked Clinton out of the circle, the aureole of goodness and trustwor-
thiness (Barlowe 21). Not only has our nation listened endlessly to broken silences,

it has witnessed silencing of sexualized, politicized women in connection with Clinton, some of whom admit that they, like Lani Guinier, had acquiesced in their own silencing, some, like Guinier, by the hope of a job. They broke their silence for what they believed to be better reasons, that is, except for Monica Lewinsky, who, like Hester Prynne, wanted to protect the man she thought she loved. Not surprisingly, the media focused on the tawdry details and political ramifications of these events. Rhetorical analyses have focused on what was spoken or written during this time. I will examine the spoken, too, but only as a means to locate the unspoken, the ways men and women used silence and silencing to protect their positions.

As I chart the narrative of this scandal, I will trace the rhetorical uses of silence and silencing that accompany each scenario, for these public performances offer rhetoricians a series of studies in purposeful and often effective silence. The legal considerations—cover-up, suppression of evidence, and intimidation of witnesses—also provide scholars new ways to consider silence and silencing rhetorically. The women involved in these cases often supplied reasons for their silences and then their speaking, reasons that, although specific, went mostly unheard. The man involved supplied reasons as well. Thus, the powerful and subordinated alike provide us with rhetorical reasons for their purposeful uses of silence. In short, this chapter analyzes the silence and silencing (and disclosure) of all the president's women.

ALL THE PRESIDENT'S WOMEN

And when we speak we are afraid our words will not be heard nor welcome, . . . but it is better to speak remembering we were never meant to survive.

—Audre Lorde, "Litany for Survival"

After Bill Clinton became president, woman after woman came forward (or was thrust forward), linking her name with his and thereby becoming a household name. Comprising a list that would come to be known as "all the president's women," Juanita Broaddrick, Gennifer Flowers, Paula Corbin Jones, Kathleen Willey, Monica Lewinsky, Hillary Rodham Clinton, and Chelsea Clinton have all taken their turn upon the national stage, some spending longer on stage than others. Hillary Rodham Clinton and her daughter would have entered and remained in the spotlight no matter what, given their position in the national order of things. But such is not the case for Broaddrick, Flowers, Jones, Willey, and Lewinsky. Had these women remained silent, they might have gone through life without having registered a blip on the screen of national consciousness. Instead, each of these women disclosed tales of sex, lies, and, in the case of both Flowers and Lewinsky, audiotapes. Not one of these stories was welcomed; not one of the women was universally believed. It was as though her motive could color her story, discolor the truth. Like Anita Hill, she should have remained silent—threats and subpoenas notwithstanding.

Again and again, the abiding Janus-question was posed: Why had she remained silent? Why was she speaking now? The same question that haunted Anita Hill would haunt most of these women (Lewinsky would be the exception, as I explain below).

Their situations at the intersection of allegedly illicit sex and private silence invoke images of Hester Prynne, our nation's cultural icon of the "bad" but desirable woman, the woman who would be punished.[2] Nathaniel Hawthorne's most famous character holds on to her dignity while she holds back her words:

> "Hester Prynne, . . . if thou feelest it to be for thou soul's peace, and that thy earthly punishment will thereby be made more effectual to salvation, I charge thee to speak out the name of thy fellow-sinner . . . ! Be not silent from any mistaken pity and tenderness for him. . . ."
> "I will not speak!" answered Hester. (Hawthorne 68–69)

As this section will attest, some of the president's women spoke publicly within a few years (Paula Corbin Jones, for instance), while others held on to their silence much longer (Juanita Broaddrick, Gennifer Flowers, and Kathleen Willey). The youngest of his sexualized women, Monica Lewinsky broke her public silence only when she faced the twentieth-century equivalent to puritanical Roger Chillingworth, Ken Starr. Chelsea Clinton, the youngest of them all, has never broken her silence about her father's behavior or silences. Her mother, however, Hillary Rodham Clinton, has "never let the American public feel that Bill had humiliated her to the point of silence. She [is] always front and center as his staunchest defender" (Olson 197).

All of these women have operated in the space between speech and silence—as well as between secrecy and disclosure—and each of them inhabited the space differently and for different reasons. Their speech and silence, then, cannot be read uniformly, as instances of superficial rhetorical display. Instead, the secrets and disclosure of all the president's women are contradictable speech acts that should be read as rhetorical forms, instantiated, as Edwin Black tells us, as "commonplaces with uncommon powers of implication and entailment" (134).

THAT'S GENNIFER, WITH A "G"

From A to G.

Although the U.S. press continues to invade the privacy of our public figures, the populist news outlets—from tabloid television and talk radio to Drudge

Reports and Oliver Stone's conspiracy-theory films—routinely invade their secrets. Spurred on, no doubt, by a reading and watching public that savors hidden scandals and longs for "the catharsis that follows discovery and *peripeteia*,"[3]
these news outlets apparently control the circulation of controversial, murky, or
intensely private (and embarrassing) news stories, making little distinction between conventional privacy and unsavory secrecy (Black 138).[4]

Threatened with unauthorized tabloid stories, Gennifer Flowers felt coerced
into breaking her silence, revealing her secrets, and cooperating with the *Star*
before an inaccurate account of her affair with presidential-hopeful Bill Clinton
hit the stands.[5] Edwin Black refers to the press's scandal mongering, which would
dog Clinton throughout most of his presidency, as the "rhetorical form of
[uncontradictable] disclosure in an epideictic mode" (138). The implications and
entailment of Gennifer Flowers's disclosures did not cease; they snowballed their
way to Monica Lewinsky and impeachment proceedings. But for the then-can-
didate and his wife, responding to the threatened disclosures was their first order of business.

Bill and Hillary Clinton arranged to speak to the biggest television viewing
audience of the year, on *60 Minutes* directly following the Super Bowl. Conser-
vatively dressed, well-spoken, seemingly upright, and holding hands, the Clintons
instantly, although only temporarily, overpowered the rumors with their com-
bined media effect.[6] They agreed to disclosure, but only within the constraints
of negotiated ground rules, which specifically prohibited the on-air use of the
"A" word (the Clintons' term for "adultery"). Thus, host Steve Kroft tossed only
puffballs, allowing the candidate to deny an affair with Flowers and describe her
as "only" as a friendly acquaintance. Together, the couple admitted to unspeci-
fied "wrongdoing" and "pain" in their marriage and earnestly announced that
they had "moved on." Admitting to pain was as far as the couple went toward
admitting any extramarital liaisons, but in doing so, they also admitted that Bill's
behavior was not a secret; it was private.[7]

In fact, Hillary firmly established what would become her trademark code of
silence, which she refers to as "the zone of privacy." Taking charge of the interview, she said:

> There isn't a person watching this *[60 Minutes]* who would feel comfortable
> sitting on this couch detailing everything that ever went on in their life or
> their marriage. And I think it's real dangerous in this county if we don't have
> some zone of privacy for everybody. . . . We've gone further than anybody we
> know of and that's all we're going to say. (qtd. in Brock, *Seduction* 255)

Bill and Hillary Clinton would not go as far as Gennifer Flowers felt she had
to go.

The woman in red speaks. A former television news reporter, nightclub singer, and Arkansas state employee, Flowers had already established a measure of celebrity in her home state before she faced the CNN camera crews and the bright lights the following afternoon at the Waldorf Astoria in New York to break her silence. Instantly, she was forever disadvantaged. Not having a professional handler (nor the strategic brilliance of Hillary), she made the mistake of appearing as the "other" woman in a scarlet suit.

Whereas Bill and Hillary had righteously told Kroft that being "any more specific about what's happened in the privacy of our life together is irrelevant to anybody besides us" (Sheehy 200), Flowers revealed that she and Bill had committed the "A" word for twelve years (1977–89); she had reluctantly aborted Clinton's child (while he was serving as Arkansas attorney-general); and after they broke off their relationship, they had remained friendly enough for then–Arkansas governor Clinton to arrange employment for her. As her story continued to unfold, Flowers embraced the opportunity to provide specific details—replete with audiotaped conversations—in the hope that by doing so, she would be believed, could control the media, and ensure her "personal safety and financial security" (*Gennifer* 107).

But without media clout and the concomitant opportunity to establish her own guidelines, the public did not return her embrace. Instead of finding herself believed, she found herself negotiating questions of condom use and instantly transformed into a late-night joke. As Black explains, a move such as Flowers's, from secrecy to disclosure, stimulates an incoherent and partially contradictory response:

> We may have a general distaste for secrecy, but it does not follow that we are uniformly comfortable with disclosure. . . . [A large] number of people would embrace the proposition not that concealment is good, but—in a variant on Pope's famous line—that knowledge can be dangerous. . . . One can inquire too far. One can reveal too much. Some things are better left unknown. (147–48)

So far as her rhetorical situation, Flowers had revealed too much in her effort to speak and control the truth.

A faithful silence? Yet even this scarlet woman would be asked why she had remained silent all these years. "'I will keep thy secret,' said Hester . . . and she took the oath" (Hawthorne 77). Prynne kept the secret; Flowers did not. Prynne remains the silent heroine; Flowers would not.

According to Flowers, she had agreed to remain silent for a number of reasons: Clinton had expressly asked her to deny their relationship; she continued to feel affection and loyalty toward him; and she wanted to get on with her own personal life. Moreover, she was wary, given what she claimed she knew about the verbal, financial, and physical intimidation (accidents, deaths, and disappearances) of other people who had crossed Clinton.[8] So she had faithfully remained silent—that is, until the *Star* broke the story of their affair, persuading her that she might as well accept the money they were offering her because they were going to run the story with or without her.

Flowers's name had arisen twice before: once, when former Arkansas state trooper Larry Nichols charged that Clinton had used state funds to maintain sexual relations with Flowers (and others), and again, when Clinton was charged with using undue influence to provide Flowers a job. When the Nichols case hit the news waves, Flowers threatened slander, a move that would come to haunt her when the *Star* story broke. That case sputtered out, but the second charge, relating to the provenience of her state job, unleashed an insatiable interest in her relationship with Clinton and compromised her disclosure as well as her silence.

Like Anita Hill, Flowers—as well as her disclosure—would be suspect. Despite her detailed reasoning for remaining silent and then for speaking out, she might be believed but never respected. If she had managed to hold her secret for years, why disclose it now? After all, "disclosure as a mediate device, as a short-range instrument, has a character different from disclosure used to achieve ultimate, conclusive aims," and the same difference applies in reverse to secret keeping (Black 138). So Flowers lost in two ways: because she sold her story to the *Star,* her disclosure was suspect; because then-governor Clinton helped her obtain and then keep a position with the Arkansas *Appeal Tribune,* her secrecy was considered to have been merely self-serving. To most observers, then, Flowers's silence and speaking out were instrumental—they helped her achieve her purpose. Because they were not ends in and of themselves (silence for privacy's sake, speaking out for the sake of openness, for instance), observers drew a moral difference.

Breaking the faith; breaking the silence. In 1992, the *Star* launched the Flowers story, and Clinton dodged the attack, successfully reaching the presidency. The silence of his women-friends was paramount to his political success. To that end, Clinton's chief-of-staff, Betsey Wright, allegedly handled the "bimbo eruptions." And, according to the testimony of several women, Clinton specifically asked them to remain silent. Under deposition, Flowers would recount the ways she had been persuaded to agree to her own silencing, to keep their secret:

> On several occasions, I discussed with Bill Clinton the subject of inquiries by the media about our relationship. He told me to continue to deny our relationship, that if we would stick together, everything would be okay. In one conversation which occurred while Bill Clinton was running for the Democratic Presidential nomination in 1991, we were discussing media coverage of Larry Nichols' lawsuit and the women who were alleged in the complaint in

that lawsuit to have had affairs with Bill Clinton. In that context he said [and she refers to taped conversations]: ". . . if all the people who are named deny it. That's all, I mean, I expect them to look into it and interview you and everything, uh, but I just think that if everybody is on the record denying it, you got no problem." ("Declaration")

In her book, Flowers writes, "I took Bill at his word when he said all I had to do was deny, deny, deny—no one could prove anything" (*Gennifer* 99). For years, she inhabited a purposeful silence that signaled her loyalty to Clinton. But as it turned out, maintaining that silence would not be possible for her.

By her own account, Flowers had agreed to deny. She had agreed to remain silent—that is, until she felt forced to speak out and admit. And once she spoke, she revealed that she had been keeping secrets. Silence and secret-keeping can appear the same, but they are not. Yet often the categories overlap until the silence is broken to reveal its character. Whereas a silence does not automatically register moral value, a secret does. Silence does not involuntarily indicate guilt or innocence, complicity or detachment, positive or negative. Keeping a secret, however, registers moral value, for secrets are a means to prevent change, maintain the status quo, exert stable control over the external world and intrapersonal tensions. A secret possesses value in that it is a mystery that can be dissipated only by disclosure. Secrets are ever susceptible to threat in ways silence is not. Therefore, Flowers's silence indicated very little, but her secrets registered as commitments.

Flowers's secrets and silence were articulated commitments to Clinton. Her silence, dependent on secrets, concerned a situation that at least two people knew about, talked about, and agreed to deny from others. According to Johannesen's twenty functions of silence, she may have remained silent because of function 11: "The person is in awe, or raptly attentive, or emotionally overcome"; function 16: "The person's silence reflects concern for not saying anything to hurt another person"; or function 20: "The person's silence reflects empathic exchange, the companionship of shared mood or insight" (29–30). But then, according to George P. Rice, everyone has "the right to be silent," "the right *not* to say what one *knows*" (352). Clearly, Flowers had reasons for remaining silent and for keeping her secret, and in avoiding the inadvertent cheapening of her story. The case of Paula Corbin Jones would be different.

Not long after the election, another Arkansas woman, incensed clerical worker Paula Corbin Jones, ignited yet another investigation. Jones did not have a story; she had a law suit, and she was shifting the focus on Clinton from adultery to "sexual harassment," one of the dirtiest words of the decade as the William Kennedy Smith trial, the Hill-Thomas hearings, the Bob Packwood resignation, and the Lt. Kelly Flinn dishonorable discharge would attest.[9] Hill's allegations, in particular, had rocked the national consciousness to the point that even the ever-leery press took sexual harassment charges seriously, awarding sexual harassment the status of an important political issue. For President Clinton, then, the arrival of Jones would change the playing field forever—as well as the program of players, many of whom had been unwillingly drafted into the game. Adultery was one thing for a president, but sexual harassment, especially as it might constitute a pattern of reckless presidential behavior, would be an entirely different ball game. As the charges unfolded, so did the silences, silencing, and secrets, all of which were used to rhetorical purpose.

PAULA JONES: NOT THAT KIND OF GIRL

> Feminists turned up their noses at the charges against Bill Clinton made by Paula Jones or joked about her "white trash" looks and manner or failed to attack those who judged her merits on class and taste. I guess this means that if one is lower ranked or lower born abuse is not abuse, a kiss is not a kiss.
>
> —Stanley Crouch, "The Huffing and Puffing Military Blues"

A Kiss Is Not a Kiss

Paula Corbin Jones never had an affair with Bill Clinton. The unmarried Paula Corbin claimed that she had been propositioned by the then-governor of Arkansas, who invited her to his hotel room, fondled her, and then exposed himself: "He asked me would I kiss it. He goes—you know, I can see the look on his face right now. He asked me, 'Would you kiss it for me?' I mean it was disgusting" (Jones).

Three years after the alleged incident, *American Spectator*'s David Brock published his anti-Clinton exposé, "Living with the Clintons," and mentioned "Paula" as a Clinton girlfriend wannabe. Clinton staffer Danny Ferguson, who had spun the story of sex and intrigue, told Brock that after meeting the governor in an Arkansas hotel room, "Paula" had offered her availability to be "Clinton's regular girlfriend if he so desired" (26).[10] Like Anita Hill, the officially silent Jones had confided to some close friends, one of whom told her about the article. Jones was humiliated. After all, as she would respond many times over the years to come, she was simply "not that kind of girl." Jones wanted a public apology—not from Clinton, but from Ferguson—and she would not be silent until she received one.

Might Someone Listen?

> There is an immense difference between having permission to speak and enjoying the hope that someone might actually listen to you.
>
> —Carol Lee Flinders, *At the Root of This Longing*

Because no one would apologize to her—not Ferguson, not Brock, not Clinton—
Paula Jones moved forward with a lawsuit.[11] Her lawsuit prompted Clinton to
prepare a public statement that he never delivered:

> I have no recollection of meeting Paula Jones on May 8, 1991, in a room at
> the Excelsior Hotel. However, I do not challenge the claim that we met there
> and I may very well have met her in the past. She did not engage in any im-
> proper sexual conduct. I regret the untrue assertions which have been made
> about her conduct which may have adversely challenged her character and
> good name. I have no further comment on my previous statements about my
> own conduct. Neither I nor my staff will have any further comment on this
> matter. (qtd. in Toobin 44)

Clinton was willing to release—but not speak the words himself—the preceding statement, distancing himself from his words, a purposeful rhetorical stance.
But Jones would not accept that: she wanted the president to speak his own
apology publicly—as well as a financial settlement.

Buoyed by the support of what Hillary Rodham Clinton would refer to as a
"vast right-wing conspiracy," Jones proceeded with her complaint, seeking
$700,000 in damages and charging President Clinton with having sexually ha-
rassed and assaulted her, conspiring with a state trooper to entice her into a sexual
liaison, and defaming her character (in order to silence her) in subsequent remarks to the news media (Biskupic).

By the time Jones's case would finally close, seven years after the alleged incident at the Excelsior Hotel, it had transformed from one of proving that she was
a good person to proving that Clinton was a bad person, from defending her
honor on the sexual front to mortifying Clinton with sexual details. In its transformation, the case snowballed into a national sex scandal that damaged an un-
told number of lives, humiliated many more women than Paula Jones and the
Jane Does, forced two Speakers of the House to resign,[12] and led to impeachment proceedings against the president.

Clinton would not settle, given his rightful mistrust of the entire situation
and a battle strategy he and especially his wife had perfected: "We've learned our
lesson about how you stand up, answer your critics, and then counterpunch as
hard as you can" (H. Clinton, qtd. in Brock, *Seduction* 253).[13] Had Monica
Lewinsky never entered the picture or the Oval Office, the Clintons' battle plan
might have worked.

You're a Smart Girl, a Silent Girl

During her deposition, Paula Jones recounted the "kiss it" episode and added
two additional and crucial transactions: first of all, after she had asserted that she

was not "that kind of girl," Clinton had assured her that he did not want her to do anything she did not want to do. But, according to Jones, Clinton then changed his strategy: even if she was not "that kind" of girl, surely she was a "smart girl," one who would keep silent. According to Jones, as she walked toward the door, to leave the hotel room, Clinton mentioned again that he knew her boss, held the door shut for a moment, and finally asked her to keep silent about the incident:

> I said, "I've got to be going. I've got to go back to the registration desk. I'm going to get in trouble." He pulled up, you know, stood up. And he was just as red as he could be. You could tell I had embarrassed him so bad because he probably expected me to do something. . . .
>
> And he said, "Well, you know, if you have any trouble, I want you to have Dave Herrington [her boss] call me immediately." And that was the second time he had mentioned Dave Herrington. And then I proceeded to go on to the door and he rushed up behind me. I started to open up the door, and he put his hand on the door to where I could not open it up any further, and he stopped me and he says, "You're a smart girl, let's keep this between our-selves." (Jones)

Jones interpreted this second incident as a threat: "He confined me for a mo-ment"; "He was threatening me [when] he said, 'You're a smart girl. Let's keep this between ourselves.' Apparently he didn't want this to get out." Jones added another layer to her initial charge: she had been entreated by Clinton to remain silent. The imperative mood of "let's keep this between ourselves" signaled the silencing of a low-level clerical worker by the governor of Arkansas.

Jones's attorneys worked hard to represent this interaction as one of textbook sexual harassment: an advance is made, rejected, and a loss follows. But Jones's attorneys could not demonstrate that they had a case, let alone verify that Jones had suffered workplace loss. U.S. District Court Judge Susan Webber Wright—after unsuccessfully pushing both parties to settle—dismissed the initial claim, ruling that "Although the governor's alleged conduct, if true, may certainly be boorish and offensive, even a most charitable reading of the record in this case fails to reveal a basis for a claim" (Nichols).[14] In other words, the plaintiff pro-vided no proof of emotional affliction or workplace punishment.[15]

The case was not settled until it had made its way to the U.S. Supreme Court. Jones dropped her sexual harassment lawsuit against President Clinton in return for $850,000 but no apology or admission of guilt.

Remaining unsettled, however, is the question of whether Clinton asked her to remain silent about their twenty-minute encounter, and, if so, what he im-plied by that request. After all, he knew what power and politics could do to a man: "Politics gives guys so much power and such big egos they tend to behave badly toward women," Clinton told his friend Mandy Merck. "And I hope I never get into that" (qtd. in Maraniss 218).[16]

But power and politics do make for big egos, especially in terms of silence and silencing. Paula Jones did not agree to the silencing: on the same day as her alleged encounter with Clinton, she told her story to two friends and two relatives. Whether she would have remained legally silent were it not for the Brock story is a matter of conjecture. What is certain is this: Jones's lawsuit ignited a series of sexual disclosures, making details of Clinton's womanizing public knowledge and common conversation.

From Unspoken to Undone

During the discovery deposition Jones's lawsuit entailed, President Clinton was required by the rules of evidence to speak to three specific charges: "the cover-up, suppression of evidence, the intimidation of witnesses in a concerted, systematic effort to prevent our client [Paula Jones] and others like her from developing cases that they might bring" (qtd. in Toobin 210). Considered comprehensively, the charges had to do with power and politics, silence and silencing.

President Clinton faced a razor-sharp line of questioning, aimed at forcing his reluctant disclosure: "Mr. President, did Kathleen Willey ever give you permission to touch her breasts?"; "Did you ever have an extramarital sexual affair with Monica Lewinsky?"; "During the 1992 campaign, did you give Betsey Wright the responsibility to deal with rumors about alleged extramarital affairs involving you?" (qtd. in Toobin 210).[17] "Did you ever have sexual relations with Gennifer Flowers?" In response to this last question, Clinton suddenly revised his *60 Minutes* performance, saying "Once [in] 1977."[18]

That last remark would open what came to be called "Zippergate." Though dressed in issues of sexual harassment, job discrimination, and silencing, the substance of the Jones v. Clinton case became, for better or worse, known by that term. Therefore, when Clinton gave his grand jury testimony, eight months later, he told them that his "goal in [that] deposition was to be truthful, but not particularly helpful. [He] did not wish to do the work of the Jones lawyers" ("Grand Jury Testimony").

Deeply invested in a plan to prove Clinton's pattern of sexual predation and intimidation of potential witnesses, the Jones phalanx of attorneys marched onward, dragging a lawsuit behind them.[19]

SEVEN JANES ALL IN A ROW

Listen to the women's voices. Listen to the silences, the unasked questions, the blanks. Listen to the small, soft voices, often courageously trying to speak up. Voices of women taught early that tones of confidence, challenge, anger, or assertiveness, are strident and unfeminine.

—Adrienne Rich, "Taking Women Students Seriously"

Ad Hominem, ad Nauseam.

Sex, sex, and more sex—whether it was Clinton's involvement in consensual sex ("Once, [in] 1977"), his allegedly crude proposition ("Kiss it"), or his sexual harassment (cf. Juanita Broaddrick, below), the gradations and variations of Clinton's alleged sexual behavior did not pose a problem for the Jones legal team. Despite their three aforementioned allegations, they focused on two specific allegations: sex and silencing.[20]

The Jones legal team set out to demonstrate that Clinton had a dark sexual past and present punctuated with a continual pattern of using his sociopolitical power to silence women. To support this argument, the attorneys' plan was to call forward "witnesses that relate to the pattern and practice issue"; in other words, they planned to bring a number of women forward, all of whom would be known as "Jane Doe," who would testify that Clinton had preyed upon them sexually and then intimidated them into silence.

The legal team limited the number of Jane Does to seven white women, reflecting on only their words and experiences, and deflecting everyone else, female and male alike—a very deliberate Burkean move. In limiting the narrative to seven Jane Does, and focusing steadily on them, the team's reflection of reality was also a selection of reality, and to this extent, it functioned also as a deflection of reality (Burke, *Language* 45). Who can say how many other women—and men—were written out of the narrative and thus silenced at the same time that these seven women were forced to speak against their will?

Of all the names circulating as Clinton "victims," lovers, acquaintances, or accusers, and of the seven Jane Does, only Paula Jones initiated her own coming forward. The seven Janes moved from silence to voice not by their own volition, but rather by means of a subpoena.

Ad Feminam, ad Nauseam

Experience is at once always already an interpretation *and* something that needs to be interpreted. What counts as experience is neither self-evident nor straightforward: it is always contested, and always therefore political.

—Joan C. Scott, "The Evidence of Experience"

Marilyn Jo Jenkins, Beth Coulson, Dolly Kyle Browning, Kathleen Willey, Gennifer Flowers, Monica Lewinsky, and Shelia Davis Lawrence—seven Jane

Does subpoenaed and accounted for. The Supreme Court decided that the case could, indeed, go forward against a sitting president. The depositions and hearings were moved (along with Judge Wright) from Pine Bluffs, Arkansas, to Washington, D.C. And independent counsel Kenneth Starr, with jurisdiction over Whitewater, Filegate, and Travelgate, suddenly found a way to expand his investigation to include Zippergate. All the (sitting) ducks (including a soon-to-be lame duck resident) were in a row.

A resistant Willey. Kathleen Willey was one of the most reluctant witnesses to speak in response to a subpoena.[21] A longtime Democratic donor, one suddenly dealing with financial disaster, Willey was positioned well enough to ask the president for paid employment. During her brief appointment with him, he allegedly groped her. Although she had kept publicly silent for several years about the incident, Willey immediately told Linda Tripp and Julie Hyatt Steele at the time. (Neither woman supported Willey when the story was eventually disclosed). When her name was circulated to Jones's attorneys and she found herself legally forced to speak publicly about the alleged incident, Willey responded like the best of unwilling witnesses: she answered every question, yet employed a rhetoric of silence, of reticence:

Q: And then what happened?
A: Then he hugged me again and said that they [the White House staff] would try to help me.

. . . . .

Q: And please describe the exact physical nature of the hug.
A: It was a hug.
Q: Is that all? Just an embrace?
A: It was a hug.
Q: Can you describe it any more fully than that?
A: Just a big hug. (Willey)

Willey expands on none of her answers, revealing nothing in her brief responses. Johannesen might say that Willey's reticence reflected "concern for not saying anything to hurt another person" (30). But that other person may have been Willey herself. After all, to speak publicly about the incident could be painful, embarrassing, even harmful to her.

As the deposition continues, Willey maintains her passive resistance to the line of questioning, even though she had negotiated the terms of her testimony well beforehand with Ken Starr's office. Her answers are flat and noncommittal:

Q: Was there any kissing involved during that hug?
A: There was an attempt.
Q: Please describe that as fully as you can.

A: He attempted to kiss me.

Q: Mr. Clinton did?

A: Yes.

Q: On the lips?

A: Yes.

Q: Anyplace else? On the neck?

A: No.

Willey's "yes" and "no" answers constitute a variation on silence, a rhetoric of withholding that appears to merge with the silence of the sexually harassed, those bereft of culturally legitimated vocabularies and interpretations. There are simply "no words to depict sexualized interactions that transpire out[side] of the contexts conventionally associated with sexuality" (Wood 353).

Willey seemed to understand that no matter what she said—or left unspoken—someone more powerful than she (the media, Starr's office, the president) would get to "assign meanings to particular events and practices" (Wood 395). That someone would also determine "how those meanings . . . circulate and acquire factual status" (Wood 395).

Everyone who was following the media coverage of Flowers or Jones would realize this fact, especially someone who had been subpoenaed. Willey seemed to know intuitively that she would be acceptable to those in power only if her speech was indirect or nonaggressive, that is, "rational." To enhance that rationality, she employs another variation on silence, a rhetoric of forgetfulness, as if not remembering could be equated with disinterest:

Q: Did you allow him to kiss you?

A: I don't think so.

Q: Was he successful in kissing you?

A: I can't remember.

Q: It could be that he was successful?

A: It could be that he wasn't. I don't remember.

. . . .

Q: Did he ever move his arms to any other portion on your body?

A: I don't recall.

Q: Is it possible that he did?

A: I don't recall . . .

. . . .

Q: What were you wearing on that occasion?

A: I don't have the faintest idea.

Q: Can you tell us whether it was dress or pants?

A: I don't remember.

. . . .

Q: Did Mr. Clinton ever place his hands on any part of your buttocks?

A: I don't remember . . .

Q: You can't categorically say he did not; is that correct?

A: Correct.

Q: Did Mr. Clinton ever seek to take either of your hands and place it on his body anyplace?

A: Yes.

Q: Please describe that . . .

A: He put his hands—he put my hands on his genitals.

Q: Which hand?

A: I don't recall.

Q: And approximately how long did that last?

A: I don't recall.

. . . .

Q: Did you resist?

A: Yes.

Q: How?

A: I just resisted.

No explanations, no elaborations—just single-word answers to the questions was all Willey would give. She endured the questioning, flaring up only when asked what she was wearing, and closed her deposition by admitting that she had wanted and offered to put "that" (the groping incident) behind her in terms of her ongoing professional relationship with the president.[22]

Though many wondered why she had remained silent for so long, few doubted that Willey was telling the truth, what very little of it she was willing to reveal through the screen of her silence. By all media accounts, she was a credible witness: to wit, she had fought the subpoena, resisted testifying, invoked forgetfulness rather than speculation, and appeared with much-commented-upon "sensible" hair, high cheekbones, and soft and halting voice (the media's code for upper-middle-class).[23] Furthermore, she had withstood a terrible blow: while she was making her way to see the president on that eventful day, her husband was committing suicide out of despair and embarrassment—a tragedy that enhanced Willey's credibility as someone who has suffered "enough."

Her self-silencing not withstanding, she appeared on *60 Minutes* to tell her story to the avuncular Ed Bradley, stammering as she explained her position of silence, claiming that she would have carried Clinton's grope "to the grave," if she had not been compelled by court to answer questions under oath. Yet on that Sunday night, she would speak out, "I just think that it's time to tell this story.

Too many lies are being told. Too many lives are being ruined. And I think it's time for the truth to come out" (qtd. in P. Baker). When Bradley asked her if Clinton had committed perjury by denying any sexual contact with her during his own deposition, Willey said, "Yes."

Silence and credibility. Although she never overgendered, outclassed, or over-powered Clinton, Willey did come out far ahead of the other women involved in the case. Not only did she look right, dress right, and talk right, but she had done the right thing since the beginning: she had remained silent, a testament to her gendered position and subordination. Like all good women, all credible women—like all *ladies*—Willey had remained silent, just as conduct manuals and cultural ideology have trained women to be: "be reserved for those occasions, where there is something going on, that you disapprove of; a grave countenance is then your best protest against the folly of those around you, and will often produce a better effect than words" (Farrar 293).[24] Following a circular argument, her silence made her credible; her credibility kept her silent; therefore, assenting to silence protects the powerful and maintains the powerlessness of the silenced and therefore the credible lady.

Yet when she was forcibly moved to disclosure, she was asked the reason she had remained silent—had she been silenced? Hers was a Catch-22 situation: she was a credible witness because she had remained silent; yet, when she was legally forced to move from silence to voice (to become a witness), the reason for her silence was challenged. Willey would say that she had never come forward, let alone filed a complaint because she "was embarrassed for the President's behavior. And I saw no benefit whatsoever in filing a complaint. I mean, who do you file a complaint with, anyway, when it's the President? Where do you go?" (qtd. in P. Baker). Left unspoken is any mention of her own personal embarrassment; instead, she emphasized her need for employment, full-time employment that she never obtained despite her persistence.

Her need for employment was the only reason she supplied for her self-silencing, for bombarding the president with personal notes after the incident, and for offering to put the incident behind her (like Lani Guinier had done some five years before[25]):

> I never hid those letters. They were my way of saying, "Hello, I'm still out here. I need a job."[26] I had made a decision that I was going to put that incident behind me.[27] I made that choice, and I'm allowed to make that choice. (qtd. in Isikoff and Thomas 22)

As for whether she enjoyed employment benefits because of or despite the incident, Willey testified under oath:

Q: Has Mr. Clinton at any time ever offered you any employment or favorable benefits in return for sexual favors?

A: No.

Q: Has he ever threatened you that if you didn't engage in sexual activity with him that somehow you would be penalized?

A: No. (Willey)

In all probability, Willey would have remained publicly silent (relatively safe and silent) like most of the other Janes had political and juridical power not forced her to assume the public voice she had avoided for so long. Willey's disclosures offered nothing to support Jones's sexual harassment suit: Willey had neither gained nor lost any employment because of the incident. She self-silenced, and she offered no support to an argument of secrets or silencing.

STARR SEARCH

The women, secretaries, stars, the wives of friends, were symbols and rewards of aggressive privilege. Sneaking around, cleaning up the mess, covering up was all part of the game. . . . it was all good fun to those who knew—part of the thrill of being inside one of the president's closer circles. Keeping the secrets was part of the price of admission, and those who knew didn't tell those who didn't.

—Richard Reeves, *President Kennedy: Profile of Power*

Spurred on by Jones's attorneys, Kenneth Starr's office tried valiantly to demonstrate Bill Clinton's longtime pattern of behavior: professional rewards for women who cooperated sexually and then remained silent; punishment for women who said no or spoke about it later. Thanks, in no small part, to the audiotapes Linda Tripp so carefully made of her young friend Monica Lewinsky, the investigation stayed the course, though it morphed from one of sexual harassment to one of impeachment. Clinton faced charges of perjury, suborning perjury, witness tampering, obstruction of justice, and abuse of power—charges that interest me only insofar as they constitute a culture of concealment, a culture of secrecy, silences, and silencing.

As the investigation moved forward, Monica Lewinsky became perhaps the most well-known Jane Doe of all time. In the process, she also became a national joke, distinguished by her blue dress, her beret, and the unvarnished details of her sexual relationship with the president. But she was not the only Jane Doe whose identity would be revealed, whose sexual relationship with Clinton would be disclosed, whose position of silence would be interrogated.

Some of the other women named in the investigation admitted to having sexual relations with Bill Clinton. Longtime Arkansas FOB (friend of Bill) and Texas attorney Dolly Kyle Browning testified that she had had an off-and-on again sexual relationship with Clinton for three decades, an assertion he denied under oath. Browning also spoke of White House attempts to silence her and threats to "destroy her" if she told her story during the 1992 campaign, when the Flowers story hit the stands.[28] Former Miss America Elizabeth Ward Gracen, who had initially denied any liaison with the president (in compliance with an alleged request from the 1992 Clinton campaign staff), admitted that she "had sex with Bill Clinton, but the important part to me is that I was never pressured. We had an intimate evening. Nothing was ever forced. It was completely consensual" (qtd. in Kennedy). As I said earlier in this chapter, former Miss Arkansas Sally Purdue came forward in 1992 with claims of an affair with Clinton, going as far as appearing on the *Sally Jessy Raphael Show*. But for various reasons, that particular show was never broadcast, and Purdue suddenly became silent and disappeared from the public eye.

Close Friends

Under oath, the other Jane Does diminished the perception that "the White House lies about everything, that [its] credibility is zero" (Michael McCurry, qtd. in Lavelle and Barnes 17). Marketing director for the Arkansas Power and Light Company, Marilyn Jo Denton Jenkins (Jane Doe 1) is the only extracurricular woman that anyone (from the Arkansas state troopers to author Gail Sheehy) claims Bill Clinton truly loved. Though both Jenkins and Clinton swore that they had a close friendship, they both denied a sexual relationship, Clinton's wildly extravagant phone bills to her notwithstanding. Silence and silencing were not an issue in this relationship.

Nor were they an issue in his friendship with Beth Coulson (Jane Doe 2), judge in the Arkansas Court of Appeals and Clinton appointee. Since she was only thirty-two years old when Clinton appointed her to a state judgeship, suspicions were raised that theirs was a *quid pro quo* sexual relationship, that he had rewarded her silence with a political appointment. But in their depositions, they, too, denied any sexual relationship, even though Clinton admitted that he had driven her Jaguar, that they had flown together to visit a mutual friend, and that he had visited her at home, alone.[29] When asked about Coulson's qualifications to serve as a judge in the Arkansas Court of Appeals, Clinton answered:

> She was an intelligent, hard-working person who was a good friend and supporter of mine. And I thought she would make a good judge. The evidence is that she did, I think. . . . [She had never argued even a single case in the

Court of Appeals], but that would put her in the same boat with every other judge. The Court of Appeals was a newly appointed court. The judges were to be elected but I had to appoint the first batch so it [the Court of Appeals] could begin to decide cases, and then there was a system for electing them. After that, they were all elected. (Clinton, "Deposition")

Jane Doe 7 was Sheila Lawrence, widow of Clinton donor and ambassador Larry Lawrence, who denied any sexual relationship with Clinton and threatened to sue political analyst Arianna Huffington for even mentioning Lawrence's name in sexual connection with Clinton. In the end, Lawrence would be better remembered for lying about her husband's war record, a nonexistent record that led to his being disinterred from Arlington National Cemetery.

The Twenty-One-Year Silence

The story of Jane Doe 5, Juanita Broaddrick, however, would startle the nation—not because it told of a forced sexual encounter between nursing home administrator Broaddrick and then-Arkansas Attorney General Bill Clinton, but because the story, kept silent for twenty-one years, was so sordid. The Jones attorneys had been aggressively pursuing the story for months, going so far as wiring one of their private investigators, who approached the unapproachable Broaddrick: "You know it was just a horrible horrible thing for me and I wouldn't relive that for anything" (qtd. in Isikoff 226). Even when faced with their subpoena, Broaddrick would not budge. In fact, she submitted an affidavit, swearing the allegation was untrue.

But when Starr offered her immunity for not telling the whole truth in her 1994 affidavit, she confirmed the long-circulating rumor that Clinton had sexually assaulted her in 1978, and she went on to provide specific reasons for having remained silent. First of all, she could not imagine that anyone would believe her, let alone take on a rape or assault charge against the Arkansas attorney general. Second, she had more to lose than just her reputation. Because Clinton's office oversaw nursing home operations, she risked losing her job, her very livelihood. And third, she was married and having an affair at the time. Therefore, disclosure could do nothing for her—at least, not in 1978.

In 1978, feminist writers and researchers were just beginning to highlight the intimate relationship between language and power; for instance, those who hold the power exercise the right to name the world, including the right to name—or not name—incidents of sexual harassment or assault. By 1993, the situation was had not much improved, at least not according to a Department of Justice study that explained the reason why it still remained so difficult to gather statistics for sexual assaults: "The perceived stigma and the belief that no purpose would be served in reporting the crime prevents an unknown portion of the victims from talking about the event" (qtd. in Faludi, Brownmiller, et al.) Thus, if men define the sexual act as one of merely exercising their power and if women define unwanted sexual acts as somehow their "fault," silence quickly surrounds an unnamed and mostly unseen practice of sexual harassment.[30]

True or not, Broaddrick's account could not shake the nation or threaten Clinton's presidency in any way comparable to the force of Jane Doe 6, Monica Lewinsky.

Jane Doe 6

> All these—all the meanness and agony
>   without end, I sitting look out upon,
> See, hear, and am silent.
>   —Walt Whitman, "I Sit and Look Out"

When the long-silenced Monica Lewinsky spoke into the public sphere on 6 August 1998, she fired up the Clinton scandal until it burned itself out in an expensive, drawn-out settlement with the Jones legal team and with an even more expensive nonimpeachment of the president. She spoke publicly then— yet she was not heard by the public until her gag ordered was lifted on 22 January 2001. In exchange for immunity (she had lied in her affidavit to the Jones attorneys), Lewinsky gave Starr her word, her words, to do with as he pleased, including posting them on the Internet and having them read by an actress on cable news programs.

Lewinsky's name was launched into media circulation when cyberjournalist Matt Drudge released her name along with an account of her relationship with Clinton and mention of audiotaped proof. Soon, the nation would know about sneaking, silencing, and secrets, which included Linda Tripp's wiring and tap- ing, Lewinksy's taped telephone conversations with both Tripp and Clinton, and Lewinsky's titillating narratives for her trusted friends and relatives.[31] But the moment her name was released, by Drudge and then by *Newsweek*'s Isikoff, Lewinsky was suddenly silent (or silenced, we may never know which, for sure). Even though she had already spilled some twenty hours' worth of beans to Tripp and would soon give more than enough "full and truthful testimony" to Starr and the federal prosecutors, she was suddenly silent.

Speaking silence. From July 1998 until January 2001, Starr had her under a gag rule—no interviews, appearances, thought pieces, no appearances on Oprah or Dan Rather (who announced on the nightly news that he was not interested in Lewinksy at all, but he would like to hear the sound of her voice). Eventually, Starr granted permission for Lewinsky to be interviewed by Barbara Walters, which I discuss below.

Starr owned Lewinsky's words, which would soon be circulated by the "Starr Report." When her words (but not her voice) were initially released, Lewinksy denied having a *quid pro quo* relationship with the president:

> I have never had a sexual relationship with the president, he did not propose that we have a sexual relationship, he did not offer me employment or other benefits in exchange for a sexual relationship, [and] he did not deny me employment or other benefits for rejecting a sexual relationship. (Lewinsky)

And the president himself would be televised nationally, wagging a scolding finger, and announcing that he "never had sexual relations with that woman, Miss Lewinsky" (Clinton, "Grand Jury Testimony").

But both of them were soon forced to revise their original testimony, Lewinsky punctuating her hours-long narrative with graphic details surrounding the stain,[32] the cigar, and the phone sex, the president going only as far as to say:

> When I was alone with Ms. Lewinsky on certain occasions in early 1996, and once in early 1997, I engaged in conduct that was wrong. These encounters did not consist of sexual intercourse. They did not constitute sexual relations, as I understood that term to be defined at my January 17th, 1998 deposition.[33] (Clinton, "Grand Jury Testimony")

In one of his few gallant moves, Clinton goes on to say that in terms of Lewinsky's original affidavit, "if she defined sexual relationship in the way I think most Americans do, meaning intercourse, then she told the truth." In other words, Clinton argued with an adolescent's logic, that they had not technically gone "all the way."

Although she was testifying before the grand jury, although her words soon circulated by way of the "Starr Report," Lewinsky was still silenced, for Starr controlled her words. His biggest worry seemed to be that she might talk out of school about his ongoing investigation. Given Lewinsky's history of disclosing details of her private life to her friends at work, her friends from childhood, and her mother, Starr's worry was a legitimate one. Still, Starr's primary purpose was to discover whether Clinton had influenced, suborned, intimidated, or, in other words, "silenced" Monica Lewinsky.[34]

A rhetorical silence of loyalty (and subordination). According to the Starr team, whether Clinton and Lewinsky shared a sexual relationship was not the issue—whether they had lied about it was. And it was only at the precise coordinates of pornographic and gynecological details that Starr might determine whether Clinton tampered with witnesses or obstructed justice in the Jones investigation, both charges being variations on silencing. So it was that if Clinton had silenced Lewinsky in any way, if he had suborned her perjury, if he had exchanged em-

ployment opportunities for her continued silence, then he had committed perjury and could be impeached.

Clinton's silencing of Lewinsky was the prime issue, even in the face of
Lewinsky's self-silencing: "I was prepared to deny the affair because of my love
for and loyalty to the President" (qtd. in Morton 206). She was willing to silence
herself, to keep their secret, out of loyalty to her president, whom she imagined
was "her" man. As she admitted, her biggest worry during her questioning and
her testimony had been how she could support Clinton through the Paula Jones
case, which she considered "bunk" (Lewinsky, "Grand Jury Testimony").

Given her loyalty, Lewinsky would never admit any sort of *quid pro quo* arrangement with the president, not sex for a job, not silence for a better job. She
had been in love: "I was in love with him"; "I never expected to fall in love with
the President"; "I liked being with him; he made me feel attractive, but I didn't
think I would fall in love with him. It was just fun and I would be lying if part
of the excitement was not that it was the President" ("Grand Jury Testimony";
"Grand Jury Testimony"; qtd. in Morton 82).[35] She supplied the Starr investigation with sexual details, but she held fast to her silence when it came time to help
the investigation develop obstruction of justice charges.

She agreed that she had remained silent on a number of issues or had given
misleading information, but she would not agree that she had accepted her silencing in exchange for keeping or getting a job. "No one asked me to lie," she
testified before the grand jury, "but no one discouraged me either." True, she and
the president had devised a cover story for why she visited his office:

> Q: You have testified previously that you tried to maintain secrecy regard-
> ing this relationship—and we're talking about obviously with the Presi-
> dent. Is that true?
>
> A: Yes.
>
> . . . .
>
> Q: And prior to being on the [Jones] witness list, you both spoke about de-
> nying this relationship if asked?
>
> A: Yes. That was discussed. (Lewinsky, "Grand Jury Testimony")

True, she had asked the president for a good job in New York, but only after
she had been fired from the White House, exiled to a job in the Pentagon that
she despised, and left with her phone calls unreturned. True, she did threaten to
tell her parents exactly why she was not returning to the White House, but it
was a "threat to him as a man and not a threat to him as president" (Lewinsky,
"Grand Jury Testimony"). Still, her threat was not a part of any *quid pro quo*
arrangement because, according to Lewinsky, it was counterfeit: "I never would
have done that. I think it was more—the way I felt was, you know, you [the

president] should remember that I sort of—I've been a good girl until now" (Lewinsky, "Grand Jury Testimony").[36]

The good girl, the silent girl. Indeed, she had followed the cultural norms of the good girl, one committed to an unequal emotional arrangement; the president himself referred to her as a "good girl." And this good girl willingly silences her self as he speaks publicly, going so far as to betray her. This good girl keeps the secrets that help her man through difficulties at the same time that he disposes of her:

> It's from my understanding about what he testified on Monday . . . that this was a service contract, that all I did was perform oral sex on him and that that's all that this relationship was. And it was a lot more than that to me and I thought it was a lot more than that.
>
> . . . I feel very responsible for a lot of what's happened, you know, in the seven months, but I tried—I tried very hard to do what I could to not—to not hurt him. (Lewinsky, "Grand Jury Testimony")

Lewinsky has taken the position of so many people who idealize the person to whom she has willingly become subordinate, she has tried not to hurt him at the same time that he is hurting her. Jean Baker Miller explains such self-silencing behavior this way:

> Many women develop a great need to believe that they have a strong man to whom they can turn for security and hope in the world. And, while it may seem improbable, this belief in the man's magical strength exists side by side with an intimate knowledge of the weaknesses to which she caters. (34)

She was a good girl, the best of girls. The president testified that "She's a good young woman with a good heart and a good mind" (Clinton, "Grand Jury Testimony"). And she was willingly silent.

Silence, secrets, and lies were the basis of the presidential scandal, yet, according to Clinton and Lewinsky both, he had not influenced her testimony (not overtly, anyway): "I never told anyone to lie, not a single time . . . never" (Clinton, "Grand Jury Testimony"). And he had not offered her a job in exchange for her silence: "I was not trying to buy her silence or get Vernon Jordan to buy her silence. I thought she was a good person. . . . And I wanted to help her get on with her life. It's just as simple as that" (Clinton, "Grand Jury Testimony"). If the president had not suborned perjury or engaged in *quid pro quo,* and if Vernon Jordan had not entered the engagement,[37] then what exactly was at stake?

It's nobody's business. For much of the U.S. public, privacy and secrecy hung in the balance. Lewinsky preserved the balance best when she rationalized her initial lies about their sexual relationship by testifying that she thought "it was nobody's business." Her intention was to preserve her own privacy, her disclosures to her friends notwithstanding. Because Lewinsky understood how negatively she had been perceived by the White House staff, she realized immediately how she would be perceived by a voyeuristic U.S. public. For her, then, the simple understanding she had with the president was this: "as we had on every other occasion and every other instance of this relationship, we would deny it" (Lewinsky, "Grand Jury Testimony"). When she visited First Friend Jordan about helping her secure a job in New York, he asked her why she wanted to leave Washington. Even to someone she suspected knew about her sexual relationship with the president, she gave "the vanilla story . . . something about wanting to get out of Washington" (Lewinsky, "Grand Jury Testimony").

Black writes that the "balance between the exposure of secrets or their preservation remains embedded in a congeries of other attitudes and is a fallible sign on those attitudes" (143). As mentioned earlier, Lewinsky initially signed an affidavit denying the affair. But as Butler teaches us, all normative regulations, including in this case a seemingly willing self-silence, contain gaps and fissures within their structure. So when she was cornered by Starr's office, Lewinsky resolved to tell the whole truth. She intuitively knew the cost of speaking out. Although she might feel a sense of release, of unburdening, the rest of the U.S. public and members of the Senate could freely pronounce her testimony "pornographic" and "gratuitous." Nevertheless, they listened and read raptly.

A new life. As the grand jury hearings wound down and the impeachment trial got going, Monica Lewinsky dimmed from view. Nevertheless, she was steadfast in taking responsibility for her own silence and her omissions; she did so for her own protection. She would not blame Clinton or Jordan, nor would she agree that there had been any kind of *quid pro quo* arrangement in terms of a job: "I would just like to say that no one ever asked me to lie and I was never promised a job for my silence. And that I'm sorry. I'm really sorry for everything that's happened. And I also hate Linda Tripp" (qtd. in Morton 322).

She was sorry for her behavior, for what it had done to her family. She also wanted to make—but was prohibited from making—a public statement before her videotaped testimony was released to the public. She wanted to apologize publicly

> to her family, to the President, to Hillary and Chelsea Clinton, and to the American people for the trouble she had caused—at least then people would be able to *hear her voice* when she was in control of what she was saying. But the plan was dropped because the Office of the Independent Counsel wanted to approve her words. (Morton 332, emphasis added)

She was not allowed to speak publicly, let alone apologize. Lewinsky endured Starr's gag order—as she faced the nation's critical and prurient gaze. She had no way of responding to her critics, defending those she loved (which, at the time, still included the president), or apologizing to the people she felt she had hurt most. Her personal life, from old boyfriends and weight problems to trysts with the president and sexual frustrations with him, had been "laid bare to the world," at the same time that Clinton was talking about "reclaiming his privacy" (Yost).

When Clinton finally went public about the reasons for his silence, he never mentioned Lewinsky or the problems and humiliation they actually shared. Instead, he successfully and sanctimoniously separated himself from her, publicly rationalizing his former silence for the sake of himself, his family, and their God:

> My public comments and my silence about this matter gave a false impression. I misled people, including even my wife. I deeply regret that.
>
> I can only tell you I was motivated by many factors. First, by a desire to protect myself from the embarrassment of my own conduct.
>
> I was also very concerned about protecting my family. . . .
>
> Now, this matter is between me, the two people I love most—my wife and our daughter—and our God. I must put it right, and I am prepared to do whatever it takes to do so.
>
> Nothing is more important to me personally. But it is private, and I intend to reclaim my family life for my family. It's nobody's business but ours. . . . (Clinton, "Transcript")

Clearly, his problems did not include Lewinsky, who was left to fend for herself. She remained silenced—even as she spoke on the March 1999 *Barbara Walters 20/20,* under carefully defined conditions.

Her first interview with Walters lasted three hours and was replete with emotions: regret, apology, love, excitement, nostalgia, but mostly nostalgic love for the way things were. Again she was a "good girl," obedient to all the guidelines Starr had outlined for her: (1) not contradict her grand jury testimony; (2) not talk about the conduct of the Independent Counsel's office; (3) not discuss her initial questioning by FBI agents and prosecutors; and (4) remain silent about any potential legal proceedings to come. But in a second interview later that year, on *Barbara Walters's Fascinating People,* Lewinsky spoke more freely, in terms of both Starr and Clinton. She had moved beyond the silences and silencing that resulted from the emotional and legal restraints of both men.

In April 2002, Lewinsky appeared on HBO, *Monica in Black and White.* She spoke freely about the events that catapulted her into the national spotlight, saying "I would do anything to have my anonymity back." Yet, she knew that there was available to her no better opportunity to "clear up misconceptions and try to answer people's direct questions." Her appearance came as no surprise. Gaps and fissures eventually break through the regulatory norms. Even Clinton knew her well enough to say, "I knew that the minute there was no longer any contact, she would talk about this. She would have to. She couldn't help it" ("Grand Jury Testimony"). Besides wanting her anonymity back, she wanted to move through her remorse: "It seems really self-centered, . . . but my stronger affinity is to my family and my friends; I'm not going to take equal responsibility for his family. I'm just not. I mean they've made choices."

AFTER THE FALLING STARR

> . . . The anger scorching me
> my throat so tight I can
> barely get the words out
>
> —Gloria Anzaldúa, "El sonavabiche"

Since the Clinton scandal has died down, much continues and will continue to remain spoken and unspoken—whether lies, secrets, or silences. At the peak of her humiliation, when her husband finally admitted his relationship with Lewinsky, the First Lady issued only one statement and that through her spokeswoman: "She's committed to her marriage and loves her husband and daughter very much and believes in the President, and her love for him is compassionate and steadfast" (*New York Times* A23).

She's committed. This icy statement refracted from a woman who, for over twenty-five years, has spoken out on public issues, even and especially when ears were turned toward her husband, seems spoken through clenched teeth and a constricted throat. Yet Hillary Rodham Clinton has prevailed and continues to speak out, even as she invokes again and again the "zone of privacy" around her family. In reality, she has it both ways: she speaks yet says nothing revealing, the most strategic response, perhaps, to a cultural double bind that offers her either speech or respect but not both. (For instance, her effort to forge national health care reform with Congress was a made-for-television disaster.) As her race for the New York Senate seat heated up, she said, "I want independence. . . . I want to be judged on my own merits. Now for the first time I am making my own decisions. I can feel the difference. It's a great relief" (qtd. in Franks 168).

Her statement implies that she is relieved to be separated from her husband— and for good reason. Even though the Clinton scandal worked to soften her image—maybe even to help her win one of New York's Senate seats—she does not like that kind of portrait of herself. Lucinda Franks writes, "Though she hates playing the victim, public sympathy has transmuted her from a scary political termagant into a woman widely admired for her courage" (173). Even though her courage was galvanized in the face of in-your-face disrespect, she managed to say that "everybody has some dysfunction in their families. They have to deal with it. You don't just walk away if you love someone—you help the person" (qtd. in Franks 174).

During her successful Senate campaign, Clinton created continuous fora for discussing her political views and her personal life, but she inhabited these spaces with the most public of personae, revealing nothing except all that she refuses to say. For example, in her first interview after her husband's confession, an interview that ironically appeared in the inaugural issue of *Talk*, Hillary Rodham Clinton matter-of-factly states, "There has been enormous pain, enormous anger, but I have been with him half my life and he is a very, very good man. We just have a deep connection that transcends whatever happens" (qtd. in Franks 174). She goes on to say, "My husband is a very good man. . . . Yes, he has weaknesses. Yes, he needs to be more responsible, more disciplined, but. . . . You know in Christian theology there are sins of weakness and sins of malice, and *this* [noticeably not "his"] was a sin of weakness" (qtd. in Franks 174, emphasis added).

The First Lady has, for years, faced that choice between speech and respect, often choosing speech and suffering the consequences of being perceived as a pushy, bitchy, androgynous Lady Macbeth. Her public silence on private matters, however, has served to offer her respite in an even stranger paradox: if she can abide the nation's pity for her forbearance, she can reap all the benefits of their admiration, a quality necessary for her election to the Senate. So whether the First Lady will ever speak out again on the issue of her damaged marriage remains to be seen (or should I say "heard"?).

She's committed, too. First Daughter, Chelsea, continues to say absolutely nothing about her parents' marriage, her father's adolescent behavior. Sheehy says that like her mother, "Chelsea did not speak of the scandal even to her closest friends, and nobody asked" (344).[38] Like her mother, she established and protected her zone of privacy.

Not only does Chelsea remain silent on such matters, but the media, since early on, have remained silent on the subject of Chelsea, a miraculous show of mass-willpower if ever there were. Of course, her parents have refused to speak about or answer questions about Chelsea since they lived in the governor's mansion, but the Clintons have been unusually successful, as such parental moves have rarely done any good.[39]

In *It Takes a Village*, Hillary writes that their family role-playing helped Chelsea control her feelings and her words, for the young family played out all the cruel, untrue, and vicious things that political opponents might use against them. The parents hoped that this early training would help their daughter control her feelings—and her tongue. Clearly, they have been successful with their daughter, just as they have been successful keeping other people for speaking about or for Chelsea. So far, only the Reverend Jesse Jackson, First Family crisis counselor, has spoken publicly of Chelsea: "In some sense, her knowledge of what has happened and yet her will to embrace [her parents] in the midst of it has been like a big piece of glue in this situation" (Gerhart and Groer).

For whatever reasons, Hillary and Chelsea Clinton continue to employ silence, and the results seem, so far, to be to their advantage. They may be withholding information, sitting in judgment, resisting the curiosity of others, strategically defending themselves, strategically advancing their ambition (particularly in the case of Hillary), protecting Bill Clinton, or feeling ashamed—and they are delivering silence. They also might be simply furious; after all, silence is one form, perhaps the only form, of socially acceptable anger. Thus, their silence might be their position—or their choice. We may never know. They may never know for sure.

OUTSIDE THE WASHINGTON, D.C., BELTWAY

In exploring silence and silencing inside the beltway, I have become especially conscious of all the ideas I have left unsaid, all the issues I have left untouched. The media's purposeful focus on intrigue, sex, and coercion works only to keep the American public from focusing on issues that truly affect them, issues such as health care, medical research funding, social security, the national debt. "Sex," "silence," and "silencing"; "cover-ups," "manipulation," and "coercion" become the operative words of D.C., the terministic screen, as Kenneth Burke would say. And as such, those terms are, indeed, a *reflection* of reality, just as they are a *selection* of reality, and, to that extent, must function as a *deflection* of reality (*Language* 45). Any terministic screen is one reality, but not reality in its entirety.

Viewing Washington, D.C., through the sordid terministic screen has been both revolting and humbling, particularly as I reviewed the questioning, deposing, and smearing, which began to take on the cast of Anne Askew's examinations, falling just short of public execution. While focusing on the so-called sexual preferences and practices of Bill Clinton, I found myself hungering for news that was truly important, truly national or international.

Coverage of the Clinton scandal usually ran with bigger, better headlines than any of the other national or international news, including Clinton's attempts to revive the Mideast peace talks. Burke would describe such a juxtaposition of headlines and stories as providing us a "perspective by incongruity," a method for gauging the situation (*Perspectives* 94). With the constant attention on the scandal, with the scandal grabbing the best spot on the front page, any talk of gun control, world peace, retirement benefits, the marriage-tax penalty, education tax credit, Head Start programs, or NAFTA was automatically and simultaneously gendered weaker, of lesser importance, if not silenced altogether.

When sex serves as the thermostat of a political climate, the climate is never a moderate one. To my surprise, I went into the research feeling impatient with

Bill Clinton and fairly flat about the investigation. But after spending time in the climate, I found myself feeling sorry for Bill Clinton and irritated by the sanctimonious prying of the special investigation. Starr and his investigative team, Jones and her legal team, the print and visual media, and the American public were all re/viewing Clinton through a terministic screen of suspicion, salaciousness, and judgment. Nevertheless, the screen was partially of Clinton's own making.

In *George,* Hillary Clinton talked about her own frustration with the media's terministic screen, recounting all the reasons she has remained silent on issues: only if she "thinks it's really important or gets new information" will she persist because she does not believe the press is truly interested (Anthony 117). Unfortunately, she may be right, as the following example attests:

> The day after she attended the premiere of *Shakespeare in Love* in December 1998, Hillary delivered a two-hour speech on international violations of children's rights. Her remarks received no coverage and were studiously ignored by the *New York Times'* Maureen Dowd, who devoted a Sunday column to the exploits of "Hollywood Hillary"—the first lady who had attended a movie opening. "There was a time when there were large and real accomplishments that she wished to achieve," Dowd wrote mockingly. "Historians will long wonder how Mrs. Clinton came in as Eleanor Roosevelt and left as Madonna." (qtd. in Anthony 111, 113)

Cappella and Jamieson tell us that the media are more interested in setting up divisions, crises, problems, antagonisms, than they are writing about resolution and agreement.

Former senator Gary Hart, of *Monkey Business* renown, echoes Hillary Clinton's exasperation, telling the same Dowd that "politicians deserve more privacy" and that "if we as a country go down this [seamy] path, we will destroy our leadership" (qtd. in Dowd). Surely, we will prevent our leadership from concentrating on leading.

Like Hillary Clinton, Hart, too, has experienced the kind of refocusing that converges on scandal and agonism at the expense of true political events, moments, and agreements. Hart went on to provide a case in point about proportionality: "I was on Fox News talking about NATO expansion and they broke in to say [Clinton attorney] Robert Bennett might not use Paula Jones's sexual history in a motion. That's breaking news?" (qtd. in Dowd).

When the American public is forced to cast its collective gaze on office, legislative, and sexual politics—when sex is politics—the American public cannot focus on politics at large, which has been relegated to the periphery. When we are forced to stare and talk about at a sustained sex scandal, we are simultaneously blocked and silenced from considering truly abiding and crucial national issues such as children's health care, national health care reform, the federal deficit, the social security system, welfare, workfare, tenure, teaching training programs, vaccine development, the minimum wage, the Paycheck Fairness Act, the Comprehensive Nuclear Test Ban Treaty, the homeless.

Those of us who would rather be speaking and listening about these issues of national and personal significance continue to be silent and silenced, regardless, it seems, of our social class, race, gender, or profession. Unlike the media and the politicians, we do not have the power to choose the national focus we would like. The media insist that we concentrate on them and their cleverness, their "stories." Some politicians and lawyers enjoy the attention; even bad publicity is publicity.

A look at the silence and silencing inside the beltway offers considerations of the power of conscientious and conscious speaking silence—and speaking out. It also offers considerations of power and control in terms of silence and speaking out.

5
Commanding Silence

This story is true, but I can't and will not say anything about it. For me to testify against anybody or even mention, try to get somebody else in trouble, is wrong, and I won't do it. 'Cause it's against my belief; it's against my religion, my culture; it's against everything that we have fought for and stood up for, and what we were told by our elders, what a warrior society is all about.

—Leonard Peltier, *Incident at Oglala*

Leonard Peltier is white America's ideal of the strong, stoic, dignified warrior of anthropological, sociological, and pedagogical analysis. And as a so-called Real Indian, he remains silent.[1] His story—and reputation as a Real Indian—began nearly thirty years ago when FBI agents entered Oglala, a "traditional" community on the Pine Ridge Reservation in South Dakota.[2] In a series of events that has never been fully explained, gunfire erupted between the agents and the Indians, leaving both agents and one Indian dead. Despite the absence of credible evidence, a jury eventually convicted Peltier of "aiding and abetting" murder, and, therefore, he continues to serve consecutive life sentences in federal prisons. Since 1989, when the actual gunman (X) offered to come forward, Peltier has remained silent, refusing to testify against X on the grounds that the incarceration of his Indian body represents justice's being served, despite another Indian's confession—hence the epigraph to this chapter.

"To be an Indian in modern American society," argues Standing Rock Sioux Vine Deloria Jr., "is in a very real sense to be unreal and unhistorical" (*Custer* 2). For centuries, the dominant U.S. culture (read "European white culture") has written and talked about Real Indians, what they are like, how they feel, how they look, what they want, what they do, what they *should* do.[3] Mainstream U.S. culture, which likes very little space between its words, has also produced extensive writings about how Real Indians use silence. Therefore, the example of a silent American Indian (warrior), of Leonard Peltier, provides a good chapter opening for the ways another culture, an Other, uses silence.

In this chapter, I will first provide a sketch of the Real Indian, the monolithic invention represented in so much anthropological, religious, sociological, and pedagogical analysis equating Indianness with silence. Then, I will outline the research findings that have labeled Indians as silent. Despite the role that English-only policies have played in that silence, Indians continue to be classified as naturally silent, more so than any other group in the U.S. For instance, D. Lawrence Wieder and Steven Pratt argue that

> When real Indians who are strangers to one another pass each other in a public place, wait in line, occupy adjoining seats, and so forth, they take it that it is proper to remain silent and to not initiate conversation. Being silent at this point is a constituent part of the real Indian's mode of communicating with others, especially other Indians. Among other things, it communicates that the one who is silent is a *real Indian*. (51, emphasis added)

I will follow up that research review with the results of my own research project, a naturalistic study of observation and interviews based on Keith Basso's foundational linguistic anthropological work of the 1970s. Over the course of several years, I interviewed many Southwest Indians about themselves and their uses of silence and silencing. After addressing this concept of the Real Indian, then, I will map out the various ways that actual speaking bodies, self-identified as Indian, have talked about themselves and the uses of spoken language and purposeful silence.

Unlike the academics I interviewed in chapter 2, who insisted on anonymity, nearly every self-identified Indian whom I interviewed for this chapter insisted that I use his or her name. I could not use all the interviews I conducted and transcribed, but the ones I do feature in this chapter offer those of us in rhetoric and composition a great deal of specific information on the dangers of overgeneralizing about any group of people, about the ontological value of silence to the human spirit, and about the rhetorical reasons for using silence and for speaking out. Most of all, these interviews remind us of the importance of establishing "rhetorical sovereignty," Scott Lyons's apt term for assuming the right to speak or not on our own terms with the other people with whom we live (449).

THE REAL INDIAN

The Real Indian is the "white man's Indian"—a deliberate fabrication of the *unreal* that paradoxically satisfies the American imagination's demand for the *real*. In *The White Man's Indian,* Robert Berkhofer writes, "Since the original inhabitants of the Western Hemisphere neither called themselves by a single term or understood themselves as a collectivity, the idea and the image of the Indian must be a white conception" (3).[4]

The white conception of The Indian (a pan-Indian identity that flattened out the thousands of distinct native societies) has evolved throughout the centuries, to be sure, but always in concert with white psychic needs (dominance, curiosity, contempt, greed), and always through the "mythic veil of mingled racism and romance" (Bordewich 3). The Indian has been alternately capitalized upon and then disparaged, in racist ways. Whether the noble savage helped protect and teach the first wave of settlers or signified the purity of the new world, whether the heathen merited systematic extermination or Christian conversion, whether the vanishing race invited charity or tourism, whether the Indian deserved to keep his land, his minerals, and his traditions or have them put to use by allegedly more-deserving whites, and whether the remaining Indian can withstand commodification or Orientalization, the Real Indian has circulated as a product of the white imagination, consigned to the twilight realm of white myth, yet always a cantilever to whiteness—just as the fiction of Indian silence has served to counterbalance white speech.

No matter how sincere, these hyperreal simulations of the Real Indian have long supplanted any actual person or tribal remembrance, for they define Indians in terms of what they are *not,* namely white European Americans.[5] As an authentic fabrication, then, the Real Indian memorializes rather than perpetuates any tribal presence. According to Gerald Vizenor, the only good Indian is the postindian, who appears among the ruins of (mis)representation and literary annihilation.[6] Whether postindian, Real Indian, or something else, those self-identified Indians are human beings, whose purposeful use of speech and silence as rhetorical arts cannot be easily categorized (as I demonstrate below).

Which Indians Are Real?

Many whites and Indians alike believe that blood quantum an Indian makes, as though the blood of different ethnic or cultural groups could be identified, separated out, and quantified. The U.S. Census Bureau counts anyone as Indian who declares himself or herself, but most federally recognized tribes have established criteria for membership, many based on blood quantum. In 1971, the Cherokee Nation of Oklahoma opened tribal membership to anyone who could prove descent from a person listed on the 1906 federal commission rolls, regardless of intermarriage and cultural assimilation, regardless of blood quantum.[7] Other tribes require that individuals be born of an enrolled mother (Onondaga and Seneca) or reside on the reservation itself (Tohono O'Odham). The Yakima tribe in Washington requires members or their parents to establish reservation residency by returning every five years as well as by having one-quarter Indian blood.

The real issue, though, is not "pure" blood or blood quantum; actually, it is the issue of distinguishing Real Indians from others, other Indians, other people. When Leslie Marmon Silko writes of her experiences as a person of mixed ancestry growing up on Laguna Pueblo in New Mexico, she explains how some of the puebloans accepted her and others did not:

It was not so easy for me to learn where we Marmons belonged, but gradually I understood that we of mixed ancestry belonged on the outer edge of the circle between the world of the Pueblo and the outside world. The Laguna people were open and accepted children of mixed ancestry because appearance was secondary to behavior. For the generation of my great-grandmother [who had married Robert Gunn Marmon, a white man from Ohio] and earlier generations, anyone who had not been born in the community was a stranger, regardless of skin color. Strangers were not judged by their appearances—which could deceive—but by their behavior. The old-time people took their time to become acquainted with a person before they made a judgment. The old-time people were very secure in themselves and their identity; and thus they were able to appreciate differences and to even marvel at personal idiosyncrasies so long as no one and nothing was being harmed. ("Fences" 2)

Silko's reminiscences speak to the issue of Indian behavior, which can in some cases override issues of mixed ancestry or mixed blood. Thus it is that Indian identity—who is a Real Indian—remains a serious question for some and a non-issue for others, as my interviews will support.

How Real Can Any Indian Be?

Can only traditionalists be Real Indians, or might the progressives who live near or on the reservation also be Real? What about the Indians who live and work in mainstream America yet remain, in various measure, connected to their home culture? How Real can any Indian be? The answers vary. For artist Maurus Chino, "Home is Acoma [Pueblo]; Acoma will always be my home." Chino told me that he believes he "was made Acoma for a purpose." He feels "special, in a way, that [he] was born Acoma," and that he is "Acoma, always."

Albuquerque-based Zuni medical technologist Todd Epaloose says that he always calls Zuni home, no matter where he lives physically. "If it was a perfect world for me," he says, "I would be back home working." But he cannot find steady employment at Zuni Pueblo, with its "100 percent graduate rate" and "100 percent unemployment rate," so Epaloose has established his career in a medical lab, where he tries to balance the conflicting demands of two cultures:

I actually feel I live in two worlds, kind of a marginal Native American (I don't know how you'd put it), pulled between two worlds. You want to be accepted in this [white] world in other people's eyes as far as being prosperous and having prestige, whether it be a title, money, whatnot—that's the way honor's [presented] in this world. So you want to get there through schooling, whatnot.

And at the same time, you go back home, and you don't want others to feel that you're any better than them, because you may be looked down upon. People might say, "You're putting yourself higher than other people." Equality is a strength among our people. I mean as far as having everybody equal, whether that be animals or human life, it's all one web of life. And if you break that [web] and try to be better than something else, then it's kind of saying, "Yeah, [I am better]."

Interestingly, Epaloose's success at the medical lab seems to sustain him culturally, despite what he perceives to be his marginal status. He continues:

I've lived in both worlds. . . . Like I said, I consider myself to be the person in between, to see the best of both [worlds]. But I have people back home that have only done that [stayed in Zuni], and it's a lot harder for them to come out to this side of the world, to assimilate, to adapt. They try, maybe they go to school for a while, and they go back because they can't handle the pressures, the different pace, maybe the ridicule. Or what is considered social status here might not be what they're after as far as being happy in life. So they go back home to what they're used to. That may, in turn, be looked down upon, too, "You couldn't make it."

Epaloose talks about the fine line of being "judgmental on either side about who does what," for he believes that "human nature's all the same." In fact, he thinks it might be because of his commitment to all humans, whatever color, that he chose his profession: "Dealing with blood, you know, is universal to all people. I'm giving life to everybody and trying to help them. There is no color but red between us all."

Rio Rancho–based Navajo artist Andrew Todacheene agrees with Epaloose that many Indians live in two worlds: "When you're growing up traditional, and you have to go to [a public or boarding] school, you really live in two worlds." And Santa Fe–based Hopi sculptor Evelyn Fredericks writes that "Indians by necessity live schizophrenic lives. We must learn to live in two worlds often at conflict with each other" (18 Jan. 2000). After a long visit with her mother and family at Hopi, she writes,

When I go out to Hopi, I make a mental shift that usually I'm not aware of. First of all, I hear the language spoken in the reality of the culture. Then that reality is superimposed (the best way I can explain it) on top of the one I just came from (Hopi is REALLY isolated). I slip into my Hopi self very easily. The difficult part is when I come back here [Santa Fe]. I've figured it's because my language and culture were initially so much a part of me that I'm never truly comfortable in this culture. After a few days of reintegrating, I can again function here. (13 July 2000)

The conflicts Todacheene, Epaloose, and Fredericks discuss center not only on the often-profound cultural differences between Indians and mainstream America, but also on issues of tribal contact, experiential cultural knowledge, careerism, identity, even wishful thinking among the Indians themselves.

Sometimes the conflicts converge on the differences between reservation Indians and urban Indians. Some urban Indians have a strong sense of tribal or puebloan identity: they lived in an Indian culture, spoke the language, and shared life experiences. Others have not—through no fault of their own. But Fredericks sometimes feels impatient with them. She writes,

> There are many people . . . who until recently knew nothing about their Indian heritage. In fact, many of these people are only guessing about their Indianness and when pressed to offer proof will probably become very defensive or angry. They tend to hang around Indian groups, go to powwows (their defining Indian experience) and will change their tribal affiliation when one or the other suits them better. I have known many people like this from college days to now. Others "feel" that they must be Indian. We [Indians] joke that with their first nose bleed, they lost all the Indian blood they had. . . . (11 May 2000)

When we were discussing the work of activist and artist Charlene Teeters, a Spokane Indian, who works tirelessly to stop Indian stereotyping, Fredericks said that using Indian names as sports team mascots

> is not an issue here [New Mexico] as far as I know, but it is in the Midwest where [Teeters] went to school. I am not offended when people use the word *Indian,* but I haven't been to anything where mascots supposedly are representing Indians. Again, it's one of those urban vs. reservation people deals where there are much larger issues facing people [on the reservation] on a daily basis. (18 Nov. 2000)

Employment, health care, education—not mascots—are reservation issues, especially for those "Indian people still living a traditional lifestyle," Fredericks told me, "most of [whom] are west of the Mississippi or—better yet—[south in] Mexico" (11 May 2000).

In *Imagining Indians in the Southwest,* Leah Dilworth argues that white America and the rest of the world continue to imagine the Real Indian as living only in the Southwest, a "'land'—of 'poco tiempo,' 'journey's ending,' and 'enchantment'—on which Americans have long focused their fantasies of renewal and authenticity" (2). Included in such fantasies, of course, are imaginings of Real Indians, "exotic, primitive people," who live "self-sufficiently in a harsh but beautiful desert landscape" (2).

Pure Indian, Certified Indian, Old Indian, New Indian, Wannabe, Outaluck, Reservation, Urban, Real—there remain many categories of Indians.

Who is a Real Indian?

No one. There is no Real Indian—just authentic simulations of the Real.

Who is an Indian?

It depends—on tribal membership, ancestry, culture, history, phenotypic presentation, and, of course, on self-identification.[8] For the purposes of my analysis, the point is not who is "more" Real so much as it is a question of my interrogating the foundational sociolinguistic, cultural anthropological research done in the Southwest and in Oregon with reservation-experienced Indians, research that generalizes about Indians' use of silence. In this context, my two-fold critical question is this: What do self-identified Southwest Indians themselves say about their uses of silence? And how accurate are the foundational research projects that have pronounced Indians to be silent?

THE SILENT INDIAN

Closely linked with the Real Indian is the silent Indian: the stoic warrior of old, so beautifully represented today by Peltier. Unless they have been fully informed by white culture, the tribal and pueblo Indians of the American Southwest are neither tethered to the Greek rhetorical tradition of public, political display nor to Western writing practices of dialectic, logical syllogisms, argument, or debate. To many of them, our European reliance on rhetorics of competition and individual prowess rings hollow, even impotent, within a cultural setting that values sharing, family, the earth, age-old agreements (i.e., government treaties), discussion, and, sometimes, silence. But whether they deliver words or silence on these and other matters, theirs is clearly the normal rhetorical display of their culture.

The common perception of silent Indians permeates popular as well as scholarly work: Indians are perceived to be fiercely silent, if not personally cold, to be solemnly dignified, if not linguistically impoverished. Marjorie N. Murphy writes, "In truth, a natural reticence to too much talk is an attribute of Indian character reflected in their rhetoric. It has its source in the whole life view towards silence and respect for the *word*" (359, emphasis in original). Murphy may be correct, yet her assertions prompt me to wonder, "a life view towards silence" and "respect for the word"—in whose language?

As the following sections will demonstrate, English-only policies coupled with other anti-Indian government policies led to the direct silencing of Indians, in both their indigenous languages as well as in English.

Silencing the Mother Tongue

Language and culture are intimately entwined and cannot be separated. Ever since Europeans first arrived on this continent, Indians have been pressured—often forced—to speak English at the expense of their mother tongue. At the end of the Civil War, President Ulysses S. Grant, by way of his 1868 Peace Commission, initiated an English-only movement as one way to end the Indian wars on the frontier.[9] By 1878, the Commissioner of Indian Affairs declared that the education of Indian children was the quickest way to "civilize" the Indian, and for efficiency's sake, education would be provided only to those children "removed from the examples of their parents and the influence of the [temporary] camps and kept in boarding schools" (Atkins xxv). This same year, Lieutenant Richard Pratt, superintendent of the first federally funded Indian school in Carlisle, Pennsylvania, claimed that the boarding school Indian students would serve as "hostages for good behavior of [their] parents," parents who would receive meager government rations and financial assistance (qtd. in Atkins 174). Thus, the systematic separation of young children from their mothers—as well as their Indian identity and mother tongue—was already in play.

By 1890, the Indian School Service nationwide followed a strict English-only policy: "Pupils must be compelled to converse with each other in English, and should be properly rebuked or punished for persistent violation of this rule" (qtd. in Adams 140).[10] The goal of the Indian schools was two-fold: to teach English and to eradicate the native languages (and concomitant cultural identifications). Students who could not speak English were to remain silent.[11]

Native languages could not survive, let alone thrive, under these conditions. Federal legislation together with local force nearly wiped out these languages.[12] Many native languages remain endangered, despite the recent movement to maintain and renew native languages and the 1990 Native American Languages Act. In *Flutes of Fire,* her study of California Indian languages, Leanne Hinton describes a conservation program in which

> elders who speak their language of heritage have teamed up with younger tribal members who are trained in education, along with other educationists and linguists, to develop teaching curricula and programs that will give children an appreciation and beginning knowledge of their languages and cultures. (235)

Besides curricula and programs, the language renewal programs Hinton describes have produced dictionaries, story collections, word games, and recordings—but no new fluent speakers, not yet anyway. Ever-evolving pilot programs are underway in the hope that these languages will survive. Ironically, the same government that worked so hard to stamp out these languages and cultures is now funding programs to preserve and revitalize them. Mrs. Anne Peaches, linguistic anthropologist Keith Basso's first Apache teacher, put the problem in no uncertain terms: "If we lose our language, we will lose our breath. Then we will die and blow away like leaves" (qtd. in Basso, *Western Apache* xiv).[13]

Any cultural observations of Indian silence—or speech—hinge upon which language is at play.[14]

There Is Silence

"There is silence," writes Acoma poet Simon Ortiz;

> You don't want that silence to grow deeper and deeper into you,
> because that growth inward stunts you,
> and that is no way to continue,
> and you want to continue.

("Right of Way" 260)

In his story about the young Acoma boy who would not speak until his grandfather "unlocked" his lips, Ortiz addresses issues of native language and cultural consciousness—and the importance of not remaining silent.[15] Ortiz is one of a number of Indian writers who address the issue of the Indian's use of silence, which is often compared with the white's use of words. And his poem and story about Indian resistance to silence run counter to long-received belief that the Real Indian delivers silence regularly and over extended periods of time.

Early in our nation's history, Thomas Jefferson described the "distinct articulation" of Cherokee warrior-orator Outcity in comparison with the "solemn silence" of his followers (qtd. in Washburn 95). The use of sign language among the six linguistic families with twenty-two separate languages of the Plains Indians also supported the myth of the silent Indian or the Indian silence.

But it was Charles Eastman, early in the twentieth century, who anchored the myth of silence in the Indian experience. An Eastland Woodland Sioux and Dartmouth-educated physician, Eastman wrote an influential memoir that celebrated the Indian's profound belief "in silence—the sign of perfect equilibrium" (89). He continues with:

> If you ask him: "What is silence?" he will answer: "It is the Great Mystery!" "The holy silence is His voice!" If you ask: "What are the fruits of silence?" he will say: "They are self-control, true courage or endurance, patience, dignity, and reverence. Silence is the corner-stone of character." (90)

Kiowa writer N. Scott Momaday extends the significance of silence for Indians in *A House Made of Dawn*. When his character Abel, also a Kiowa, relocates to Los Angeles, he attends a religious service at the Holiness Pan-Indian Rescue Mission, led by "The Right Reverend John Big Bluff Tosamah," who preaches an appreciation for silence: "The Word did not come into being, but *it was*. It did not break upon the silence, but *it was older than the silence and the silence was made of it*" (97, emphasis in original). In his sermon, he also emphasizes the

Indian's appreciation for both the carefully spoken word as well as the silence that creates and surrounds each word: "Consider for a moment that old Kiowa woman, my grandmother. . . . You see, for her words were medicine; they were magic and invisible. . . . She never threw words away" (96).

When Navajo Lisa Arviso Alvord, now a physician, moved from Crownpoint, New Mexico, to attend Dartmouth College (and then Stanford Medical School), she went into what she can now only describe as "complete culture shock": "I thought people talked too much, laughed too loud, asked too many personal questions, and had no respect for privacy. . . . We were taught to . . . value silence over words" (Alvord and Van Pelt 27). And Chicksaw Linda Hogan, describing how an eagle feather helped her locate her granddaughter's precious umbilical cord, writes that "when we are silent enough, still enough, we take a step into such mystery" (453).

But Ortiz does not find that same mystery in the silence of everyday life. In fact, his poetry resists the notion that Indians tend to seek and appreciate silence; in "What I Mean" he describes a silence not of the Indian's choice:

We didn't talk much.
Some people say Indians are just like that,
shy and reserved and polite,
but that's mostly crap. Lots of times
we were just plain scared
and we kept our mouths shut.

(327)

White writer Peter Matthiessen, too, explains some of the reasons Indians are perceived to be voluntarily silent. In Indian-populated states, Indian silence is

less a reflection of antisocial tendencies than of the racism and punitive attitude toward Indians, whose "crimes" mostly relate to alcohol, who are jailed regularly because they cannot afford bail, and who are often convicted because—until recently—they rarely attempted to defend themselves in court. (34)

The silences Ortiz and Matthiessen describe are the enforced silencings of the Others who do not want their words to get them into (more) trouble with a more powerful person. Many writers connect silence with the Real Indian, but Ortiz and Matthieson connect it with real people.

There Is Silence—and Research to Prove It

"Most American Indian tribes," writes Richard L. Johannesen in "The Functions of Silence," view silence as a "worthwhile element in the human communication process," for it reflects reverence for careful language use, prevents the promiscuous use of words, facilitates effective listening, and serves as the cornerstone of character, constituted by the virtues of "self-control, courage, patience, and dignity" (27). As he surveys the functions of silence, Johannesen makes casual reference to Indians and silence. Other white academics, Keith Basso, in particular, have produced landmark studies, dedicated entirely to Indian silence. In the following sections, I provide an overview of this research, a close reading of Basso's conclusions, and then the richly varied results of my own research project into the uses of silence and silencing by Southwest Indians, a project modeled after Basso's own.

"To give up on words." Linguistic anthropologist Keith Basso has been publishing on the subject of Indian silence for nearly forty years. In his latest book, *Wisdom Sits in Places,* Basso writes, "Over a period of years, I have become convinced that one of the distinctive characteristics of Western Apache discourse is a predilection for performing a maximum of socially relevant actions with a minimum of linguistic means" (103).[16] In other words, in his investigations into the relationship between Western Apache speech and silence, Basso has found that "a few spoken words are made to accomplish large amounts of communicative work" (103). The "minimalist genius of Western Apache discourse" leaves Basso "silent in its wake" (104). Now finding himself silenced by their laconic expression, Basso was earlier in his career fascinated by their silence, particularly those that meaningfully inhabit the Western Apache language and culture.

In 1970, Basso published "'To Give Up on Words': Silence in Western Apache Culture," his foundational investigation of Western Apache silences from which Basso deduces a "number of situations—recurrent in Western Apache society—in which one or more of the participants typically refrain from speech for lengthy periods of time" (214). These specific acts of silence are encouraged and deemed appropriate by all participants who understand the ethnography of communication within their specific culture—and in response to six specific, socially ambiguous *situations:* (1) when meeting strangers, (2) during courtship, (3) when greeting those returning from a long absence, (4) while getting cussed out, (5) during mourning, and (6) during ceremonials.[17] According to Basso, the function of a specific act or delivery of silence varies only slightly for the Western Apache—but always in response to situational uncertainty and unpredictability.

Although he warns that "standard ethnographies contain very little information about the circumstances under which verbal communication is discouraged," Basso feels that the reasons Western Apaches refrain from speaking in certain situations might provide a transferable framework for understanding the spoken and the unspoken in other Indian cultures of the Southwest, which are the focus of this chapter ("To Give Up" 227).

Transferring/translating the framework. Following Basso's suggestion, then, I conducted a series of interviews on pueblos and reservations, in urban and rural settings with Indians identified with various pueblos and tribes. I wanted to know if Basso was right, if his framework for understanding attitudes toward and practices of silence had relevance to other Southwest Indian cultures. All the while, though, I kept in mind two important precepts supplied by Evelyn Fredericks. The first had to do with overgeneralizing about Indians:

> The problem with people like Basso, who I understand studied the Apache, a group totally unlike my cultural group (Hopi), is that there are too many generalizations. There are many Indian groups in this country alone, some still practicing their traditions, and other groups almost totally acculturated. (18 Jan. 2000)

The second precept had to do with preparation, not so much my preparation for asking questions; rather, what I needed to do to hear the responses. To that, Fredericks wrote,

> My only advice to someone seeking to learn about Indians is to get to know Indian people, go to their reservations, and see how different everyone is. There, you will then feel the similar undercurrents, the similarities of Indian cultures (because there are definite universal feelings, values) that we as Indian people can value in each other's culture. (18 Jan. 2000)

With Basso's research model and Fredericks's two admonitions in mind, I proceeded to talk—and listen—at length over the course of several years with Southwest Indians about their purposeful uses of silence and silencing.

The arrangement. Never did I interview anyone during our first meeting. Interviews were always carefully arranged, days, weeks, even months in advance.[18] Most interviews lasted well over an hour, and the taped interview itself took place during a much longer social meeting or a series of social meetings. I transcribed all the interviews, word for word. And never did I pay anyone for his or her interview. In fact, when I met Maurus Chino for our interview, the first thing he asked me was how much I planned to pay him. When I replied, "Nothing," he laughed and said he was teasing me. Both he and Andrew Todacheene had experience with anthropologists who paid for interviews, and both of them said they would not have agreed to be interviewed if I had offered to pay, let alone had I been an anthropologist.[19]

I knew some of these Indian people before I ever began this study of silence; others I was introduced to through mutual friends. Since the interviews, I have developed a measure of friendship with some but not all of the Indians I interviewed, relationships that clearly surface during the course of the interviews.

Most of the interviewees insisted that I publish their names, while a few wanted to remain anonymous. I quote long passages from some interviews and nothing from many others. And just as Fredericks cautioned, the responses to my queries were richly varied. Some of the responses confirm Basso's hypotheses; others do not.

Talking about Silence

Every person I interviewed knew we were going to talk about Indian uses of silence before we got started. At the beginning of each interview, I asked them to self-describe (name, age, cultural affiliation, family, employment, and so on) in such a way as to distinguish themselves from the others I was interviewing. Often, just these initial instructions would provoke responses about silence. For instance, after describing himself as a "Navajo male, forty-three years old," a "silver worker," an "artist," Andrew Todacheene moved immediately into his perspectives on silence:

Among Navajos generally, when we come to the age of seven years old, . . . we're generally taught by our mothers the basics of discipline . . . language, and discipline. From there on, we are told specifics in our culture about Navajo idealisms, beliefs, history, and respect. And discipline as behavior. . . . When we're taught something, we're always asked not to break in or interrupt. . . . We're always taught to listen and watch what's around us.

When I met Kevin Saavedra on the Acoma mesa, he said, "I was born and raised here. . . . I'm in my early thirties and have three boys. And I am an artist. My whole family is famous for our pottery making; we're known for our fine lines." He continued, connecting silence with his intricate pottery painting:[20]

Speaking as a native American, I feel that silence is a form of meditation, not just as our culture but as our religious culture, our Catholic religion.

[Silence] plays a big part of our everyday life. . . . We use it as a form of meditation on our artwork; we do concentrate on our pieces when we're working, even though there are people outside. You can hear what's going on outside, but you're still concentrating on one piece. Your mind is focused; you're focused on your individuality—that's what you're focused on. There's things happening outside, but you're not paying attention; you're just centered on that, that piece of pottery.

Zuni Todd Epaloose spoke for his people: "The only time we'd purposefully use [silence] would be out of respect and courtesy. As far as conversations go, we tend to listen more first and tend to be silent until we totally understand that the person talking to you is done." He continued,

We are all different in our ways, but the majority of Zuni people were brought up to listen rather than be outspoken or aggressive, if you will. So personal space, silence to us, is more showing respect or courtesy rather than [it is] in this culture.[21] [In white culture,] you're taught to look people in the eye, to show that you're present, and [to use] close proximity, show aggression, just to make yourself known. Whereas I think in our culture, we back off on personal space; we don't look people in the eyes, just because it's a sign of disrespect or [that] you're invading someone else's personal space. So we have a tendency to be withdrawn and listen more until we know for sure that the person we're having a conversation with has said everything there is to say. I mean that there's a lot of hand gestures.

Usually, when you're speaking with an elder, you stay there for quite some time [until] he or she lets you know, "I've said my piece now." There, in turn, it's your turn to speak. So in that way, I think, silence is used more as a sign of respect.

After I initiated the interview with Earl Ortiz (brother of Acoma poet Simon Ortiz), he described himself as a "full-blooded Indian from the pueblo of Acoma," who has lived in Albuquerque for the past twenty-five years, where he works as a "land surveyor for the Bureau of Indian Affairs." He continued by describing his purposeful use of silence in terms of his own personality rather than his pueblo affiliation:

When I want to be silent, I usually want to keep something to myself. I don't want to express it. Maybe it's a character defect. I don't express myself when I feel emotional pain, so I'll usually keep it to myself. And it's real hard for me to express something that's affecting me painfully, so I use silence, you know, in that way, to keep it to myself. You know, [I] just don't want anybody to know some things. . . .

Leila Moquino O'Neal's response resonated with Ortiz's in so far as she spoke personally:

I'm thirty-eight years old, and I'm from Santo Domingo Pueblo, . . . and I'm an artist. I make Native American jewelry, and I work down in Old Town [a section of Albuquerque]. For me, using silence purposefully would be . . . when I don't want to hurt anybody's feelings or keep my opinion to myself, [to] think before I open my mouth.

Forty-five-year-old Maurus Chino (nephew of Earl and Simon Ortiz) is self-described as "fairly educated by tribal standards" with a bachelor of fine arts degree. Currently, he supports himself as an artist. Chino has lived on and off Acoma as well as in other states. But no matter where he lives, he says, "Acoma will always be my home, and I go there often." Although Acoma is his home, always, he warns me, "You certainly cannot tell just by talking to me how the Acomas are because I'm not the same as every other Acoma. Everyone's a little bit different."

Like Todacheene and Saavedra, Epaloose tended to speak for his cultural group: "I should state that I'm speaking on behalf of most Zuni people." Ortiz, O'Neal, and Chino, on the other hand, spoke only for themselves. And Fredericks told me in no uncertain terms that she "could not in good conscience presume to speak for everyone." These seven people, self-identified with five specific Southwest Indian cultural groups, each responded in a different way.

Situational Silences

When I offered up Basso's six situations for silence, the responses were richly varied, even when they harmonized. As I read through Basso's assertions, one by one, in every interview, I described the types of situations in which, as one of Basso's original informants had put it, "it is right to give up on words" (qtd. in Basso, "To Give Up" 217).

When Meeting Strangers. The first of Basso's assertions is that when Western Apaches meet strangers, whether Indians or whites, they do not speak, because "the establishment of social relationships is a serious matter that calls for caution, careful judgment, and plenty of time" (218). In response to this assertion, the refreshingly outspoken Chino said,

> I think that to be truthful that anthropologists are full of bullshit. I think they misunderstand people a lot, and . . . they make their own views without talking to the people. At times, people are silent because it's different growing up in a cultural background and going to a completely different culture. And a lot of it has to do, too, with Indian people, especially in the Southwest, when they speak their languages it's difficult to make that transition from their own tribal language as opposed to English.

Earl Ortiz responded that Basso's assertion might be true, "to a certain extent, but I don't think it's really totally true." And then Ortiz proceeded to remind me of our initial meeting at a Santo Domingo feast day: "When I first met you, [well] it depends on how that person comes at you. Now I was attracted to you because of your demeanor and the way we greeted each other. And I'[d] never met you." I reminded him that he had been standing with Chino, who was selling his inimitable red-glazed pottery that day, and that I had greeted Chino, whom I had known for a couple of years. "Didn't it help, too," I asked, "to have Maurus [Chino] as an intermediary?" He responded with "Um hm, Maurus knew you."

Todacheene seemed nonplussed by Basso's assertion that strangers are met with silence:

> That's not true. How can you learn each other's tribe, position, status, or how one thinks by just being silent?
>
> We're always taught to . . . extend your hand and shake hands, and always introduce yourself. With Navajos, you give your clan system and that will enable the other person to get the idea of whether you're related to them [and through which family member]. Clan systems are very friendly, an extreme way of knowing who your relatives are. As one realizes, Navajo clans started out with four and have evolved into over 250 clans.
>
> My clan is To dich 'ii'nii, and the problem that I had within my mom's clan is that the majority of Navajo people I meet are either related to me through my mom's side, or they're my uncles, or I'm theirs. . . . How can one . . . know who one is by just being silent? That doesn't make sense because you need to know who your families are in terms of clanship and relationship boundaries.

Unlike Todacheene, O'Neal described her response to strangers in terms of herself and then her family, in particular her powerful grandmother with whom O'Neal spent much of her younger years:

> When I meet a person, I'm silent until I get good vibes from the person; then, I can open up and start talking with that person. If I don't feel the good vibes, then I stay silent. . . . I feel people and their vibes, basically. . . . And my grandmother was very much like that.

I drove out to Grants, New Mexico, one morning to interview three sisters, all of whom are Acoma Pueblo affiliated, Annette Romero, Danielle Victoriano, and Billie Wanya.[22] Thirty-six-year-old Romero told me that "when you meet someone for the first time, you kind of do have that silence, and you got to know how they present themselves. From there, you may break the silence, or they'll approach you." Thirty-three-year-old Wanya answered,

> I think I would rather approach [strangers] than have them approach me, so they won't see us Native Americans being so quiet. Anyway, sometimes we are. I don't know why. I guess we're just afraid that what we say—we might be put down for what we say. I think that's why we're quiet at times when we're getting to know someone.

Epaloose echoed Wanya's response, even as he adds texture in response to the assertions that Indians are silent when whey meet strangers. The notion of "personal space" permeates all of Epaloose's responses, and this one is no different:

I would agree with that assertion, I mean, going back to personal space and not wanting to tread on anybody. . . . With strangers, especially, you haven't established anything.

And traditionally, way back when, you were amongst your own people, and when you met strangers, well, there's a lot of beliefs in mysticism and witchery. You don't want to fall into evil's hands, so of course, you would be withdrawn and careful. . . .

. . . With the aggression of looking people in the eye or getting close and making your presence known, in my [Zuni] culture, that would be a violation of your personal space. It puts you on guard, and you say, "Watch out for this person," especially if it's a stranger who is coming up to you and saying, "Hi, how are you," and I don't know you.

Epaloose addressed the idea of the aggressively friendly stranger in much the same way as Laura Kaye Jagles.

Jagles, an English teacher from Tesuque Pueblo, responded to the prompt by detailing her general view about "some Indians" and then about her own experience at the Bread Loaf Summer School of English, where she was working on her master's degree during the summer and making good grades:[23]

Well, I wouldn't say that if I meet up with a stranger, I'm not going to talk to them. I guess it would depend on what [Basso] means by silence—body language or eye contact—because I know some Indians don't make eye contact. And that, in a way, could be a form of silence: I'm not going to make eye contact with you.

When I asked her if she was talking about Indians from her pueblo, she answered,

No, I'm talking about others. But I might look at them, make eye contact, say hi, but I am going to keep my distance.

[Keeping my distance was] one thing I think Andrea Lunsford was concerned about when they first came to campus: I wasn't doing the same things that everyone else was—the parties, you know. I wasn't into that because a lot of times (now, I'm making a generalization), people from the East Coast, white people, are fake. I would rather observe and take my time, like the second thing [Basso says] about [friendship] being a precious thing, so being cautious about it.

But I'm not completely silent if somebody comes to talk to me—they do. But I'm still worried about somebody asking me stupid questions, get[ting] the information and leaving, and then not talk[ing] to me the rest of the time. I feel like I'm being used, and so that's one of the reasons I eventually end up making friends during the middle period, when all the other people are . . .

getting into spitspats and whatever. At least [spitspats are] something I can avoid by keeping my distance.

But for Andrea, and some of the other people, they're concerned that I wasn't going to stick with the program. But indeed I was. I was more worried about this B-minus thing, [because] if you get a B-minus or below, you don't get credit. And I'm like, well, what's the purpose of being here?

Jagles's insightful response can be read on several levels: she responds in terms of what "other Indians" do and then about what she herself does in that situation. Finally, she moves into a specific situation in which she felt pressured to hurry into friendships. Because they are "fake," white people tend to rush friendships, sometimes leaving Jagles to feel "used." Jagles's opinion of some white people's attitudes toward friendship (they hurry and then end up having "spitspats"; they "use" people) runs concurrent with Basso's findings.[24]

My next prompt moves away from total strangers and seeming friendships with strangers to developing relationships with stranger-acquaintances, who might be white, Indian, or some other cultural group.

During courtship. Basso argues that "during the initial stages of courtship, young men and women go without speaking for conspicuous lengths of time" ("To Give Up" 218). Whether they are at large public gatherings or in situations where they find themselves alone, young people are reluctant to speak to each other. Of course, as their relationship develops, young people get to know each other and talk more and more. But early on, protracted discussions are discouraged: "This is especially true for girls, who are informed by their mothers and older sisters that silence in courtship is a sign of modesty and that an eagerness to speak betrays previous experience with men" (219).

When I posed this scenario to the people in my study, the results uniformly diverged from Basso's results for two obvious reasons: I did not interview any Western Apache, and, even if I had, courtship patterns may have changed dramatically over the last thirty years. In fact, when I posed this assertion to the three Acoma Pueblo sisters, Romero, Victoriano, and Wanya, they broke into laughter, and only one responded: "Well, probably in the old days," said Romero, "way back then, way before 1978, way before our times." She went on to ask if Basso had paid everyone he interviewed. If so, she surmised, "they gave him the answers he was [looking for] . . . so they could get the money."[25]

Saavedra, father of three and husband to Victoriano, also dismisses Basso's assertion, saying that he disagreed

because there will be love and affection and all that, but you've got to get to know one another; you just can't read each other's mind. It would be nice, but you can't do that. You have to get to know one another. There is a focus point; you've got to be focused on one another. You've got to trust one another; you're not going to get trust from silence. You've got to get to know the other in a courtship.

Chino, ever-admonishing about cross-cultural research, responded again with, "I think that anthropologists are full of bullshit." He continued with,

That's certainly not the way that [courtship] is perceived. I mean, certainly in my own experiences with courtship, I've never [seen] someone who is silent in that manner. . . . But it's different when a person from another culture studies another culture. And I've not seen [silence during courtship] to be the case.

Epaloose seemed to be puzzled:

I'm not sure how silence—I mean, you'd have to interact somehow to let the other person know where you're coming from. I mean, I don't know how you'd use silence as far as that's concerned. I'm not sure what his point is.

Earl Ortiz, father of two grown daughters, laughed, saying, "Ah, that's funny. . . ."

I was married. I remember my courtship as being anything but silent. . . . Maybe if it was an Indian married to an Anglo, from totally different cultures, that might be the way it was. But I got married to another Indian, not from my same tribal affiliation (she's a Navajo). But . . . I don't know.

I've always been a silent, quiet person, but it wasn't because of the courtship.

Like Ortiz, a never-married, younger pueblo woman brings up the idea of a cross-cultural courtship, saying that "the courtship would depend on whether the Indian was with an Indian or a non-Indian." She continued, thoughtfully:

It also depends on the experience that the individual has, whether it's a male or a female. Most likely, the female will be silent more so than the man. Because I know when I first dated a pueblo guy, I was really shy. [But] I wouldn't say that I was silent, because one of the reasons why he was interested in dating me was because I wasn't [silent] and that I voiced certain things. But I think [my speaking up] ended up being an issue because I wasn't silent about going further, . . . being physical. . . . And when he started planning out our whole lives and where we were going to go to graduate school, . . . I said, "No, I don't want that." So that was what severed the relationship. (Anonymous XIII)

But it was Navajo Todacheene who spoke at length about silence during courtship:

> Hmm. Well, that's pretty interesting. There's no merit in making an assumption that way because a lot of tribes—plains, pueblo people, Athabaskans, Apaches, and Navajos—have the same concept of clanship, kinship. They have to know who they're dealing with. You need to know who you're going to be courting for marriage or courting for a relationship.
>
> If I met a woman and I was interested in carrying on a relationship or getting married, the first thing we'd have to know in Navajo culture is whether I was related to her. Again, you need to discuss your clan background, who your parents are, who your grandfathers are, what your clan on your father's side is, his mother's clan, his father's clan. . . . If you're silent in . . . courtship, you might . . . be committing a cultural crime that is very taboo among your parents. Otherwise than that, your parents' or your family's honor is at stake because people are going to say, "Oh, there goes Mr. Todacheene; he met this girl, and they were silent. And he didn't know who she was. And it's funny because his parents didn't tell him that he should talk to her; otherwise than that, it's funny because he married his own clan sister." That's a crime in its own part.

Todacheene's wise reference to clan relationships is an important response to Basso's basic assertion, and a feature of courting that Basso also mentions: "Among the Western Apache, rules of exogamy discourage courtship between members of the same clan and so-called 'related' clans, with the result that sweethearts are almost always 'non-matrilineal kinsmen'" ("To Give Up" 219n5).

Upon returning from a long absence (or, better said, greeting those returning from a long absence). For the Western Apaches, the common type of reunion involves boarding school students and their parents. Basso writes,

> As the latter disembark and locate their parents in the crowd, one anticipates a flurry of verbal greetings. Typically, however, there are few or none at all. Indeed, it is not unusual for parents and child to go without speaking for as long as 15 minutes. ("To Give Up" 220)

According to Basso's informants, parents remain silent in order to see if their long-absent children have been changed for the worse by living with whites. Parents are especially anxious to know if their children have lost respect for their parents and their native culture.

Basso's assertion is underpinned by a long literary tradition of depicting homecoming as an ambiguous situation. In one of the earliest and most popular accounts of an Indian girl's homecoming, *Stiya, A Carlisle Indian Girl at Home*, Stiya returns to Hopi after a five-year absence:

My father and mother, who were at the station waiting for their daughter, rushed in my direction as soon as they saw me, and talking Indian as fast they as could tried to help me from the train.

. . . I had forgotten that home Indians had such grimy faces.

I had forgotten that my mother's hair always looked as though it had never seen a comb.

I had forgotten that she wore such a short, queer-looking black bag for a dress, fastened over one shoulder only, and such buckskin wrappings for shoes and leggings.

. . . I am thoroughly disgusted this moment at the way the Indians live. . . . (Embe 2–3, 20)[26]

Stiya's story paves the way for homecoming silence and for resisting homecoming recidivism. Although her parents enthusiastically greet her, they are met by her shock and barely disguised disgust. As her story unfolds, so does her growing disdain for them, their home, their food, their way of life.[27] Other parents would be more cautious about allowing their children to attend Indian boarding schools.

In *Civilization, and the Story of the Absentee Shawnee,* Thomas Wildcat Alford writes that his homecoming was a "bitter disappointment" (111). "No happy gathering of family and friends greeted him"; instead, he was received "coldly and with suspicion," for they immediately noticed his change in manner, speech, and dress. Clearly, they understood his disapproval of them, for he writes: "Instead of being eager to learn the new ideas I had to teach them, they gave me to understand very plainly that they did not approve of me" (111). His parents greeted him with silence, realizing full well that their son had been adversely changed by his white schooling.

It might be easy to assign homecoming silence to the days of Indian boarding schools, but the scenario persists in popular twentieth-century writing as well, such as when the main character in Sinclair Browning's *The Last Song Dogs,* part-Apache private investigator Trade Ellis, heads for the San Carlos Apache Indian reservation in Arizona, and her grandmother, Shiwóyé, greets her with silence, for Ellis had not been on the reservation for a while.[28]

Given this literary support and Basso's research, I wanted to know what kind of responses I would receive, especially since the situation seemed to stimulate mutual fear: the people greeting the returnees are afraid that the returnee has changed (become white), and the returnees seem to be afraid of the same thing. The fear that a prolonged absence could somehow rob one of one's Indianness or that one might surrender one's Indianness during that time casts doubt on the actual importance of blood quantum and family training to Indian identity. It is evident that Indianness has less to do with blood chemistry and genetics than with maintaining a distinction between Indians and outsiders.

When I spoke with various Indians about this socially ambiguous situation, the responses ranged widely. Jagles talked about the first time she left home for an extended period of time, to attend Allegheny College in Pennsylvania. She received a good deal of advice, most of which pertained to her return to Tesuque Pueblo:

> In my [journal], I talked about the different things that happen before you leave. You just get blessings. . . . You just bless each other, father, son, holy spirit, you know, and the family that you go visit gives you food or money or whatever. . . . "Don't forget that we'll always be here," from people older, and some people younger will tell you a little bit like, "Oh, will you write to me?" and things like that.
>
> One time I was leaving, and one of my cousins tells me, he says, "Don't come back; don't come back and just shake my hand. I want you to come back and hug me."
>
> And I said, "Why are you saying that?"
>
> And he said, "because your cousins who left before you, they come and shake your hand, not even touching your palms, just the fingertips."
>
> Like this [Jagles demonstrates]. Like they're more assimilated . . . and better than the people at home. And I said, "Don't worry about that; I'm not going to be like that." And when I came back, and I saw him, I gave him a hug to let him know that I am not like my cousins and stuff like that. . . .

Epaloose, a Zuni, simply agreed with the assertion that returnees are met with silence, saying, "There's a lot of that." He extended his response to incorporate the tensions he and others feel when they try to live in two cultures, native and white:

> It may not actually be a silence; it may be brought forth right out. And they will come right out and say, "Well, you're doing all this well, but are you trying to act better than us? Why aren't you at home doing your responsibilities there, doing your duties to your culture and your religion?"

Speaking as a participant in two cultures, O'Neal also confirmed incidences of homecoming silence:

> I feel that's true. Sometimes [the Santo Domingo people] don't want to know what [the returnees] have experienced as far as white man's way. They don't want to know about it; they don't want to talk about it. They're afraid the person might have changed more into thinking white, being white. They feel he took a part of them out and gave [it] to the white man. So rather than talking to him, they'd rather not know. Period. That's how I feel.

Todacheene, speaking as a Navajo, initially disagreed. Then he remembered what happened "when the Pima Indian guy, Ira Hayes, went to war. . . . He saw such a horrible time with a lot of killing that he witnessed that he came back and didn't want to talk about it. Maybe that applies to Indian veterans."[29] So far as Navajo civilians are concerned, Todacheene did not think the homecoming silence applied:

> I've been gone from the reservation since 1983, and I went to the East Coast and the West Coast and traveled extensively. But when I went back home, I always told my parents, you know, what I've learned and experienced, where I was, what I've done, and what I've witnessed.
>
> Due to the fact that I was raised traditional, my dad always took care of me, . . . [so he wants to] find out, you know, what my travels were like to match what he learned through medicine men. . . . So when we speak, I tell him what I witnessed, [and] he says, "Yes, that's the way this man from . . . Chinle Camp said that you were O.K., and that you were safe" (due to the fact that my parents were always worried about my safety, and if anything happened to me, they would at least want my body to be brought home).
>
> But in the meantime, there's no merit for a person [Basso] to say that about silence because families always want to know how their kids reacted in the real world environment. Being American Indians, most . . . families like to know how their sons and daughters did in school, how they achieved, what their plans are going to be like, whether they're going to remain or they're going to leave, whether they're going into the military, if they're going to stay, and so forth. Otherwise than that, I can imagine a son or daughter coming home and remaining silent and totally frustrating the parents because [the parents] don't know what their family's future is going to be like.

Speaking from atop Acoma mesa, Saavedra disagreed with Todacheene's assessment, saying that silence does indeed accompany a homecoming: "Yes, that's very true, and it's called jealousy":

> They get jealous because you've left the reservation to better your life. And they think, "Well, he's going out to Phoenix to be a technician or something." [But] when you come back, you're coming back to your culture. You never leave home; you're always welcome at home. Always there's a home for you in Acoma.

Saavedra's wife and two sisters-in-law responded to Basso's assertion of homecoming silence by saying, "You don't know *our* family" (Romero). They disagreed with Basso, and also, to a certain extent, with Saavedra. The sisters recalled Romero's return from Phoenix after a long absence, saying,

We talked to [Annette Romero] right away because we hadn't seen her for the longest time. She moved away from us, and the only reason why she came home was because of our mother's illness. We all banded together; that's the only way our family has survived is by banding together as a family. (qtd. in Romero)

The response of Earl Ortiz, also an Acoma, had a slightly different slant:

I go home every now and then for tribal ceremonies. I don't participate in the dances; I visit my relatives. . . . I like to go home to visit my sisters and see the family there.

And I guess maybe in a certain way, [the homecoming silence] is true because when I greet people up there [on the mesa], I almost have to reintroduce myself because people really don't know me. And so I guess there is a certain amount of silence regarding when a person is gone. . . . [But] they don't really hold it against you for what you've become. At least I haven't felt that.

Chino's thoughtful answer provided texture for the homecoming situation, for he gave yet another perspective on silence in this situation:

I don't think that's completely true. In my own experiences, when I've gone away to school, different times in my life, certainly you do get treated a little bit different when you come back to your people, but . . . I was never given that silent treatment. I was always treated a little bit different, as if I wasn't completely Acoma anymore.

Maybe people speak to me in a different manner, but I was never given the silent treatment, especially, from what I've experienced, the tribal leaders. It was my peers who treated me a little bit different but never the people.

Since he continued to equate silence with disapproval, turning away, not waiting to see, I asked him some other questions, especially about who he was referring to as his "peers." He replied,

My peers are people in my own age group, people that I went to school with, my peers at home. At the time, during my generation, it was still a little bit unusual for people to go off to the university. The younger generation, almost all of them go away to school of some sort. So when I got back, they all treated me a little bit different.

But maybe I wasn't completely Acoma anymore, and I had to prove to them that I was still the same person. [But] I don't recall any people turning away from me or being silent with me in that manner.

These considered responses to Basso's third assertion both vary and overlap: some Southwest Indians mention talking immediately, while others mention a homecoming silence, not unlike that of Western Apaches. In every situation, however, the ambiguity of the situation resides with the people who are arranging for the homecoming—not the returnee—who wonder if the returnee will be distant and unfamiliar.

Getting cussed out. Not to be taken literally as an exercise in profanity, this expression is used to describe "any situation in which one individual, angered and enraged, shouts insults and criticisms at another" ("To Give Up" 221). The person or persons who are on the receiving end are often—but not always—the reason for such a display. But whether innocent or guilty of provoking the "cussing," the response to it is generally silence. After all, Basso explains,

> Individuals who are "enraged" *(hashkee)* are also irrational or "crazy" *(bini' édih)*. In this condition, it is said, they "forget who they are" and become oblivious to what they say and do. . . . In a word, they are dangerous. ("To Give Up" 221)

When I posed this scenario, Chino immediately said, "No [that's not true]." He continued,

> I mean, it's so stupid to make these kinds of generalizations about the people. Certainly, there are going to be some people who are going to be silent in situations like that, and the Indian people that I know of are no different. I mean, some of them are not going to say anything . . . because they're just going to reach a point that you'll wish you hadn't pushed them that far. People are just that way.
>
> As a whole, I've never encountered a situation like that, whether it was a schoolyard dispute or even a disagreement with another tribal member, as I am now as a forty-five-year-old man. There are some that are going to be quiet; they are not going to say anything, and there are some that are just going to say their mind. So, it's very dangerous; it's dangerous for people of influence, especially that are educated and that other people listen to because they publish their opinions. It's dangerous for those people to make generalizations of that sort, I believe.

O'Neal agreed with Chino: "I don't believe that's true." And then she laughed:

> The angry person is just expressing himself. Some people deal with anger in a silent way. I do. I don't want to hurt a person; I just stay silent. I just listen to what he has to say—he or she. I'll think through it, maybe talk to that person after I've thought through about what he or she has said. I don't think that [anger] makes them crazy; it's just them, that's how they express themselves.

Others, however, felt that the anger and response to anger were true: "I agree with that," said Epaloose. As he continued to analyze the response to anger, he said

Sometimes, just hearing and listening is enough for that person. . . . So I guess the initial reaction would be stay back; this person is irrational; he's not thinking straight. Let's wait until the situation calms down. Whether people are having . . . problems [or] coming right out and voicing their opinions, we listen to them first.

Interestingly, Epaloose equated keeping silent with respectful listening.

Todacheene also equated silence with respect, which is learned in the Navajo family:

Indians don't fight verbally; he has a point there. Most Indians, most Navajos and Apaches that I know, are taught not to talk back to people, not to answer with menace, not to give a bad impression that they come from a family where talking back and responding rudely is how the family is. Most Indian families, before the 1980s, were like that because a lot of families had a lot of respect.

Jagles, too, mentioned Tesuque family training, but her training differed from Todacheene's:

My response to anger . . . comes out of how well somebody knows how to vent their anger or emotions. . . . In my family, we're told not to cry, and the girls weren't supposed to show anger [because it wasn't ladylike]. Girls could cry, and we could pout and all that stupid stuff. So when my anger would boil up, I wouldn't say anything; I wouldn't show any action at all until my teenage years. That's when I learned how to punch the wall, which probably wasn't the best thing to do—but it helped.

Later in his response, however, Todacheene spoke of meeting anger with silence; he conflates anger with fighting and dismisses them both as bad things:

Fighting doesn't get you anywhere, . . . so most Indian people just remain silent, due to the fact that they don't want to inflict any pain, or they don't want to hurt. It's not that they don't want to fight back or talk back, it's just that most Indian people can size people up. . . . When you get reprimanded or have a personal comment made against you, it'll hurt. Because most Indian people can be really nasty. . . . But most Indian people generally have the respect of not fighting, due to the fact that no good comes out of it at all. Maybe it's their religious training that keeps them in harmony; . . . fighting takes you out of this harmony.

Although Epaloose is Zuni, parts of his response also resonated with Todacheene's:

We only deal with the way things are, the way the world is, accept it as that, and say, "Move on." So I think . . . it takes a lot more to get people in my culture angry. . . . The stress levels are higher, [but] the tolerance levels are a lot higher. But at the same time, we may hold too much in, until it actually bursts.

The last section of Todacheene's rich and complex response on anger met with silence has to do with using silence to calm down:

Maybe [fighting] relieves some people, but, generally, traditional Indian people like to be silent for a while before everything settles down. Then it comes to sitting down at the table and discussing one's problems or family problems or community problems or whatever. Power and influence [in] Western culture has become trapped; [whites] settle their problems through the court system.

Saavedra's response, though more personal, aligned with Todacheene's, both in terms of family training and in terms of using silence during the cooling-off period:

I see hatred among Native Americans who are fighting among each other; there's jealousy. They get mad at small things, which shouldn't be. . . . There's a lot of provoking going on, as people are trying to establish their lives. . . . They'll not want to sit down and talk about it; they'll want to fight. But there's no silence. You'll make up afterwards if you're relation. But we've never done that [fighting] in our family; we're closer than that.

[When my wife and I fight,] the truth comes out. You're so mad inside, so filled up with anger, resentments, maybe, but there is silence afterwards during the healing process. You never go to bed mad. That's what our grandparents told us. If there's some argument, or you're mad at your kids, tell them, but never go to bed mad.

Perhaps Earl Ortiz's response to Basso's assertion is the most useful. Not anchoring the silent response in Indian culture, let alone any particular pueblo or tribal culture, or specific family training, Ortiz explained the response as a basic human one: "It's the same for any culture: when someone's pissed off, really mad, and doesn't want to be interrupted, stay away, keep your mouth shut, and you'll live longer."

During mourning. Basso refers to this category as "being with people who are sad," a sometimes-prolonged period following the funeral or wake. The reasons Basso's informants supply for the use of silence are three: for the mourners, speaking requires an "unusual amount of physical effort" ("To Give Up" 222); verbal communication is unnecessary at this time; and intense grief is akin to intense anger in that it warps people's personalities.

My informants provided a range of responses, as usual, beginning with Saavedra, who disagreed with Basso and yet rehearsed the link between silence and healing:

I disagree, because there is a healing process, which is four days for us—and that's a lot of mourning. There's a lot of family in the home; there's a grieving period for the whole family. And the spirit world is taking your spirit, which gives you four days in each four directions. You have two in each direction, and that last day, you're going straight up.

And there's a lot of silence. The kids don't really know what's going on. The elders know what's going on; they're just preparing [for their own passing]. There's silence there. Silence in the elders. My generation, age group, we're not preparing; we're seeing the future. We'll be next [living out the future as elders].

There's a lot of work involved. You try not to be mad at one another; we try to get along. There's a lot of commotion at times. As I said, it's a healing process.

They're never forgotten; we visit their graves. We don't talk about how they died because most of them died from old age or from being diabetic. We tell the kids that they're sick because they don't understand. [There's no taboo for talking about how someone died] in our culture, but in other cultures, it might be taboo. The Acoma culture is not afraid to talk about our deceased because they live on with us through our whole lives.

Todacheene, too, disagreed with Basso's assertion, saying it "doesn't make sense," at least not anymore, not with the heavy Western influence on Navajo culture. Despite Western influence, however, Todacheene mentioned the significance of the four days:

No, that's not true at all, because, speaking for Navajos, what I would [have] miss[ed] was when my grandfather died and everybody participated in his funeral and burial. In the old days, Navajos' bodies were put in between crevices of rocks or buried where nobody knows where they were buried, but today, as Western culture has a lot of influence on Navajo society (a lot of Navajo people are . . . Catholics, Mormons, Pentecostals, Christian Reformed . . .), and a lot of these taboos that one learns about Indians are not true today. . . .

When a person dies, for four days, you can't do anything supposedly bad: spouses can't make love; couples can't make love; there's no sex. But in that time between, . . . a lot of Navajo people get together, the whole family: cousins, distant cousins, relatives, nieces, uncles, grandchildren—everybody [stays] up all night, talking about that person, how good he was, what they did [together], what he learned, where he was raised, who his family was, what he did for a living, the good side. Everything comes out, how bad he was, how he cheated, if he went to church. Everybody tells about their experiences with that person. And after that evening, the [deceased's] name is usually not said.

. . . You know, you can't have a funeral and be silent. There's a lot of things to discuss; there's a lot of things to do in the mourning. There's a lot of things to be done; there's a lot of things that need to be reminded for to be done; there's a lot. There's basically too much to be done not to talk about [it].

O'Neal, on the other hand, agreed with the assertion, saying that "Native Americans do stay silent when they're mourning":

But after a while, they start talking about the person, like white people do. What he did, or what she did, or how that person was a good person, whatever. But during mourning, yes, everybody does stay silent, Native Americans or white people. I know I do.

Epaloose, too, agreed:

There are certain rituals that need to be done, and it's not like a single act of mourning, like one day. It could carry on for years, and then you're done. It all depends. Time heals each person.

So, I mean, everybody takes responsibility for the death, and they do the rituals that need to be done, and they carry them out. And there's not as much interaction. I don't know if that's good or bad; it works both ways, depending on the person. Some people need comfort and reassurance, and others just need the time to be alone. It could go both ways.

Earl Ortiz's explanation of the Acoma tradition converged with Basso's:

Yes, even though we mourn for the person that's passed away, we go through a traditional ceremony for them, which everyone participates in, but only a few people actually do . . . the blessing for that person. The rest of the people watch or pray silently within themselves.

Wanya, also from Acoma, said that "for the person they're mourning, the person they've lost, I think it's all right for them to be silent because they're hurting. [The deceased] are gone; they're going to miss them." Victoriano interrupted, "But everybody else talks among themselves and talks to other families, saying, 'Hello, how are you,' greeting each other, making sure everybody's family is good and strong." And Romero interjected, "Everybody gets together and brings dishes, food. And everybody talks." Wanya spoke again, "I think it's better to be together and to talk than to be sad, because the person you have lost, I don't think they want you to be mourning over them and to be sad. [They want you to] just move on and take care of your family and be strong." Victoriano agreed.

Jagles addressed the issue of silence and mourning by discussing two different situations of mourning, that which accompanies a slow and painful death and that which accompanies a sudden death:

> I think that [might have been] the way a long time ago or something. In a lot of ways, it would depend on how that person died, because if that person was an elder and you knew so-and-so was going to die, it was easier to joke around and say, "Oh, you remember when he—." The way we would help each other get through [my grandfather's death] was to talk about the funny things he did, the way that he was cussing and trying to combine Spanish and English, like *sonavabiche,* and . . . what else did he say? [We would tell one another] different things that he would do, not to forget about those things, and that it really wasn't sad even though my mom told me not to cry. . . .
>
> But just talking to my mom and my sisters and the family while we were preparing his things, it was a lot more helpful than to just be silent and wonder what everybody is thinking. So I don't think [what Basso says]. And a lot of times, too, I mean it's kind of funny, but you would hear laughter, and we'd just be laughing.
>
> But say, for instance, when my aunt, who we didn't know was going to die—I think in that situation because we were in shock, we didn't know what to say. She had a heart attack after a gall stone removal. I think she had epilepsy, so she might have had a seizure that triggered it. Just the shock of it, but also talking about, when people came to see her, "Oh how did it happen?" Then having to explain it was helpful, but the shock of it made it more uneasy than my grandpa's. So . . . even though he says silence, it just doesn't make sense to be silent during mourning.

But Chino said, in no uncertain words, "He is just full of shit." But as he continued, he tempered his views, mentioning the silence that is in play and also alluding to the four days' movement of the spirit:

> I mean, when people are silent, it's because . . . of the nature of what is going on. When you are in mourning, you are silent because you are respectful of the event that has happened to you. I mean, it's very hard. So, yes, people are silent, but it's because of how you want to respect . . . their life and your life, and because of the prayer of continuing from the person's passing to the time, four days, before they go back to the spirit world. So they're still within this world. So, yes, you purposefully keep things down so to speak. I mean you're not out there making all kinds of noise, or it's a time of reflection.

The responses to Basso's fifth assertion were particularly interesting in that most of the informants conflated a prolonged period of mourning with the mourning immediately following the death. As I reread my prompt and the transcripts of all the interviews, my prompt seems clear. Maybe it was not—or maybe these people could not respond to my prompt, so they responded in whatever ways made sense to them, according to their own experiences and observations. However, no one responded according to Basso's observation, that is, in terms of how the bereaved might be disturbed or unstable, like an angry person.

During ceremonials. According to Basso's informants and his observations of over seventy-five "curing ceremonials," everyone is silent while they are "being with someone for whom they sing" ("To Give Up" 224). From the moment the ceremonial is about to begin until the final chant the next morning, everyone must remain silent except for the medicine man or his aides. Basso explains this necessary silence in terms akin to those surrounding an angry person or a grieving one: people undergoing ceremonial treatment are perceived "as having been changed by power into something different from their normal selves":

> They are regarded with caution and apprehension. Their newly acquired status places them in close proximity to the supernatural and, as such, carries with it a very real element of danger and uncertainty. These conditions combine to make "being with someone for whom they sing" a situation in which speech is considered disrespectful and, if not exactly harmful, at least potentially hazardous. (225)

Not surprisingly, I did not receive many responses specific to curing ceremonies—nor should I. After all, as Laguna-affiliated Paula Gunn Allen reminds me, native people, "particularly Pueblos," are "protective toward their traditions" ("Problems" 56). I did, however, receive a number of rich responses that coupled silence with ceremonials in general.

Todacheene's response was the only one that mentioned curing ceremonies:

> When medicine men are hired to do specific diagnostic situations for families, individuals, [or] children, mostly the families sit in silence. The medicine man and the apprentice and the head of the family do a lot of the talking, but it's in low whispers, . . . [for] instructions have to be given about how to deal with ashes, about [where] water needs to be placed, how much wood needs to be there. And generally when a song or prayer is done, everybody sits in silence and waits and listens to what the prayer brings.
> In other words, if a family is doing harm to another family, and this individual is brought in and a ceremony is done, [then] everybody is silent.

Because you can hear, [or so] they say, witches come around. You can hear footsteps; you can hear noises; you can hear bird calls—that's a reason for silence because you need to know what you're dealing with. So from then on, the medicine man, the apprentice, and the head of the family or members of the family know how to deal with [evil], how to react or counter-react to evil that was drawn out, or how the goodness was used to combat evil. It goes back and forth [between goodness and evil], and generally silence is employed a lot. And it's very important that no noise or no interruptions are made to cross-yield the effects of the ceremony.

Epaloose did not speak to a specific kind of ceremony, but he did speak to the importance of silence on the part of participants:

[Basso's observation about using silence during ceremonials] is true, and it should be. There's a purpose in ceremonials, and there's a purpose to why you're doing it. And it [silence] is a sign of courtesy and respect, all going back to why you're there and why you're doing whatever ceremony it might be. The actual goal is not to be there as a spectator but to be part of it and to rejoice. And I guess if you're outspoken and laughing and whatnot during a ceremony that it's a sign of disrespect, and you're actually violating that purpose of the ceremony, whatever it is.

Jagles, too, responded in terms of audience participation, whether the audience uses silence or words: "In parts of it, you are silent; [in] other parts, it's almost like you're reassuring the individuals that are in charge of it that you're aware." She continued:

You say something that makes them know that you're awake and aware of it, and you also say something that gives them a little bit more strength in whatever they're doing, like when somebody's preaching, a lot of the men will say, "*ho wah na mu*," like "That's the way it is." Almost like "Amen" or "That's right." You know how black people say, "That's right, Sister, keep talking." Well, it's kind of the same thing.

Chino's response also aligned with Epaloose's in that Chino, too, discussed the importance of silence with ceremonies in general, but he also discussed fasting:

Yes, people use silence during ceremonials; it depends on whether that person is a participant in some way—say you're fasting. By fasting I mean that there are certain things that aren't allowed during that time, [that the person is] not necessarily fasting for food. So one of the things that they ask you when you do fast is that you do fast from outbursts of anger. . . . So you keep yourself calm, and you reflect on why you are fasting and [about] the holiness. . . . You're quiet in those times, but by being quiet, I don't mean that you don't say anything. You go on with your daily life, and you speak to anyone who is going to speak to you. It's not as though you live a life of a monk, but you are fasting. What you do is become reflective in those times.

O'Neal said that remaining silent during ceremonials is "a must." "You have to stay silent and respect the ceremonies that are going on. Anybody talking or laughing, not putting their whole selves into the ceremonies, are asked to leave or go home, whatever; that's part of the respect." She then distinguished between public ceremonies—harvest, feast, and corn dances, for instance—and private, pueblo-only ceremonies:

> [Dances are] offered for anybody, open to the public, so there might be more talking there. As far as the non-Indians, it's understood that they are going to talk and express their feelings about the ceremony. But most of the native Americans that are watching the dances are just silent, just watching and meditating at the same time.

She continued, this time expressly mentioning white visitors:

> Or if a white person's watching any dances in the pueblo, respect that, be silent, don't ask a stranger, especially a Native American, any kind of questions when it comes to their dances, ceremonies, whatever. Wait till you get with a friend that's from the pueblo reservation and then ask in private. Otherwise, you might offend that person. They might ignore you; they will be silent—not to be rude; they just don't want to answer you right there and then.

Romero and her sisters agreed that they remain silent during ceremonials in order to "watch them dance and show respect and hear them." Wanya piped up to say that "the only time you hear noise is when the kids make noise or when people greet each other with our Kerésan language." The sisters talked about how they all dance and how they are all supposed to speak their language on the mesa.

But Earl Ortiz's minimalist discourse reflects Allen's caveats about protecting the ceremonies. When I asked him about Indians being silent during curing ceremonials, he replied, "So are white people." After a reflective pause, Ortiz continued; he provided general information about ceremonies, but nothing specific:

> There are different types of tribal ceremonies that we use. Like you could split them into two distinct situations; where the non-Indian is invited and then only our Acomas, like in October and July.

The [ceremonials] that are just for our own people are fairly silent. We don't cheer or clap; we don't outwardly express ourselves during the ceremonies. We pray within ourselves. We pray [to] help the spirits, pray for whatever, everything, silent. Whereas on the other occasions, where non-Indians are invited, there may be food stands, vendors, [or] carnivals involved, which is more lively, more colorful. We [might talk among ourselves] in other religious ceremonies where only our tribal members participate, but [our talk] is not as outwardly expressed as [that of] the other non-Indian participants.

Allen warns that informants should keep ceremonials private; Devon Mihesuah writes that "some informants may not be culturally aware, yet naive researchers may take their word as truth just because they are Indians" (*Natives* 3).[30] There is also the possibility that some Indians may respect the silence without knowing the specific reason for the silence. It is impossible for me to draw a line between what these people might not know about their cultural legacies and what they do not want me to know about them. I tend to believe that they told me what they wanted me to know and that is all. I dropped the subject and talked with them about their uses of silence, in general. Interestingly, many of them turned immediately to the subject of silence and schooling.

Talking about School and Silence

Basso's foundational work on the Cibecue Apache influenced a number of closely related studies of Indians at school, school being yet another ambiguous setting where silence is often employed. Two representative studies are Gary Plank's research on the linguistic practices of Navajo schoolchildren and Susan Philips's analysis of the classroom practices of Warm Springs Indian schoolchildren. I used these studies as the basis for my interview questions about silence and schooling. On the whole, the responses I received aligned with Plank's and Philips's conclusions.

Plank writes that for the Navajo population with which he works, silence is a "form of communication," not "merely the lack of speaking," and that "silence serves a purpose for the non-speaker" (4). Plank goes on to say that "the Navajo child is unlikely to *ask* a question in the classroom. Also, the Navajo child is not apt to *answer* the question presented by the teacher" (5). For Plank (and Basso as well), the reason Navajo students do not speak out in school is because they have been socialized at home in two very important ways: (1) they should not distinguish themselves from their classmates; and (2) they should listen and watch their teacher, not question or answer him (5).

Plank's assessment of Navajo schoolchildren is echoed by Alvord, who writes about cross-cultural discomfort at school:

As I mentioned earlier, Navajos are taught from the youngest age never to draw attention to ourselves. So Navajo children do not raise their hands in class. At a school like Dartmouth, the lack of participation was seen as a sign not of humility but lack of interest and a disengaged attitude. (30)

Alvord goes on to say,

The very thought of exhibiting my skills and knowledge before others was disturbing: I could not bring myself to participate in class discussions and debates, or to volunteer answers to professors' questions, although it was expected. The same problems I had encountered at Dartmouth were even more exaggerated here [at Stanford]. I didn't feel comfortable raising my hand in class, I wasn't competitive enough about test scores and projects, and I didn't like to draw attention to myself. I lacked the "right stuff" that every med student needs: a competitive edge. Yet it was hard for me to behave any other way. Silence is a normal part of Navajo communication; words are used sparingly and weighed carefully. It took me a long time to be comfortable with the non-Navajo style of learning. (39)

Plank, however, does not concentrate so much on the discomfort of Navajo students as he does on the discomfort of their white teachers, one of whom said,

It felt real uncomfortable cause I would remember things like driving one of the kids (students) down to the clinic (a 15-mile drive) and there wouldn't be a word spoken all the way down. I would say something like, "So where are you going?" And he'd say, "The clinic." Then I'd try to talk to him and say something and there would be no response or very little. No conversation. They'd get out and say "Bye." They wouldn't even say thanks or anything. (qtd. in Plank 8)

Although it is difficult, if not impossible, for me to decouple a generational silence from a cross-cultural silence in this situation, Plank addresses it culturally: "Navajo children feel fine with silence, it is the [white] teacher who is uncomfortable and uninformed about the use of this behavior" (7). During our interview, Todacheene's response attests to that statement:

We're always taught to listen and to watch what's around us. Basically it's the teacher who does the speaking while we, as young people, learn to listen and comprehend in a silent nature. This is all done through the teaching period—which extends from thirty minutes to several hours to six hours maybe even several days, depending on the nature of the teaching.

Susan Philips writes about the listening behavior of Warm Springs Indian children, who like many Navajo children remain silent while listening. Their behavior often confuses white teachers who expect eye contact or at least nodding or "mm hmms" at appropriate junctures (*Invisible* 52). Some teachers describe such silence as the "Indian students' *failure to participate* in classroom discussions and school activities" ("Participant" 374, emphasis added).

When Epaloose recounted to me his perceptions of his own classroom silences, he imagined how his teachers regarded him, saying

> There are situations where I've probably been looked at to be more passive or withdrawn where in actuality what I was really doing was listening, be it in class, or seminars, or whatnot. You know, when other people raise their hands and promote conversation, I'm more one to sit back and listen to everything first—and then present myself if I have any questions.
>
> I don't know. People look at it as passive, but like I said, it's more a sign of respect rather than being laid back. I know at an early age, being with the language difference and everything, I was kind of looked at as being slow and not taking initiative. In first grade or so, they probably thought that there was something wrong, that I needed special attention, but in actuality, I just needed [things] explained in my way. I guess [my way] would be the Zuni cultural way or how things were presented—or even [across] the language barrier.
>
> In first grade, I came . . . from Head Start in Zuni . . . to Albuquerque, to Zia Elementary, so it was quite a big difference. [I went] from speaking my mother tongue to speaking English. But the thing is, back then, there wasn't the patience and dedication for cultural diversity; then, if you couldn't get your point across, they thought that person was slow.

Although they understood student silence as culturally specific, the white teachers in Philips's study did not stop talking to listen themselves. Feeling that there was little to no classroom interaction, they kept talking, without interruption, while their Warm Springs Indian students (the listeners) continued to remain silent.

Remembering back to how his own school experiences intersected with his home culture and advice, Acoma member Earl Ortiz told me,

> You know, I was thinking when I was coming over. You know, when we were growing up, our elders, especially our mother and father, especially our mother, she was always telling us, "Be quiet. Listen. And you will learn." In Indian, she would tell us that constantly. When you go to school, be silent, listen, and you will learn. She never said anything about speaking up.

Ortiz's memories substantiate Plank's and Philips's strong assertions about Indian uses of silence at school, assertions based on Basso's initial work. Despite this research and the testimony of various Southwest people, I am both energized and discomfited by these assertions—especially when I consider how so many of us whites see (and want to see) so-called Real Indians in the first place and how very little American Indian scholarship—written by Indians—is read by these researchers or most white people in general.

INDIANS SPEAKING OF THE SILENT INDIAN

In *Off the Reservation,* Allen writes that she sees Indians as "best kept silent" rather than silent on their own terms. She explains the silence that is often perceived as emptiness in her description of pueblo pottery: "A truly beautiful clay pot from Acoma or San Juan Pueblo signifies *on the emptiness it surrounds*" (173–74, emphasis added). Acoma poet Simon Ortiz describes the Indian's purposeful use of silence, particularly in comparison with their friend Agee, "a hero," who "was talking. I mean talking," which "may not sound like a big deal":

> Some people say Indians are just like that,
> shy and reserved and polite,
> but that's mostly crap. Lots of times
> we were plain scared
> and we kept our mouths shut.
> I mean Grants and Milan and the mines
> between Haystack and Ambrosia Lake,
> all that area used to be Indian land—
> Acoma land—but it was surveyed
> by the government and stolen
> at the turn of the century
> and there was plenty to say
> but we didn't say it.
> I mean being Indian wasn't the safest
> thing to be in town
> so we didn't say much, much less
> be in Grandma's Café arguing
> with white miners who made jokes
> about squaws and called you chief.
> I mean Agee was talking.

("What I Mean" 327)

The subject of Indians using silence purposefully constituted a good deal of my interview time, particularly when the Southwest Indians with whom I spoke talked about using silence to nourish themselves or protect their culture, especially from inquisitive, often unthinking whites. Chino, for instance, reinforced his opinion about the necessity of using silence to preserve his cultural ties:

What binds [Acoma people] is our beliefs, our language, and our culture, but the [individual] people are different. . . . I've seen the culture anthropologists to be the most prejudiced, just full of it. They've put lies into the people's minds, and the people tend to believe it because it's written, so it must be true. And it is not. Because when the anthropologists go to different places, they have what [are] known as informants. And a lot of the informants are paid, and you know they're going to tell whatever [the anthropologists] want to hear. And a lot of it even has to do with protecting the cultural identity, and so they're going to say something misleading so that the anthropologist doesn't fully understand the religious practices or something [having to do with our sense of] nature. So they're going to be deliberately misleading. But for the most part, they're all paid.

Jagles also talked about keeping silent on things she and her pueblo do not want everyone else to know about, about sharing a silence (or a secret) as a way to protect their culture:

Well, I would give an example from [Bread Loaf] this summer, where I would choose not to talk about certain things that the class was talking about. What they were talking about was sacredness and the difference between something being sacred and something being a secret. They thought the only way that something could be sacred was if it was secret. [This was my] Cultures of American Southwest class, [which was] mostly white, and an Alaskan native and myself . . . along with the professor, who was just, you know, pretty much observing the discussion. And so were we, the Alaskan native and myself.

There were so many things I wanted to say, but then at the same time, . . . I could do either one: I could choose to remain silent, or I could vocalize my opinions about it. But at the same time, I could also hear my mom saying, "Well, you shouldn't even refer to certain things that we have because if you refer to certain things then that means that we have them."

[I'm] talking about certain ceremonies and stuff, so if you refer to them, then somebody will automatically [think], "Oh, Tesuque Pueblo does have such and such a thing." But if you don't talk about them, if you don't refer to them, then [the knowledge of the ceremony] stays limited to the knowledge of the people living in Tesuque Pueblo. Otherwise, nobody knows about it. So, in a way, that secret is already secret because of what [the Tesuque people] think of it as. So the secretness of what [the class] were talking about doesn't really make it sacred.

And the reason why they started that discussion was because Simon Ortiz came, and he talked about ruins and about some people [who] came to the village and asked what they should do about the pottery they found in this particular ruin location near Acoma. He said, "Leave it there." And the councilmen told them to leave it there, to leave it alone. And then that's when one of the [white] students said, "Well, why don't you mark where these things are so that nobody will go in?"

Ortiz said, "Well that defeats the purpose. Then more people will be inclined to go look and try to find stuff."

So that's why [the white students] got into the conversation of what is sacred, "Is it just because it's secret?"

I wanted to tell them, "No, because if you think something's precious and sacred to you, it doesn't necessarily have to be secret. It could just be among your family, or it could be among your community, like a church [for communion, baptism, marriage, funerals, which are sacred but not secret]. It could be a public place; people can go in there, whatever. [The white students] could contain it or keep their own perceptions of what that is because they're never going to know or understand it. . . .

So my decision was to stay silent, for two purposes: one, my mom's saying, "Well, don't refer to it a whole lot because that means we have it"; and the other one was to see how the discussion was going and to see what everybody had to say.

In addition to using silence to protect their culture, the people in my study also told stories about using silence for self-protection, nourishment, and respect.[31] The stories ranged from the easy silence linked with morning prayer to the darker silences of abuse. All of them were the silences important to the individual. For instance, Chino clarified for me his use of silence as respect:

I stop to think about my answer before I speak. Because as I've learned within my time on this earth, so many times in my youth, I spoke without thinking. Because I want to live my life in a better way, I try to think before I speak. I don't know if this has anything to do with culture: it just has something to do with the way I want to conduct my life.

And other uses of silence are . . . when I want to ask somebody—it's probably a cultural thing—when I go to ask somebody's help, an elder. And if it's a formal request, there will be a short time, a respectful silence, before I just start talking to that person and ask. I always wait after I've asked that other person to respond, and in that time, there's often silence. Or when I'm going to pray, I usually have a bit of silence before I begin my prayer. And for me, that's a measure of respect to the creator who I'm praying to.

Chino punctuated our conversations about his uses of silence by invoking the dangers of cross-cultural study, particularly when the researcher does not truly respect the other culture or worse yet does not even talk with representatives of that culture: "When a person from one culture studies another culture, they get a different perception, often a wrong one."

And O'Neal, from Santo Domingo, told me that she wished Indians used silence in some of the ways white schoslars romanticized. Although she thought it would make for a kinder lifestyle, she thought that most Indians used silence and language the way white people do, as individuals: "Everybody uses silence differently," she told me, "I'm not too sure about anybody else":

> I use silence in a lot of different ways. First of all, in the morning, when I get up, I use silence to meditate, to pray. When I'm deep in thought, I use silence. If I'm ready to make a decision in life, I stay silent; that way I think through exactly what I'm going to do and see if it's the right choice.
>
> I also use silence when I'm angry because I don't feel like opening my mouth to hurt anybody, so if I'm angry, upset with anybody, I use silence. . . . That's how I do it.

O'Neal spoke freely and thoughtfully, but only about herself, not about her entire pueblo. She ended our interview by saying, "Silence, to me, is very powerful—spiritually, mentally, and physically."

A woman from a northern pueblo (who preferred to remain anonymous for this interview) explained some of the other reasons for keeping silent:

> And there are some other issues—I don't know what the percentage is because nobody ever does research, and nobody ever talks about how many individuals are sexually molested within the reservation because of the silence. So unfortunately that did happen to me. . . .
>
> It happens too often, and nobody talks about it. It's more [than] cultural values that make a child not want to talk about [molestation]. A child [does] not question adults' molestation because you're taught [to] respect your elders, don't question what's going on, and don't ask questions. [Usually it's someone who's being kind to you in some other way,] or they're teaching you different things about the culture that you find really special, because some [adults] don't choose to do that [teach you those special things].
>
> Or it's a type of relationship where you don't [even] have to ask questions because [the adults] are giving you the [special] information. So I think the cultural values of respect your elders, don't ask them questions, and they are all perfect—[well,] that's not true.

All of the people I interviewed told stories like these, stories that speak to the importance of narrative (of Burkean selection, reflection, deflection of reality) in getting to the truth. As Silko explains, telling stories is much more significant than "telling a once-upon-a-time story":

> I mean a whole way of seeing yourself, the people around you, your life, the place of your life in the bigger context, not just in terms of nature and location, but in terms of what has gone on before, what's happened to other people. So it's a whole way of being. . . . (qtd. in Barnes 71)

Thus, these stories interinanimate to argue a truth, a truth about Southwest Indians (as individuals and as a group) and their uses of silence and their perceptions of silencing. Early on in my research, Chino, in particular, urged me to avoid reading the work of white researchers and, instead, to talk with even more Indians and read scholarship written by Indians, to listen to many stories—all as a way to get to the truth. Mihesuah also insists that white scholars can find Indian voices—if they bother to look (*Natives* 5). And he argues for the necessary reinforcement provided by multiple perspectives: "Works on American Indian history and culture should not give only one perspective; the analyses must include Indians' versions of events" (1). "There is no one Indian voice. Different members of one tribe may have different interpretations of the same stories" (3). As I quickly discovered, many individuals can tell recognizable or wildly divergent versions of the same stories, the same truth. It all depends on the individual.

Who Can Say, Anyway?

But stories themselves, even overlapping ones, remain contested sites in postmodern scholarship, given the absence of a master narrative of uncontested truth. Still, despite these postmodern complications, all of us academics continue to read and write stories, for, as Vizenor tells us, stories are "more than survival, more than endurance or mere response"; they have "the power to make, re-make, and un-make the world" (qtd. in Powell 396). In many important ways, these interview stories provide what Keith Gilyard would call a "grand counter narrative to be posed against dominant, western European ideologies" ("African American"). Besides, as Carroll Smith-Rosenberg writes, if we "relinquish our grasp on the world behind words," if we "deny the knowability of the world, we lose that aspect of the world we are . . . committed to knowing" (32)—in my case, Southwest Indians' use of silence.

In "Rhetorics of Survivance," Malea Powell argues that such stories help Native people "reconceive our history, to re-imagine Indian-ness in our own varying and multiplicitous images, to create and re-create our presence on this continent" (428). Creek poet Joy Harjo reminds readers that memories substantiate all stories:

Remember you are all people and all people
are you.
Remember you are this universe and this
universe is you."

("Remember")

And as I mentioned earlier, Lyons speaks of *rhetorical sovereignty,* the "inherent right and ability of *peoples* to determine their own communicative needs and desires in this pursuit, to decide for themselves the goals, modes, styles, and languages of public discourse" (449–50, emphasis in original). For Lyons, then, all the people I interviewed have a right to tell their stories of silence and silencing and to use silence and silencing rhetorically, as the means to achieve their own goals. Lyons writes that rhetorical sovereignty—as a right, a theory, a practice, and a poetry—is the right to speak, and speak like the people with whom we live (467). For the people I interviewed, rhetorical sovereignty also includes the right, theory, practice, and poetry to remain purposefully silent, to be silent like the people with whom they live, and to use silence as a means of communication.

NOT THE LAST WORD

Although I believe that some Southwest Indians do regularly employ silence in some socially ambiguous situations, I cannot make more of a generalization than that. Basso's research findings sometimes hold firm—and sometimes leak. It is tempting to compare Southwest Indians' use of silence with that of whites, but I do not know of a comparable study that investigates the connection of silence and whites and those six situations. It seems evident, however, that some Southwest Indian families still teach silence as respect (whether as young children learning to remain silent or as adults who cushion a request with silence). I can go so far as to say that while many white people show respect by speaking, using a spoken ("Sir," "Ma'am") language of respect or a body language of deference, many Southwest Indian people might show respect by a "stilling" or a "silencing" of the self. In either case, it all depends on the individual.

As I read and reread my transcriptions of these interviews, I was struck by the sometimes cryptic language these interviewees used. Of course, it can be difficult to be taped during an interview; it can be even harder when the prompts are pointed and sometimes laughable (the silence-during-courtship prompt, for instance). Although these responses were always comprehensible to me, I do wonder if some of these individuals purposely omitted words and phrases that a white person might have automatically included. In other words, were these Southwest Indians employing the power of omission, of silence? Was there first-language interference? Both? Neither? I do not know.

The beauty of the interviews was that no Indian person I spoke to was surprised that white academics often consider them to be silent. For whatever reasons—privacy, respect, caution—each Indian person could speak at length about his or her purposeful and rhetorically effective uses of silence, sometimes as a member of a tribe or pueblo, but always and foremost as an individual.

6
Opening Silence

I catch the pattern
Of your silence
Before you speak.
I do not need
To hear a word.
In your silence
Every tone I seek
Is heard.

—Langston Hughes, "Silence"

In *De Oratore,* Cicero pronounces delivery "the dominant factor in oratory; without delivery the best speaker cannot be of any account at all" (3.56.213). Quintilian writes that "the nature of the speech we have composed within our minds is not so important as the manner in which we produce it" (11.3.2). And when asked to list the three most important components of rhetoric, Demosthenes is said to have replied: "Delivery, delivery, delivery" (Quintilian 11.3–6). Well, what if the delivery is silence, silence, silence? How does the delivery of silence unsettle, resist, transform, and enrich our idea of a rhetorical delivery, or the tradition itself?

Those of us trained in rhetoric have most likely learned *the* history of rhetoric, that history of aristocratic, agonistic, and, most of all, eloquent males. In the last fifteen years, however, that history has been unsettled and transformed by the inclusion of "other" rhetorical practices and theoretical contributions. White and nonwhite women and men of nearly every social class and theoretical stripe continue to be written into the rhetorical tradition. (The scholarly contributions of Kermit Campbell, Jessica Enoch, Keith Gilyard, Michael Hecht, Karyn Hollis, Ronald L. Jackson II, Susan Kates, Randall A. Lake, Karen Lunsford, Jaime Mejía, Keith D. Miller, Gwendolyn Pough, Elaine Richardson, Joy Ritchie and Kate Ronald, Blake Scott, Wendy Sharer, Kathleen Welch, and Morris Young, to mention just a few and omit far too many, come immediately to mind.) Just a walk through the book exhibits at the meeting of the Conference on College Composition and Communication, the National Communication Association meeting, or the Modern Language Association meeting will provide a wondrous array of thought-provoking, tradition-modifying new publications that speak back to, resist, and transform histories and theories of rhetoric.

The verbalized or *spoken* continues to make its way into our articles, conference presentations, and books, but as Carole Blair and Mary Kahl have so eloquently argued, the rhetorical tradition cannot be rewritten with new characters without a concomitant reevaluation of the rhetorical theories that also inform that tradition. And although we have made some headway, we have yet to seriously probe our own disciplinary silences and silencings, the *unspoken*. Theorizing the unspoken is an even newer disciplinary concept. The push toward a more inclusive rhetorical tradition, however, is paving the way for further investigations into silence and the unspoken.

Patricia Bizzell, coeditor of *The Rhetorical Tradition,* surely one of the most successful rhetorical projects of our academic lifetime, writes that the feminist project, in particular, continues to present the "most trenchant challenges to traditional scholarly practices, opening up exciting new paths not only in the material scholars can study, but also, and perhaps ultimately more significantly, in the methods whereby we can study it" (5). To open the silences of "other" rhetorical traditions, whether they are feminist, ethnic, collaborative, or unspoken, our scholarly community must continue to explore new paths and use new and "other" methods. The work of Lisa Ede and Andrea Lunsford provides a case in point.

For more than twenty years, Ede and Lunsford have employed other methods in order to resist traditional rhetorical conceptions of singular authorship (as well as audience). To do so, they write in *Singular Texts/Plural Authors,* they had to open the silence that until then had deadened the sounds of collaborative authorship: that silence was "the pervasive commonsense assumption that writing is inherently and necessarily a solitary, individual act" (5). Their own methods and practices of collaboration—of delivering words together—helped them open up that assumption, particularly since their "own experience as coauthors" had generated so much dissonance in their profession:

> What seemed natural to us, however, seemed anything but natural to our English department colleagues. Some in our field cautioned us, for instance, that we would never receive favorable tenure decisions or promotions if we insisted on publishing coauthored articles. Even those who did not caution us about the dangerous consequences of our habit professed amazement at our ability to write together, questioning us in detail as though we had just returned from a strange new country. (6)

Their experience provides an lesson for all of us who are working to enrich the rhetorical tradition: we must locate, discover, stumble over, and then open up silences. Since the publication of that book, Ede and Lunsford have worked steadily to configure methods for developing, sustaining, and rewarding collaborative delivery—a no-longer silenced rhetorical practice, but one they are still explaining and defending ("Collaboration").

Brenda Jo Brueggemann's *Lend Me Your Ear* is another important project that has opened silence, in particular the silence of deafness. Once she pierced the silencing of her own deafness—once she "came out" as deaf, Brueggemann developed methods for listening to the vibrant rhetorical world of deafness and deaf education:

> It was not until I had embarked on my "coming out" as a deaf person that I considered my rites of passage and dwelled on my acts, both deliberate and unconscious, both past and present, of passing. Because my coming out was a midlife event, I had much to reflect back on and much to illuminate ahead of me. This passing through an identity crisis, and the rites of passage involved in uncovering the paths of my lifelong passing as "hearing," took place in a hall of mirrors. Later I would come to know this place as the art and act of rhetoric. (82)

When she opened the silence of her own deafness, she simultaneously rerouted the path of rhetorical delivery from leading only to the "good man speaking well" to providing options for the "good man or woman speaking, writing, and *signing* well."[1] After examining various rhetorical constructions of deafness, Brueggemann suggests "space for a rhetoric of silence, as well as time for a rhetoric of responsive and responsible listening that matches our rhetorical responsibilities for speaking—time for a rhetoric that lends its ear" (17). Krista Ratcliffe's current project does just that.

Ratcliffe's "Rhetorical Listening: Identification, Gender, and Whiteness," is another transformative rhetorical project, one that opens the silences surrounding codes of cross-cultural conduct. That silence broke open for her when she was finishing up *Anglo-American Challenges to the Rhetorical Tradition(s): Virginia Woolf, Mary Daly, and Adrienne Rich*. Ratcliffe's white editor asked her to call a black scholar for advice about adding a chapter on a black woman. Ratcliffe did not make the call, but the editorial advice provoked Ratcliffe's thinking: how might whiteness inform the theories of Woolf, Rich, and Daly. Because whiteness (as a functioning cultural category that informs identity) is invisible to most whites, Ratcliffe wondered how whites could learn to see what we/they are socialized not to see. "Then it struck me," Ratcliffe writes, "Perhaps we could hear it. That lead me to Fiumara, Heidegger, the divided logos, and listening" (12 Apr. 2003).

Ratcliffe imagines listening as a productive pathway to rhetorical invention, writing that the "rhetorical listening [she] is promoting is a conscious performance that has four functions":

(1) it promotes *understanding,* (2) it proceeds from a *responsibility logic,* not a guilt/blame one, (3) it locates identification in discursive spaces of *commonalities* and *differences,* and (4) it accentuates commonalities and differences not only in *claims* but in *cultural logics* (or ideologies). Rhetorical listening enables us to hear textual strategies associated with a h(ear)ing metaphor, such as tone, rhythm, voice and silence. (27 Mar. 2003, emphasis in original)

Ratcliffe goes on to write that her project "offers new rhetorical concepts (rhetorical listening, non-identification) and new rhetorical tactics (eavesdropping, listening metonymically, and listening pedagogically)." Thus, she transforms the same rhetorical tradition that she is resisting, just as Bizzell, Blair, and Kahl would have her do.

As I have demonstrated throughout *Unspoken,* silence and silencing also provide new pathways and new methods for expanding the rhetorical tradition. After all, people use silence and silencing every day to fulfill their rhetorical purpose, whether it is to maintain their position of power, resist the domination of others, or submit to subordination—regardless of their gendered positions. Each one of these rhetorical situations offers the participants a chance to readjust relations of power. And just as important to my purpose, each rhetorical situation offers observers an opportunity to analyze how those readjustments are being attempted and successfully achieved or why the attempts might have failed. Any readjustment of rhetorical power is a rhetorical transformation. Still, the transformative power of silence is not always obvious; that is, it is not obvious if rhetoric can only be delivered by words or if rhetoric can only be about establishing power, disciplinary beliefs a number of rhetorical scholars are currently working to unsettle.

We live inside the act of discourse, to be sure, but we cannot assume that a *verbal* matrix is the only one in which the articulations and conduct of the mind take place—regardless of the measure of inward or outward persuasion. After all, as Ortega y Gasset reminds us, "People leave some things unsaid in *order* to be able to say others" (246, emphasis in original). Any theory of rhetoric must also have a concomitant theory of silence, and we need to educate ourselves to this fact. We will need to resist rhetoric as we learned it in order to transform it, realigning our perceptions of the spoken and unspoken in ways that recognize silence as an integral component in the making and delivery of rhetoric, as persuasion, understanding, invitation, or something else.

TOWARD A RHETORIC OF UNSPOKEN RESISTANCE—AND TRANSFORMATION

At the same time that a rhetoric of domination is being resisted, a

new rhetoric that challenges power-over must be formulated in
the strategy of empowered action.

—Sonja Foss and Cindy L. Griffin

In "A Feminist Perspective on Rhetorical Theory," Sonja Foss and Cindy L.
Griffin argue that many women have trouble understanding traditional rhetorical theory because of its inherent patriarchal bias, which embodies the "experiences
and concerns of the white male as standard" (331). Using feminism as their foot-
hold, they write (together with Karen A. Foss) that the very nature of feminism
itself "opens up choices and possibilities" and "is rooted in choice and self-determination and does not prescribe one 'official' position" (Introduction 3). Cheris
Kramarae and Mercilee Jenkins support their assertion when they write, "Since
language systems are social constructions, they *are* open to alterations to fit women's
needs" (148, emphasis in original). Thus, for these feminist scholars, rhetoric
cannot be concerned solely with the traditional pursuit of verbal persuasion.

To prove their point, Foss and Griffin juxtapose the rhetorical theory of Starhawk, feminist writer, activist, and practitioner of Wicca, with that of one of the
most influential rhetoricians of our time, Kenneth Burke. Using a method they
refer to as "re-sourcement," Foss and Griffin place these different rhetorics alongside each other, not exactly as Burke does with his "perspective by incongruity,"
but rather as reflection and negotiation (Burke, *Attitudes* 308ff., Foss and Griffin,
"Beyond"). Thus the authors offer Starhawk's rhetoric of inherent worth, power-
with, and empowered action in dialectical tension with Burke's theories of hierarchy and domination, which have long dominated the discipline of rhetoric.

Like Starhawk's rhetorical theories of inherent worth and empowered actions,
a rhetoric of silence can also resist the discipline of rhetoric, for it too can serve
both "resistance and creation—acts that refuse compliance with the destructive
rhetoric and those that create alternatives to it" (Foss and Griffin, "Feminist" 337).
In "Arts of the Possible," Rich writes about the possibilities that silence holds,
saying that "it is not always or necessarily a denial or extinguishing of some reality" (324). She continues to describe the ways silence links with creativity: "It can
be fertilizing, it can bathe the imagination, it can, as in great open spaces—I think
of those plains stretching far below the Hopi mesas in Arizona—be the nimbus
of a way of life, a condition of vision" (324). And she writes about the ability of
silence to empower linguistic action, in her case that of a poet:

> The matrix of a poet's work consists not only of what is there to be absorbed
> and worked-on, but also of what is missing, *desaparacido,* rendered unspeak-
> able, thus unthinkable. It is through these invisible holes in reality that po-
> etry makes its way—certainly for women and other marginalized subjects and

for disempowered and colonized peoples generally—but ultimately for all who practice any art at its deeper levels. (324)

For those rhetors who practice the art at its deeper levels, a rhetoric of silence, as a means of rhetorical delivery, can be empowered action, both resistant and creative. However, as I made clear in every case, whether having to do with academics, with political participants, the characters in tabloid-like political drama, and with Indians, silence continues to be, too often, read as simple passivity in situations where it has actually taken on an expressive power and has, in fact, transformed the rhetorical situation itself. In every chapter, I demonstrated the ways silence, whether choice or im/position, delivered positive or negative abilities, fulfilling or withholding traits, harmony or disharmony, success or failure. I also demonstrated the empowered action and creativity of the silent rhetors, all of whom were practicing the art of rhetoric at its deepest levels.

Silence can deploy power—as in the case of academic department chairs, a U.S. president, an independent council, Southwest Indians in prayer, and, to some extent, Anita Hill. It can defer to power—as in the case of traditionally disfranchised peoples, political hopefuls, the sexually harassed, Southwest Indians in prayer, and, to some extent, Anita Hill. It all depends. As I have said earlier, silence is not always empowering or patently engaging, but the purposeful delivery of silence can speak volumes, as it did in the case of the department chair who nominated his colleague for a research professorship, the committee chair who disapproved of the junior faculty member, the Indian woman who will not speak to strangers, Bill Clinton, Lani Guinier, and Anita Hill.

The delivery of silence can be a way of taking responsibility all the while refusing to be compliant (as in the case of the black female academic who wrote her way into academic success); it can be a way of refusing to take responsibility all the while appearing to be compliant (as in the case of the black male academic who experiences silencing on a quotidian basis). On the other hand, resistance and creation (or transformation) can take the form of breaking silence, of "speaking the unspeakable . . . and allowing secrets to become common knowledge" (Foss and Griffin, "Feminist" 337). Anita Hill, Lani Guinier, and most of the president's women have done just that.

Throughout *Unspoken,* I resisted a rhetorical discipline constituted solely of purposeful language use and insisted that it also include the purposeful uses and deliveries of silence. And as I hope I have made clear, I have used an interpretive framework that shapes language and silence as reciprocal rather than as opposites. By doing so, I can figure silence as a rhetoric, whether it is used for domination, persuasion—or, maybe best of all, rhetorical listening that leads to understanding.

Both the spoken and the unspoken can resist domination; both the spoken and the unspoken can invite consideration. In "Beyond Persuasion: A Proposal for an Invitational Rhetoric," Foss and Griffin redirect the traditional end of rhetoric. Instead of persuasion, they pursue "invitational" rhetoric, "an invitation to understanding as a means to create a relationship rooted in equality, immanent value, and self-determination" (5). These scholars define invitational rhetoric in feminist terms, though they hasten to say that it can be used by women, men, feminists, or nonfeminists. "What makes it feminist is not its use by a particular population of rhetors but rather the grounding of its assumptions in feminist principles and theories" ("Beyond" 5).

Invitational rhetoric, then, which asks only that a listener listen, and in response, that the rhetor listen—both sides taking turns at being productively silent—transforms the rhetorical discipline from one of persuasion, control, and discipline (on the part of the rhetor) to a moment of inherent worth, equality, and empowered action for (rhetor and audience alike). As one feature of invitational rhetoric, a rhetorical silence of careful listening can transform the interactional goal of rhetoric, which has traditionally been one of persuasion to one of understanding (an interactional goal Guinier was clearly after). After all, Royster wants us to remember that "voicing at its best is not just well-spoken but also well-heard" (40).

The uses of productive rhetorical silence will expand the discipline of rhetoric to include silence as a rhetorical art of empowered action. A productive rhetorical silence carries some of the weight of Ratcliffe's rhetorical listening as well as Eugene Glendin's "absolute listening" (118–22) in that all three actions stimulate the formulation of a new way of being rhetorical. As I have mentioned before, Kalamaras's *Reclaiming the Tacit Tradition* also offers silence as a rhetorical action, as well—not as a new way but as an age-old way that we might do well to reconsider. For Kalamaras, meditation is a means of contemplating the truth as well as a stopping point before affixing meaning and words. Silence is an action, then, but one of a different kind.

He makes his point even more clearly in "Meditative Silence and Reciprocity," where he draws on the work of two leading compositionists, James Moffett and Charles Suhor, both of whom have written at length about the advantages of introducing silence into the writing classroom. For Moffett, meditative practices can help students develop "inner speech as fully as possible and at the same time learn to suspend it. They must talk through to silence and through stillness find original thought" (240). Suhor argues, "When we are most successful, our students have a sense of well-being which is intimately linked with the inexpressible, the ineffable—that is, with silence" (11). Kalamaras complicates their work, however, in seeing the benefits of silence in the classroom. For him, meditative silence is a beneficial practice in and of itself—just as writing is. And the practice may be more beneficial to teachers, "as a guiding principle in their pedagogical theories," than to students ("Meditative" 23). After all, the "practice of meditation" (what I call "silence") offers practitioners "trust in intuition, ambiguity, and chaos as well as trust in the reciprocity and interpretative quality of experience" ("Meditative" 23). I imagine that Pat Belanoff might agree—to various degrees—with Moffett, Suhor, and Kalamaras, too, as she has recently demonstrated some of these new means of empowered rhetorical action when she writes about silence as reflection, meditation, and contemplation, three activities that can be attached to thinking through or thoughtful uncertainty. And Anne Gere, too, writes of the ethical and political resources of strategic silence, a rhetoric of silence, especially in the classroom. The resources of silence that these scholars herald appear in every chapter of *Unspoken*.

Rhetors using silence can use it to think through a problem and even enhance their needed isolation or sense of uniqueness. But rhetors using silence can also use it to reflect on what the rhetor or audience is saying and thereby invite understanding. Most of all, rhetors using silence will not be participating in the traditional rhetorical discipline of combat and dominance; they will be sharing perceptions, understandings, and power. They will use silence to embody new ways to challenge and resist domination and hierarchy at the same time that it disrupts and transforms it. Mere spoken language cannot do justice to the shape and vitality of a rhetoric of silence. After all, speech and silence are inextricably linked and often interchangeably meaningful. Thus silence is not, in itself, necessarily a sign of *either* domination *or* subordination; and silencing, for that matter, is not the same as erasing. I have said it before: like the zero in mathematics, silence is an absence with a function.

AFTER WORDS AND SILENCE: ROOTS FOR RHETORICS OF SILENCE

It is all too easy to take language, one's own language, for granted—one may need to encounter another language, or rather another *mode* of language, in order to be astonished, pushed into wonder, again.

—Oliver Saks, *Seeing Voices*

A rhetoric of silence is, indeed, another mode of rhetoric, joining the multiplicity of rhetorical deliveries (verbal, written, electrified, signed) that we already take for granted. Honoring such multiplicity, according to Trinh T. Minh-ha, is a primary rhetorical method for disrupting hegemonic thought. For Trinh, the best rhetors and rhetorics do not settle "down with any single answer" (qtd. in

MacDonald 116). Multiplicity can be achieved when rhetors cross conventional genres and categories: they can "resist simplistic attempts at classifying, . . . the comfort of belonging to a classification, and of producing classifiable works" (Trinh, *Moon* 107–8). In the section that follows, I will honor Trinh's call for multiplicity by offering a number of possibilities for developing further rhetorics of silence, rhetorics that disrupt the hegemony of rhetoric as spoken-only to allow for rhetorics of the unspoken.

The list of categories I am offering is incomplete; the categories themselves blur at the boundaries, overlapping and leaking. But these loose categories are roots for rhetorics of silence, starting places for it to grow in rich and complex ways, at the hand of a number of scholars in various fields.

Ratcliffe's work on listening provides one of the most tantalizing starting places for developing such a rhetoric. Her work, influenced as it is by Gemma Corradi Fiumara's *Other Side of Language: A Philosophy of Listening*, Martin Heidegger's "Phenomenology and Fundamental Ontology: The Disclosure of Meaning," and Royster's "When the First Voice You Hear Is Not Your Own," resonates with a number of other works on listening as well, with only Royster's being overtly linked with rhetoric.[2]

Religion offers numerous pathways toward rhetorics of silence. In *Let Your Words Be Few*, Richard Bauman explains the Quakers' deliberate silence as suppression of the earthly self, since "God manifests himself not to the outward man or senses so much as to the inward, to wit, to the soul and spirit" (David Barclay, 1831, qtd. in Bauman 146). At the intersection of silence and religion are many valuable resources—none of them linked to rhetorical studies, but all of them linked with self-discovery and self-realization as he indicates:

> God is in the silence, available only with the suppression of the outward, speaking self. The highest, purest reach of the contemplative act is that which has learned to leave language behind, for the ineffable, God, lies beyond the veil of language. Silence permeates the solitude of religious contemplative life, just as it permeates all contemplative lifestyles. (Bauman 146, emphasis in original)

Anthony Storr's Solitude: *A Return to the Self* offers further support for the importance of silence: "The capacity to be alone, to deliver and receive silence, becomes linked with . . . becoming aware of one's deepest needs, feelings, gifts, and impulses (21).

Storr's book joins a long history of religious/contemplative writings that consider the value of silence. Thomas Merton's work, of course, could be considered, as well as the writings of Frank Bianco, Patricia Hampl, William Johnston, Kathleen Norris, Henri J. M. Nouwen, Saint Teresa, and Albert Soesman. That the silence of religious solitude and contemplation might enrich rhetorics of silence seems clear. How such a link might be made remains an invitation.

"What are the notes between the notes? Graces, or grace notes," writes Bernard MacLaverty (33). Further along in his novel by the same name, he continues,

> Grace notes—notes which are neither one thing nor the other. A note between the notes. Notes that occurred outside time. Ornaments dictating the character of the music, the slur and sound of it. This is decoration becoming substance. (133)

MacLaverty's book-length treatment of "grace notes" strikes a chord for figuring rhetorics of silence as they contribute to music. Steven Katz's groundbreaking work *The Epistemic Music of Rhetoric* offers a pathway into such a study, through consideration of John Cage's brilliant musical compositions as well as those of John Tavener.

In "Cultural Uses and Interpretations of Silence," Charles A. Braithwaite offers several warrants about the uses of silence by various ethnic group, warrants that grow directly out of Basso's foundational research, which I outlined in the previous chapter. Braithwaite applies his conclusions (or warrants) to a wide range of other ethnic and cultural silences: those of American Indians, Japanese Americans living in Hawaii, Japanese, rural Appalachians, the Anang of Nigeria, the Maori of New Zealand, and so on—silences that all merit further examination. Closely related to Braithwaite's research study is the dissertation project of Vorris Nunley, who is working on a theory of "hush harbor" rhetoric, a hush harbor being a safe site (surrounded by a protective silence) for African American rhetorical performance. Closely linked with David Harvey's *Spaces of Hope,* Nunley's project will connect culture, race, space, ethnicity, rhetoric, and silence.

Finally, I am hopeful that further research on rhetorics of silence will be rooted in the classroom. As Moffett, Suhor, Kalamaras, Belanoff, and Gere have demonstrated, silence offers space for teachers and students to contemplate and strategize, grace notes, so to speak. But theirs is not the only work stretching to connect pedagogy, rhetoric, and silence. In *Without a Word: Teaching Beyond Women's Silence,* Magda Gere Lewis writes that she is

> fusing an examination of that silence which cannot be spoken with an understanding that silence which offers the possibility of a transformative politics . . . in search of a pedagogical practice that might address women's silence not as an absence but as a political act. (3)

Lois Weis and Michell Fine, on the other hand, are in search of a pedagogical practice that addresses the silences of their students—gifted, Native American,

African American, resistant, disruptive, gay or lesbian, working class, and poor—in their collection of essays entitled *Beyond Silenced Voices*. In *Teaching with Your Mouth Shut*, Donald Finkel argues for the value of self-silencing, of leaving space for students (and colleagues) to fill, of creating silences that become opportunities for student responsibility. Peter Elbow provides a collage on silence, writing that he has "always been interested in people who don't write or talk—the silent ones" (174).

> *When* they say something, their words often seem remarkably powerful: more umph, more conviction, more presence—their words more "gathered up." I think I see it even in small versions: if we sit in silence for a while, there is apt to be more gathered energy and focus in what we say. Is this really so? (174)

Elbow's consideration of silence as an important pedagogical element plays out beautifully when rehearsed in Anne French Dalke's *Teaching to Learn, Learning to Teach*. Tapping her Quaker practices, Dalke enriches her investigation into her own teaching and learning with silence, the practice of silence. She knows she has been trained to talk more than her students, so she encourages them to speak at the same time that she learns to inhabit a fruitful pedagogical silence. But when she discovers that she overtalks her coteacher, she backs off, too far at first. Throughout her study, she marks the passages of location that eventually lead her to a nourishing balance of the spoken and unspoken. Dalke writes,

> When silence is embedded in our speaking, we may better hear what is said and better give it voice; moreover, silence alone may be fuller, richer, more replete than language can ever be, an evocation of that which is too full to be spoken, so deep that it defies expression. (109)

Dalke's book is one of several—and I hope more to come—that demonstrate the power of classroom silence, especially when it circulates as a creative or ethical resource.

FINALLY

A rhetoric of silence has much to offer, especially as an imaginative space that can open possibilities between two people or within a group. Silence, in this sense, is an invitation into the future, a space that draws us forth. There is not one but rather many silences, and like the spoken or written, these silences are an integral part of the strategies that underlie and permeate rhetoric. Thus, silence is at once inside the spoken and on its near and far sides as well. In a hallway, a committee meeting, a courtroom, at a news conference, on a mesa, a reservation, a pueblo, or in a classroom—silence is a linguistic art, one that needs only to be named in order to be understood.

Notes
Works Cited
Index

Notes

Preface

1. The Picard and Dauenhauer books helped me secure this opening chapter, along with Deborah Tannen and Muriel Saville-Troike's coedited *Perspectives on Silence*.

2. Dale M. Bauer and S. Jaret McKinstry, Patricia Hill Collins, Elaine Hedges and Shelley Fisher Fishkin, bell hooks, Carla Kaplan, Kris Ratcliffe, and Eve Sedgwick have all demonstrated the ways silence and voice are gendered positions, whether gender resonates with race, sex, sexuality, age, or class. Their work provided me a set of varying perspectives by which to evaluate *Unspoken* as did the nonverbal communication work of Laura Guerreo, Joseph DeVito, and Michael Hecht; the silence work of Saville-Troike; and the political analyses of Lani Guinier, Anita Hill, and Emma Coleman.

3. To that end, the sworn depositions of Dorothy Broaddrick, Dolly Kyle Browning, William Jefferson Clinton, Gennifer Flowers, Paula Corbin Jones, Monica Lewinsky, and Kathleen Willey have informed my thinking on silence and silencing as have the political analyses of various print and news journalists.

4. Keith H. Basso's work with the Cibecue Apaches laid a foundation for Susan Philips's work with the Warm Springs Indians and Gary Plank's work with the Navajos. Although my findings did not correlate directly with theirs, the work of Basso, Philips, and Plank informed my own interviews with various American Indians of the Southwest.

A Word (or Two) on Terms and Categories

1. Gerald Vizenor argues that the "post Indian turns in literature . . . are an invitation to the closure of dominance in the ruins of representation"; after all, he writes, all tribal referents have been predicated on "colonial arrogance" and mere "simulations of the tribal real" (63).

2. In *White Women, Race Matters: The Social Construction of Whiteness,* Ruth Brandenburg writes that whiteness is a

> complexly constructed product of local, regional, national, and global relations, past and present. Thus, the range of possible ways of living whiteness,

for an individual white woman in a particular time and place, is delimited by
the relations of racism *at that moment and in that place*. And if whiteness varies spatially and temporally, it is also a relational category, one that is cocon-
structed with a range of other racial and cultural categories, with class and
gender. This coconstruction is, however, fundamentally asymmetrical, for the
term "whiteness" signals the production and reproduction of dominance rather
than subordination, normativity rather than marginality, and privilege rather
than disadvantage. (236–37)

Brandenberg's definition of whiteness, then, resonates with my reference to it as
a gendered presence, masculine in its insistence on and expectation of subordination. Clearly, white resonates that way for the Indian man.

3. Writing about "The Sounds of Silence" conference she had attended, which
dedicated an entire day to the "social construction of race and gender and oppression," Williams writes:

I think: my raciality is socially constructed, and I experience it as such. I feel
my blackself as an eddy of conflicted meanings—and meaninglessness—in
which my self can get lost, in which agency and consent are tumbled in constant motion. This sense of motion, the constant windy sound of manipulation whistling in my ears, is a reminder of society's constant construction of
my blackness. (*Alchemy* 168)

4. Lee and Kathy Marmon, of Laguna Pueblo, told me that they began home-
schooling their son, Leland, because he was only one-eighth Indian and thus did
not qualify to attend Laguna Indian School. Once Kathy began the homeschool-
ing project, the school relented—but it was too late. Their story left me wondering how Leslie Marmon Silko, Lee's eldest child, had fared early on, given that
her blood percentages would have been the same as Leland's. Silko writes that
her father (one-quarter Laguna) had "wandered over all the hills and mesas around
Laguna when he was a child, because the Indian School and the taunts of the
other children did not sit well with him" ("Interior" 166). She attended a BIA
(Bureau of Indian Affairs) school at Laguna through fifth grade, at which time
her mother (Virginia Leslie) drove her and her sisters into Albuquerque (sixty
miles each way) every day for their schooling. Now the most famous Indian writer
in America, had Leslie been Indian enough to attend the reservation school without being taunted?

Who qualifies as "Indian," however misleading the term itself is, remains a
legal issue. In *The Rights of Indians and Tribes,* Stephen Pevar writes

Some federal laws define an Indian as anyone of Indian descent, while other
laws require one-fourth or one-half Indian blood in order to be considered

as an Indian for purposes of those laws. Still other federal laws define Indian as anyone who has been accepted as a member of a "federally recognized" Indian tribe. (12)

However the term is contested, "Indian" has the virtue of clarity in its vagueness; Indian is by far the most commonly used term among natives themselves and their organizations: the National Congress of American Indians, the American Indian Movement, the Indian Health Service, and so on.

1. DEFINING SILENCE

1. While feminist and "minority" presses and publications continue to provide venues for this ever-widening range of voices, investigations into various kinds of silences may be a newer endeavor, as my own surely is. Just a quick search on Amazon.com reveals 1,962 books with "silence" in the title.

2. Or *zoon phonanta,* man the speaking animal.

3. The rules of conversation are written for equals. The only problem with the rules is that many conversants are not considered truly equal, for reasons of class, gender, race, religion. In "When the First Voice You Hear Is Not Your Own," Jacqueline Jones Royster writes forcefully about voicings that go unheard by those privileged by power and authority.

4. One of Royster's big questions is this: "When veils seem more like walls . . . who has the privilege of speaking first?" (36).

5. In *Talking Power,* Robin Lakoff reminds us that silence-as-power shifts in the courtroom:

the [mostly silent] judge has most of [the power] while the trial is in session, but the [always silent] jury (which enjoys none of the observable signs of discourse power) ultimately is the most powerful participant. Here those who do the most talking and determine topics (the attorneys) arguably have less power than anyone else. . . . (44)

6. During the Middle Ages, however, civic drama featured the life of the Virgin, a talkative, active participant in religious life. One portion of the N-Town cycle centers on her life, as does an extant portion of the "Ludus Coventriae," which delivers the only complete life of the Virgin. All the medieval cycle plays highlight her life with both visiting angels and a measure of verisimilitude, including her public conversation, questioning, and arguing.

Yet the Virgin Mary is not silent in practice for Catholics. Indeed, she intercedes with God on behalf of the prayerful.

7. Pat Shipman is my next-door neighbor and good friend. Over numerous dinners together, she related these experiences to me. Her *Taking Wing* won the Phi Beta Kappa prize, and *The Wisdom of the Bones* won the Rhône-Poulenc prize.

8. Originating in the *Wall Street Journal*, 30 Apr. 1993, the epithet was repeated in over three hundred articles in print media around the country.

9. His list is based on the works of Hugh Duncan, Paul Goodman, Alice Greene, Karl Jaspers, Joseph Lebo, Joost Meerloo, Robert Oliver, Walter Ong, Robert Scott, Geoffrey Wagner (29).

2. ENGENDERING SILENCE

1. Pagels writes that "the absence of feminine symbolism of God marks Judaism, Christianity, and Islam in striking contrast to the world's other religious traditions, whether in Egypt, Babylonia, Greece, and Rome or Africa, Polynesia, India, and North America" (97).

2. *The American Heritage Dictionary* (1981 edition) defines grammatical gender as "any set of two or more categories, such as masculine, feminine, and neuter, into which words are divided according to sex, animation, psychological associations, or some other characteristic, and that determine agreement with or the selection of modifiers, referents, or grammatical forms."

3. Showalter writes that

despite its unifying appeal, the concept of a women's language is riddled with difficulties. Unlike Welsh, Breton, Swahili, or Amharic, that is, languages of minority or colonized groups, there is no mother tongue . . . spoken by the female population in society, which differs significantly from the dominant language. (255)

Linguist Sally McConnell-Ginet writes that "there is absolutely no evidence that would suggest the sexes are preprogrammed to develop structurally different linguistic systems." The many specific differences in male and female speech, intonation, and language use that have been identified cannot be explained in terms of "two separate sex-specific languages" but need to be considered instead in terms of "styles, strategies, and contexts of linguistic performance" (qtd. in Showalter 255).

4. What became a frequently anthologized essay started out as comments by the same name presented at "The Personal and the Political Panel," Second Sex Conference, New York, 29 Sept. 1979.

5. As Bourdieu states, "It is not hard to imagine the weight that the opposition between masculinity and femininity must bring to bear on the construction of self-image and world-image when this opposition constitutes the fundamental principle of the division of the social and the symbolic world" (*Logic* 78).

6. I hasten to add that not all wives play the subordinate role in conversation; not all wives are at the mercy of silencing. Some wives use silence, sometimes against silence, as the following woman attests: "In my family—a matriarchy—

as you know—silence and control and quietly doing what you want [are] the power responses (vs. ineffectual rantings and loss of temper, which [are] ignored)—like playing your cards close to the vest" (Anonymous x).

7. There's a loss of status, unless the person staying silent already holds conversational power, as in the research of Fishman and DeFrancisco and the examples that follow.

8. She goes on to say that

If the ritual by which the institution confers its most purportedly meaningful sign of recognition is marked by a refusal to communicate, what kind of significance does that then imply for tenure itself? Not being ADDRESSED is really not so tragic in countless situations, but it was highly ironic in the context of a ritual (tenure) that presumes to address . . . the very heart of an institutional rite of passage, by which the institution was to confirm upon me a certain sort of legal identity; a kind of "sign of recognition" was passing through an awful silence of no recognition. This was "awfulness" in several of its senses: the "awe" of not being addressed; not one upon whom address is conferred is in a sense being cast into a place of non-being; awful in the only sense that what could inspire it—I could hardly think—would be some kind of absolute god-like assumption; aweful in the sense of terrifying, surely.

9. Such turf battles are widespread within English departments, if not between composition and literature, then between literature and theory, or literature and cultural studies, or cultural studies and rhetoric. The iterations are endless as are their nation-wide occurrences.

10. In *Genie, An Abused Child's Flight from Silence,* Russ Rymer documents one of the most compelling stories in recent times. In 1970, Genie was discovered in a small back room of her home, where she had spent long hours tied to her potty chair since age 2, and left wordless. Her case of sustained abuse (of epic proportions) and linguistic deprivation caught the attention of linguists, cognitionists, scientists, and host of social-services people, which may be the reason that her care became so fragmented and finally useless. Victor, the wild boy of Aveyron, became the subject of Jean Marc Gaspard Itard's study in the early 1800s. Like Genie, Victor, too, remained linguistically retarded. These two stories are played out in Charles Maclean's retelling of Kamala and Amala, the wolf-children discovered and then reared by Rev. Joseph Singh and his wife in Bengal. Amala died early after her "capture," and Kamala never exceeded the linguistic developments of Genie or Victor. Writing as Jean-Claude Armen, Jean-Claude Auger tells of the gazelle-boy of the Spanish Sahara, who supposedly lived out his life in the wild. These are all cases of language subordination far beyond the realm of double-voicing.

3. Witnessing Silence

1. In one of his most famous passages, Burke says, "It is so clearly a matter of rhetoric to persuade a man by identifying your cause with his interest" (*Rhetoric* 24).

2. Ratcliffe's definition follows:

A performance that occurs when listeners invoke both their capacity and their willingness (1) to promote an *understanding* of self and other that informs our culture's politics and ethics, (2) to proceed from within a *responsibility* logic, not from within a defensive guilt/blame one, (3) to locate identification in discursive spaces of both *commonalities* and *differences,* and (4) to accentuate commonalities and differences not only in *claims* but *cultural logics* within which those claims function. ("Rhetorical" 204)

3. On 27 June 1991, Marshall, the first African American ever to serve on the Supreme Court, resigned after twenty-four years of service:

My Dear Mr. President:

The strenuous demands of Court work and its related duties required or expected of a justice appear at this time to be incompatible with my advancing age and medical condition.

I, therefore, retire as an Associate Justice of the Supreme Court of the United States when my successor is qualified.

Respectfully,
Thurgood Marshall (A13)

4. Two months before Hill's testimony, Maya Angelou wrote "I Dare to Hope" for the *New York Times*. Even this liberal looked for a silver lining in the appointment of a man known for his "audacious actions as Chairman of the Equal Employment Opportunity Commission [which] were anti–affirmative action, anti-busing and anti-other opportunities to redress inequality in our country" (34). But because, and only because, Thomas had been poor and was black, she hoped he could be "won over again": "The prophet in 'Lamentations' cried, 'Although he put his mouth in the dust . . . there still is hope'" (35).

5. Dr. Joycelyn Elders writes that her harshest feelings about the Thomas-Hill hearings "are reserved for the sight of someone like Thomas taking Thurgood Marshall's place" (Elders and Chanoff 303). She goes on to write,

In my opinion, Thomas is a man who has sold out his black people in order to be accepted by the white establishment. Having him on the Supreme Court

is the worst thing that has happened to African Americans in recent memory.
. . . Putting a Clarence Thomas up to replace an individual of Thurgood
Marshall's stature just violated everything I believe in. It made me know that
my government would stick a knife through my heart and tell me it was good
for me. (303–4)

6. In the body of this chapter, I will refer to the entire "Statement of Anita F.
Hill to the Senate Judiciary Committee October 11, 1991," which is cited in my
bibliography.

7. It's important to note that at the time of their interaction, Thomas was chair
of the EEOC, the last recourse for victims of sexual harassment.

Although sexual harassment became a legal cause of action under Title VII
of the 1964 Civil Rights Act, guidelines were not codified until 1988. In 1980,
the Equal Opportunity Employment Commission came only as far as to devise
Interim Interpretive Guidelines on Sex Discrimination. The 1988 EEOC Guidelines, published one year after Hill had departed, provide the current juridical
parameters; they are slight revisions of the tentative ones:

> Harassment on the basic of sex is a violation of Title VII. Unwelcome sexual
> advances, requests for sexual favors, and other verbal and physical conduct
> of a sexual nature constitute sexual harassment when (1) submission to such
> conduct is made explicitly or implicitly a term or condition of an individual's
> employment, (2) submission to or rejection of such conduct by an individual
> is used as the basis of employment decisions affecting such individual or (3)
> such conduct has the purpose or effect of unreasonably interfering with an
> individual's work performance or creating an intimidating, hostile, or offen-
> sive working environment. (sec. 1604.11)

8. Jamieson attributes this term to psychologist Gregory Bateson, "who formulated the concept of the double bind in an examination of schizophrenia,
assumed that it was primarily mothers deploying double binds who induced
schizophrenia in their sons" (5). Drawing one of her most compelling examples
from the early seventeenth century, Jamieson tells us that

> In 1631, in *Cautio Criminalis,* Julius Friedrich Spee identified one no-win situ-
> ation in which prosecutors placed women accused of witchcraft. The suspected
> witch was submerged in a pond. If she drowned, she deserved to; if she didn't,
> she was a witch. In the first case, God was revealing her nature; in the sec-
> ond, the devil. Under torture, women either did or did not admit to com-
> plicity with Satan. If they did, they were executed for their crime. If they didn't,
> their silence was attributed to solidarity with Satan, and they too were marched
> off to the stake. (3)

"Although he didn't know it," Jamieson continues, "Spee had identified a trap set for women throughout history. When our foremothers overstepped prescribed boundaries, they confronted situations constructed to ensure that they were guilty until proven guilty" (3). And so the situation seemed to be for Anita Hill.

9. In *Speaking Truth to Power,* Hill explains Senator Orrin Hatch's belief:

> Virtuous women are seldom accosted by unwelcomed sexual propositions or familiarities, obscene talk, or profane language. Accordingly, since virtuous women so seldom experience harassment, the numerous claims must be raised by women without virtue and thus society should not be concerned about it. (151)

Hill believes that Hatch was referring to Phyllis Schlafly's widely accepted reasoning, that sexual harassment was not a real problem because "men hardly ever asked sexual favors from women from whom the certain answer is no" (qtd. in Phelps and Winternitz 130–31).

10. As I said in my preface, I am purposely using "nonwhite" as my semantic option in this chapter, given Anita Hill and Lani Guinier's positioning as nonwhite females who resisted the domination of white males. See Middleton, and Dyer for why nonwhite is the better semantic choice.

11. Resonant with Morrison's assertion that white America *depends* on blackness and a perception of black subjugation to construct white identity and maintain its power, Judith Butler writes that Hill was doubly oppressed (by race and sex), her race becoming a convenient way to represent sexuality pornographically:

> Just as the racialized scene of Thomas and Hill allows for the externalization of sexual degradation, so it permits for a purification in prurience for the white imaginary. African-American status permits for a spectacularization of sexuality and a recasting of whites as outside the fray, witnesses and watchers who have circuited their own sexual anxieties through the publicized bodies of blacks. (*Excitable* 83)

12. Tijuan Murray writes that "in the United States a black wom[a]n's sex is detestable, something that the mainstream culture wants forgotten. It is unthinkable, horrific, black sin. And people crusade against it, against us, as if their very lives depended upon our destruction" (397). Murray's assertion that mainstream culture wants to forget black female sexuality at the same time that it constantly invokes it, such as in the Thomas-Hill hearings, echoes Burke's notion of the paradox of negativity: "In one sense," he writes,

> there is a paradox about "don't." For the negative is but a *principle,* an *idea,* not a name for a *thing.* And thus, whereas an injunction such as "thou shalt

not kill" is understandable enough as a negative *idea,* it also has about its edges the positive *image* of killing. (*Language* 10)

What better way not to think of a black female's sexuality than to talk and talk about it—in great detail—publicly?

13. Higginbotham continues:

Senator Arlen Specter accused Professor Hill of perjury to Congress—a punishable federal offense—without producing the least bit of evidence to back up his charge. Senator Orrin Hatch, waving over his head a copy of *The Exorcist,* managed to suggest quite seriously that Professor Hill was as demented as the character in the novel who was possessed by the devil. Senator Simpson, recalling the McCarthy witch hunts, made the vague and sinister announcement that he had reams of compromising letters about "this woman" coming out of his every pocket. . . .

The Hill-Thomas hearings represented a sequela of attitudes that in some ways were not very different from those of the antebellum "statesmen" and "judges" who regarded all women, and particularly black women, as inferior persons. *Thus, Anita Hill was treated far more harshly by the Senate committee than she would have been had she been white, and Clarence Thomas was treated far more generously than he would have been had the victim been a white woman.* (32–33, emphasis in original)

14. By focusing on Hill as the only opposition, Bush people could more easily deflect and silence the very real hesitation of various civil rights organizations, the NAACP, the National Urban League, the Congressional Black Caucus, and the American Bar Association, all of whom could name a number of infinitely better qualified black jurists, namely Amalya Kearse, who was serving on the federal appeals court in New York. She, however, was a moderate, which did not fit into Bush's plan. No one could come up with a better qualified *conservative* black nominee, given Bush's purpose. Besides Thomas's being conservative *and* black, his record as a legal scholar, though meager, exhibited reliable hostility to civil rights, affirmative action, environmental protection, and women's freedom of choice.

15. A special issue of the *Journal of Applied Communication Research* featured twenty first-person narratives by communication professionals about their experiences with sexual harassment. One woman wrote that

When Anita Hill went public, the incidents from my own past came back all too vividly—I understand intimately how someone could go years without telling anyone about such events, how shameful and painful they are to remember, why a woman would be reluctant to file a complaint. ("Our Stories" 388)

16. Only later did Hill move herself to Oral Roberts University, the University of Oklahoma, and finally to Brandeis, where she currently teaches. In 1997, Hill was "relieved" of her position as Oklahoma College of Law professor, under circumstances that have never been clearly explained. To me, the circumstances seem suspiciously akin to a "hostile" work environment (see *Speaking* 326–41). During the years that Hill had chosen to remain silent, her reputation was not at issue, her faculty appointment was not at stake.

17. I am grateful to Ratcliffe for enumerating some of the reasons for silence (*Anglo-American* 123); I take responsibility for the inferences and specific connections to Hill.

18. Reno's integrity has yet to be at issue, so her declaration seems to be sincere, believable, correct. In comparison is President Bush's declaration that Clarence Thomas was the "best person for this position," which few people believed (qtd. in Hill and Jordan xix).

In an interesting, yet hardly surprising, twist, Robert Bork's nomination to the Supreme Court a couple of years before had been "opposed by more than 200 law professors. That letter got a lot of press" (Garrow 28).

19. The following passage provides a clear, contextualized example of Guinier's legal scholarship on the complicated issue of voting rights:

> In Virginia, where Douglas Wilder is the first black elected Governor since Reconstruction, some commentators have interpreted his victory as a "new black politics." *But cf. Ayres,* "Virginia Governor Baffles Democrats with Crusade for 'New Mainstream,'" *New York Times,* Oct. 14, 1990, at A22, col. 1 (Wilder considers himself "a governor who happens to be black, not a black who happens to be governor.") . . . Others see Wilder's win as the triumph of a single-issue constituency in the wake of recent Supreme Court decisions on abortion. In either case, given the narrow margin of victory, Wilder's ability to govern on other issues important to the black community is considerably vitiated . . . . ("Triumph" 1109n.151)

20. In an interview given after her nomination was withdrawn, Guinier explained once again her point about authentic representation:

> The whole notion of racially polarized voting was an effort to measure why some members of the legislature were unresponsive to the needs of their minority constituents, although these constituents were exercising the franchise. And the reason, according to the courts, was that these legislators could get elected time and again without the necessity of any support from the black or Latino community.
>
> It's that ideal of having a legislature that is integrated, but also responsive, that really animates my work. (qtd. in Garrow 31)

21. When asked about being the "Condom Queen," Elders wondered what the term meant and writes, "If I could get every teenager who engages in sex to use a condom, I'd gladly wear a crown of condoms on my head" (304). Helmsley's nickname drew attention to her Jewishness.

22. Opponents were combing her law review writings and quoting her liberally out of the rich contexts she had created for her legal opinions, thereby feeding the media (who became dependent on these unfair, acontextual, and biased spins) with fuel for her soon-to-be failed nomination.

23. Cappella and Jamieson's research findings indicate that Americans trust neither politicians nor the media. The public tends to see the media as part of the problem, not part of the solution. They write, "[P]eople have strong opinions about media practices, believing that they choose stories that are more strategic than substantive and, once chosen, tend to slant the stories toward more strategic and sensational frames" (227).

24. Smear campaigns are relatively easy to initiate in the United States, for as Cappella and Jamieson remind us, the "press is preoccupied with conflict" and especially with press coverage that enhances strategy-for-personal-gain at the expense of the public good (31).

25. She writes, "Inspired by the work of James Madison, I explored ways to insure that even a self-interested majority could work with, rather than 'tyrannize,' a minority" ("Who's Afraid" 41)

26. Guinier was not the "first." Solicitor General-designate Drew S. Days had been a full-time civil rights lawyer at the time of his nomination. Days had been Guinier's superior when she worked in the Civil Rights Office during the Carter administration.

27. It was not Guinier's job to defend herself; the White House has an in-place press presence that counters negative campaigns and accusations.

28. Hillary Rodham Clinton also cut Lani dead when the going got tough. Guinier writes about the First Lady's initial strong support, which included, among other things, fierce handholding and confidential admonishment to "organize." But when Guinier's chips were down, the First Lady passed her in the hallway with a "Hi, Kiddo." Friends since their Yale law school days, the Clintons have not spoken another word to Guinier since then. Silence can, indeed, cut both ways: Bill Clinton silenced Guinier; both Bill and Hillary Clinton employed silence.

29. Cf. his 14 May proclamation that he "would never have appointed anybody to public office if they had to agree with everything" he believed in (qtd. in Apple A8).

30. If she found his endorsement of personal friendship or promise of personal loans insulting or patronizing, she has never said so publicly. One does

wonder, however, if Clinton would have made such a public financial gesture to a white or nonwhite man. She has, however, spoken about her public humiliation and frustration, some of which has to do with "the manner in which the president of the United States would treat a friend" as providing "an insight into his character as a human being . . . [and] an unexpected peek into his character as leader" (*Lift* 113).

31. For instance, when asked if her voting ideas could be translated to South Africa, Guinier replied, without hesitation:

> The majority should rule, but it should rule in a way that is respectful and that recognizes the interests of the minority in being part of the governing coalition. The minority has to feel that the government is legitimate in order to go along with its policies. (*Lift* 45)

32. In "Lani, We Hardly Knew Ye," Patricia Williams would write that

> for all the ballyhoo, Guinier is a distinguished career civil-rights advocate, whose fairness and equanimity are celebrated, who has argued and won cases before the Supreme Court, and who holds tenure at one of the most conservative law schools [Penn] in the country. If she is the radical crackpot fringe, one wonders if the Mainstream is really a mirage after all, a powerful fantasy concocted by that wacky fun-loving knucklehead Clint Bolick. (28)

33. Her Yale professional colleague Harlon Dalton supported her public views that very day, quickly affirming the necessity of talk:

> She was trying to . . . expand the universe of possible remedies, and . . . we ended up with this non-debate about it. Her senate hearings would have been a conversation about what democracy looks like in a multi-cultural society in the 1990's, and I think that's a conversation we need to have. (qtd. in Applebome)

And he does not leave unsaid his final dig: "Instead, the Senate and the President ran away from it."

34. See Burke's *Philosophy of Literary Form* 203, *Attitudes Toward History* 317, and *Permanence and Change* 283 ff.

35. This marvelous title of gendered power differential was originally coined by the Quakers, who distributed an influential pamphlet by the same title during the war in Indochina.

36. "Lift Every Voice and Sing," written by James Weldon Johnson in 1900 to commemorate Abraham Lincoln's birthday, is the unofficial National Negro Anthem.

37. Since her dis-appointment, Guinier has moved from the University of Pennsylvania to become the first nonwhite female to become a tenured profes-

sor at Harvard Law School. In addition, she has published three books, all of which have provided her even greater opportunities to talk and listen to the American public. *Tyranny of the Majority*, a collection of her most controversial and dense legal arguments appeared first, allowing her words, for the first time, to speak for themselves and providing her (through her book tours) an opportunity to speak for herself in words and terms that laypeople in America can understand. *Lift Every Voice* recounts her nomination process, including the silencing of her expertise and the silencing of the civil rights movement itself. Finally, in *Becoming Gentlemen* (coauthored with Michelle Fine and Jane Balin), she addresses education at elite law schools, an education that shuts down the genuine deliberation necessary to understanding, interpreting, implementing, and writing law as well as the silencing of both nonwhite and white women within the system.

4. ATTESTING SILENCE

1. The U.S. Senate acquitted Clinton on all four counts—perjury, subornation of perjury, obstruction of justice, and witness tampering. Two of the votes, though, were close: 55–45, not guilty on charges of perjury; 50–50 on obstruction of justice charges.

2. Just as I began writing this section, I received a copy of Jamie Barlowe's *Mob of Scarlet Scribblers: Rereading Hester Prynne*. I am grateful for her provocative, insightful, and thorough examination of Hester Prynne's place on our cultural landscape.

3. A sudden change of fortune or reverse of circumstances.

4. Black establishes an important difference between "private" and "secret":

A private life is simply one shared only with intimates, conducted without attracting notice. There is an expectation that everyone will have a private life. But a secret life is one attended by potential scandal, one in which there is a disparity between appearance and reality, between reputation and character. . . . The secret life is usually concealed even from one's intimates while a private life is lived among them. (145)

5. As I move into various alleged Clinton romances and dalliances, I want to delineate some marked differences between the way the U.S. press and other national presses cover the lives of public figures. While the U.S. press was tirelessly investigating the secret sexual escapades of Clinton, the French press respected the private sexual life of French president François Mitterand. For instance, when Mitterand was buried, the French press witnessed the first, official public appearance of Mitterand's long-time mistress and their child. At the invitation of his family (his widow, two sons, and grandchildren), Mitterand's

mistress and only daughter were included in the private burial services—an appearance that went without further comment. Although the French press had known about the second family for years, little mention was ever made of it because it was not a secret; it was private.

In Spain, news coverage of the royal family is overwhelmingly positive despite occasional tabloid mentions of the king's alleged lovers and long-time mistress. As in France, the mainstream press concerns itself with the political workings of the nation. Political sex scandals "wouldn't get a second reading here. In Spain that kind of thing is considered a private [not a secret] matter," a leading Spanish journalist writes (qtd. in Anderson 115). The journalist concedes that the Spanish press participates in self-censorship on such matters. Neither the British nor the American press is so accommodating.

6. It is important to note that Hillary has enjoyed the easy access and expert abilities of television writer-producers Harry Thomason and Linda Bloodworth-Thomason, best known for *Designing Women* and *Picket Fences,* as well as the television-appearance advice of media specialist Mandy Grunwald.

7. In *Hillary's Choice,* Gail Sheehy writes that the Clintons' media consultants offered "polls showing that 39 percent of voters would have reservations about voting for a candidate who had been unfaithful—but that percentage diminished if the wife had known about it and accepted it" (199).

8. Flowers emphasizes her need for personal safety: "Giving myself maximum visibility was crucial. . . . People who posed a threat to Bill Clinton had a habit of ending up hurt or dead, and if I could prevent it, I wasn't about to become another statistic because of all this" (*Gennifer* 107).

9. Catherine MacKinnon's 1979 *Sexual Harassment of Working Women* became one of the most influential writings of the century as the basis for what would become workplace conduct legislation. Arguing that gendered power differentials nullify the weaker party's "consent," MacKinnon blurs the boundary between consensual sex and sexual harassment, particularly in terms of workplace or work-related sexual activity. Her landmark work mightily influenced the introduction of evidence (against the president) during the Paula Jones trial.

10. Four years later, Brock would write President Clinton a letter of apology for introducing Paula Jones to the world, saying that "the troopers were greedy and had slimy motives, and I knew it" ("The Fire" 64).

11. She had missed her chance to file a formal sexual harassment complaint under federal law, which requires action within 180 days of the alleged incident, so she filed a civil suit under Arkansas law, which gave her until 8 May 1994, three years after the encounter.

12. In the spotlight of sexual McCarthyism and the congressional ecstasy of sanctimony, both Bob Livingston and Newt Gingrich resigned their positions.

13. B. Clinton felt that a settlement would equate with an admission of guilt; moreover, he and Hillary knew from experience that if they paid, they would continue to pay; if they fought, the opposing side would eventually relent.

14. Wright warned both parties that Clinton's consensual sexual relationships were not news:

> I have been a lifelong resident of Arkansas. I'm aware of Bill Clinton's reputation for womanizing. . . . But he doesn't have the reputation of being a harasser. He doesn't. And you're not going to be able to find a jury with twelve people who have never heard that Bill Clinton is a womanizer. But I don't believe before this case was brought he ever had a reputation for doing anything other than just chasing skirts. You know, just having a good time. (qtd. in Toobin 209)

15. Although it is true that Jones didn't receive flowers on Secretary's Day and was moved to a desk closer to her boss, she received every merit and cost of living raise she was eligible for, and left her state job of her own volition. Her deposition reveals how very little Jones understood about her own employment record (her hourly wage, her government ranking, her job title), a severe handicap in a workplace harassment claim (see Jones).

16. In his own deposition (a "discovery deposition"), Clinton would deny ever meeting with Jones, let alone making any untoward sexual advances:

> Q: Now, Mr. President, you've stated earlier in your testimony that you do not recall with any specificity the May 8th, 1991 conference at the Excelsior, is that correct?
>
> A: That's correct.
>
> Q: If that is true, sir, how can you be sure that you did not do these things which are alleged in Ms. Jones' complaint?
>
> A: Because, Mr. Bennett, in my lifetime, I've never sexually harassed a woman, and I've never done what she accused me of doing. I didn't do it then, because I never have, and wouldn't. (Clinton, "Deposition")

17. Clinton, "Deposition." Clinton's answer to this question was "Along with the other charges that were made against me."

18. Clinton, "Deposition," 17 Jan. 1998.

19. "Drag a hundred dollars through a trailer park, and there's no telling what you'll find" (James Carville, qtd. in Stout 34).

20. Writing in response to this move, Anita Hill predicted that the Jones team's decision to

> pursue the legal claim in such a manner [via the media] [would be] a bad one for Ms. Jones. As a private citizen with limited public exposure, she does not

have the resources to handle the kind of media barrage that she will encounter if she attempts to settle this issue through the media. Moreover, I question the strategy of insisting that the case be tried during Bill Clinton's second term as president. I believe Ms. Jones will fare better as a plaintiff in a
suit against a former president than in a suit against a sitting president. Like
or dislike Bill Clinton, many prospective jurors have a respect for the office
that will put her at a disadvantage in issues of credibility. (*Speaking* 303)

Hill comes close to imagining the sex-circus to come.

21. I assert her reluctance even in the face of Toobin's and Isikoff's claims that
Willey had placed anonymous phone calls to the Jones legal team: "There's something you should know. I had a [incident] similar [to the Paula Jones incident]
happen to me when I worked at the White House in 1993" (qtd. in Isikoff 107).
Willey resolutely denied placing any such calls.

22. The rest of her testimony can be found in her deposition.

23. Katie Roiphe writes,

Have you noticed that Kathleen Willey's name almost never appears without
the word "credible" in close proximity? . . . Certainly Kathleen Willey's accusations are no more or less serious than Paula Jones' and her story is no more
or less riddled with contradictions and ulterior motives, but she looks right.
She sounds right. With her sensible hair and high cheekbones, she has the
slightly generic quality of a "Good Morning America" host; she could be your
mother, your sister, your third-grade teacher.

Michael Isikoff and Evan Thomas write, "With her sad, handsome face, her
Democratic Party credentials, and a certain middle-class, middle-aged dignity,
Willey seemed more credible to many ordinary people than Paula Jones or Monica
Lewinsky" (22).

24. I am grateful to Jane Donawerth for providing me materials from the
conduct manuals she investigated in the Library of Congress's Rare Book Room.

25. Guinier told Vernon Jordan to pass along her message to President Clinton,
"I would like to meet with him privately, so we can begin to put the petty things
behind us and move on to the important policy issues" (*Lift* 144).

26. As her enthusiastic yet banal letters of support repeatedly indicate, she was
loyal and she desperately needed a job; thus, many of her letters, such as the
following, are forthright, yet unrealistic, requests for employment:

October 18, 1994

Dear Mr. President,

Thank you so much for taking the time to meet with me. Since I've seen you, I have had the opportunity to talk with Mel French, Harlan Lee, the assistant chief of protocol, and Craig Smith. I hope to meet with Leon Panetta next.

As I said to you, I have invested almost three years with your campaign and administration and am not very willing to depart yet. I would like to be considered for an ambassadorship or a position in an embassy overseas. I now find myself with no encumbrances, with Shannon away at medical school and Patrick in college in North Carolina.

I feel confident that I would represent you and our country well if given the opportunity and hope you will consider my request.

Please accept my best wishes for your historic trip to the Mideast next week—I don't need to remind you of my willingness to help you in any way I can.

Fondly, Kathleen

Given her lack of education and specific job-related experience, the results of her White House job applications are not surprising. Furthermore, all her correspondence to the president and members of the White House staff—informal bread-and-butter notes and quasi job applications alike—were written by hand. Never once did she use a computer. Although handwritten notes remain the etiquette standard, handwritten job applications are entirely inappropriate and speak to Willey's lack of experience.

27. See Willey's deposition, 14 Mar. 1998.

28. For complete details, see Browning's 1998 sworn declaration.

29. "The fact that her husband was not there was incidental. She was a friend of mine, and I would go by and see her from time to time. I hadn't been visiting with her in a long time. Sometimes I saw him when she wasn't there. He was a friend of mine, too" (Clinton, "Deposition").

30. Wood reports that

in one of the first national studies ([Safran], 1976), a shocking 92% of 9,000 clerical and professional women claimed to have experienced some form of sexual harassment on the job. In 1987, the U.S. Merit Systems Protection Board discovered that 42% of the women working for the federal government (ironically, including those very agencies specifically charged to protect civil rights) reported having been sexually harassed in the workplace (Edmunds, 1988). (350)

31. Best-known worst-friend Linda Tripp became Lewinsky's primary confidante, but others included old friends, her aunt, mother, former therapists, and former lover Andrew Bleiler. Like Tripp, Bleiler would appear on national television, profiting financially from his self-righteous narrative of the Lewinsky-Clinton relationship.

32. Had it not been for Tripp's intervention in preserving this stain, Lewinsky might have been no more than a tabloid headline, "Intern Transferred for Stalking President," the spin the White House was giving her, anyway. In an odd twist of events, Clinton's DNA-proved semen stain catalyzed her transformation from stalker to temptress.

33. The mandated definition set down by the Jones attorneys included the following:

> For the purposes of this deposition [and all subsequent ones, as it happened], a person engages in "sexual relations" when the person knowingly engages in or causes—
>
> 1. contact with the genitalia, anus, groin, breast, inner thigh, or buttocks of any person with an intent to arouse or gratify the sexual desire of any person;
> 2. contact between any part of the person's body or an object and the genitals or anus of another person; or
> 3. contact [intentional touching, either directly or through clothing] between the genitals or anus of the person and any part of another person's body. (qtd. in Toobin 218)

It is important to note that definitions two and three were struck from the record, leaving only the first definition, which excludes kissing. Clinton seems to have interpreted it as excluding his receiving fellatio or participating in phone sex.

In his testimony, Clinton goes on to say:

> But they [the encounters] did involve inappropriate, intimate contact. These inappropriate encounters ended at my insistence in early 1997. I also had occasional phone conversations with Ms. Lewinsky that included inappropriate sexual banter. I regret that what began as a friendship came to include this conduct, and I take full responsibility for my actions. While I will provide the grand jury whatever other information I can, because of privacy considerations affecting my family, myself, and others, and in an effort to preserve the dignity of the office I hold, this is all I will say about the specifics of these particular matters. . . . (Clinton, "Grand Jury Testimony")

34. Interestingly, Lewinsky agreed: "by signing the affidavit I was in effect putting on my team jersey, to be on the president's side" (qtd. in Morton 206).

35. At the time of her final testimony, however, she declared her feelings for the president to be "mixed."

36. Earlier in the day, Lewinsky testified before the Grand Jury that

> a lot of other people might have made a really big stink . . . and would have

talked about what kind of relationship they had with the President so they don't lose their job. . . .

37. The *Washington Post* led with this paragraph:

Independent counsel Kenneth W. Starr has expanded his investigation of President Clinton to examine whether Clinton and his close friend Vernon E. Jordan, Jr., encouraged a 24-year-old former White House intern to lie to lawyers for Paula Jones about whether the intern had an affair with the president, sources close to the investigation said yesterday. (Schmidt, Baker, and Locy A1)

38. When prodded by those closest to her to release her feelings, Hillary Clinton allegedly said, "I'm not going to talk to you and get you subpoenaed" (qtd. in Sheehy 319).

39. Consider the media coverage of Britain's young Prince William as he negotiates the young-adult lifestyles and behaviors; or the wild and fully documented behavior of Monaco's Princess Stephanie; or the constant surveillance of John F. Kennedy Jr., whose own mother advised Hillary Clinton on the virtue of privacy as the best and only way to keep children, particularly First Children, out of the spotlight and away from the microphone.

5. COMMANDING SILENCE

1. I addressed my choice of terminology in the note on terms and categories. Fergus M. Bordewich writes that *Indian* has the virtue of clarity:

It remains by far the most commonly used term among Natives themselves and the established form for organizations such as the National Congress of American Indians, the radical American Indian Movement, and the new National Museum of the American Indian, for such agencies as the Bureau of Indian Affairs and the Indian Health Service and as part of the official name of most modern tribes. (19–20)

By using the term *Indian,* I am following the lead of scholars, such as Anishinaabe Gerald Vizenor, who use this term ironically to point out its misapplication: "The word *Indian* . . . is a colonial enactment, not a loan word, and the dominance is sustained by the simulation that has superseded the real tribal names" (11). Berndt C. Peyer notes that the term's implication of a universal identity for often very different cultural groups has become a point of rhetorical strength for Indian tribes. Some of the Indians I interviewed referred to themselves as Indians, others as Native Americans, and still others by their tribal affiliation.

2. "Traditional" Indians are characterized by their cultural and political attitudes, which turn toward Indian rather than white. Whether "full-blood" or

"mixed-blood," traditionals have resisted Bureau of Indian Affairs (BIA) assimilation into poor white culture and, therefore, have been excluded from any measure of BIA rewards.

3. After ironically reporting how many of his white friends and colleagues claim to have Indian "blood" (usually a Cherokee grandmother), Deloria observes that many more white people claim to understand Indians:

> Understanding Indians is not an esoteric art. All it takes is a trip through Arizona or New Mexico, watching a documentary on TV, having known *one* in the service, or having read a popular book on *them*. . . . Anyone and everyone who knows an Indian or who is *interested,* immediately and thoroughly understands them. (*God* 5)

Although I have familial connections to one Indian community in particular, I do not claim to be Indian nor do I claim to understand "all Indians." I write as a white woman—from my cultural location—who has known and interviewed individuals who self-identify as Indian.

4. In fact, Christopher Columbus manufactured the Indian immediately upon his arrival in American five hundred years ago. Thinking he had reached the West Indies, he called the inhabitants Indians:

> But really they were Arawaks, and they had as much in common with the Iroquois of the northern woodlands as the Iroquois had in common with the Blackfoot of the western Plains or the Haida of the Pacific Coast. In other words, when Columbus arrived in America there were a large number of different and distinct indigenous cultures, but there were no Indians. (Francis 4)

Fergus Bordewich writes that each of these native societies had

> its own unique history, its own systems of ethics and aesthetics, and its own cosmology, each speaking a language that, as often as not, was completely incomprehensible to groups that lived just a few miles away. Few of them were organized in their modern tribal form, and fewer still were known to each other by the names that we associate with them today. (33)

Had an Indian claimed to have discovered the European—a monolithic culture including, say Holland and Turkey—the pronouncement would have been equally absurd.

5. Vizenor writes that "tribal realities are superseded by simulations of the unreal" (8). Deloria writes that to be an "Indian in modern American society is in a very real sense to be unreal and unhistorical" (*Custer* 20). And in *Off the Reservation,* writer Paula Gunn Allen compares the western world's view of

women to its perception of Native people, with both groups gendered feminine (and, not surprisingly, silent):

> Certainly, the language used to designate the one is frequently employed to designate the other. Both are close to nature, irrational, intuitive, mystical, culturally focused, domestic, dependent entities, at one with flora and fauna, and best kept silent, dependent, and enclosed—for their own protection. (9)

6. In "A Word (or Two) on Terms and Categories," I wrote that the word *Indian* is a simulation in the literature of dominance; only *postindian* is the absence of invention, the end of representation. My use of Real Indian will always signify with the irony of simulation. Serious tribal matters, final-word interpretations, or definitive definitions are neither the mission of or within the expertise of this white English professor.

That said, I appreciate Vizenor's irony, but I wonder if any of the Southwest people I interviewed for this study would. I detected no irony whatsoever when they spoke of their tribal or puebloan affiliations; they regularly referred to their people as "the people." They used irony when describing how white people perceive Indians, but not about their own self-perceptions. They also used irony when discussing members of the Wannabe tribe and many other such whites.

7. I do not have access to the 2000 census figures, but from 1980 and 1990, the number of Indians jumped by "78 percent in New Jersey, 66.1 percent in Ohio, 64 percent in Texas, 62 percent in Virginia, and 58.3 percent in New York, with similar figures recorded almost everywhere in the country. In 1990, nearly 2 million Americans listed themselves as Indians in the U.S. census" (Bordewich 54–55).

8. As chair of the Conference on College Composition and Communication, Keith Gilyard delivered a compelling address that focused, at one point, on the importance of knowing one's own identity. He talked about an inebriated Indian man, and how this man was treated at the bus station. At one point, the man turned to Gilyard and asked him if he was "Injun." Gilyard said, "Naw, I ain't Injun":

> En route to New York City[,] I thought about this "Injuness" and of my great-grandfather, Toby Townsend, the 6'6" Cherokee shop owner who refused to labor in the fields for anyone else. Good image. I also thought about the "Trail of Tears," the seizure of Cherokee lands. Poignant image. But I recalled reading that the Cherokees were the most assimilationist of the Indian nations. Not the image I want to romanticize. So then I considered how Indian scouts aided the confederacy, but also how Blacks served in the U.S. Army as agents

of genocide against Indians. But that was all mental exercise, perhaps useful in widening and deepening perspectives about family history and the world. However, I knew my primary identity. Not a single bad thing has ever happened to me because someone pegged me for Indian. When I arrived in New York City, I tucked my wallet in my shoulder bag and tried not to appear threatening to the NYPD. ("Literacy" 270)

Despite his "Indian blood," Gilyard knows his primary identity is that of a Black man.

9. The *Report of the Indian Peace Commissioners* reads as follows:

By educating the children of these tribes in the English language, these differences would have disappeared, and civilization would have followed at once. . . . In the difference of language to-day lies two-thirds of our trouble. . . . Schools should be established, which children should be required to attend; their barbarous dialect should be blotted out and the English language substituted. (16–17)

10. In his 1900 account of Indian school life, Francis La Flesche reports the hardship he and his friends endured when they "encountered a rule that prohibited the use of [their] own language, which was rigidly enforced with a hickory rod, so that the new-comer, however socially inclined, was obliged to go about like a little dummy until he had learned to express himself in English" (xvii). These students were effectively silenced.

In a letter to Pratt written on behalf of her great-grandfather, contemporary Diné writer Laura Tohe writes about the assimilationist policies that her teachers enforced when she attended school in the late 1950s:

Besides teaching us to read, write, and count in English, she was instructed to wipe out *Diné bizaad* through shame and punishment. We still bear painful memories for speaking our native language in school and that legacy is partly why many indigenous people don't know their ancestral language. . . . We learned quickly that if we didn't want to be punished and shamed in front of our classmates we had best speak our language in private, far from the ears of the teachers, or stop speaking; most chose the latter.

Ironically, the Diné language was successfully utilized as a secret code during World War II. Without the Code Talkers, the war might have had a substantially different outcome for America. (Introduction x–xi)

11. In 1887, the U.S. government continued to sponsor the suppression of Indian languages (and cultures); J. D. C. Atkins, Commissioner of Indian Affairs, wrote (with no trace of irony) that as the Indians

are in an English-speaking country, they must be taught the language which they must use in transacting business with the people of this country. No unity or community of feeling can be established among different peoples unless they are brought to speak the same language . . . .

The instruction of the Indians in the[ir] vernacular is not only of no use to them, but is detrimental to the cause of their education and civilization, and no school will be permitted on the reservation in which the English language is not exclusively taught. (xxi–xxiii)

The U.S. policy against "foreign languages" reverberates today, for we continue to ask immigrants and indigenous minorities alike to give up their language for English.

12. Furthermore, this government-sponsored suppression was, for centuries, coupled with genocidal activities from relocation and forced marches to contagion and massacres that sharply reduced the Indian population in the United States, from an estimated ten million in 1492 to just over two hundred thousand in 1900, and then up to 1,878,285 in 1990. Without extended families of native speakers, without children learning their native language as their mother tongue, native languages—and thereby cultures—simply wither away:

> Okay, you children listen. If he won't tell you, then I must. You must know your language first. Yes, we must know the white man language to survive in *this* world. But we must know our language to survive *forever.* (Aunt Gladys, qtd. in D. Wilson 38, emphasis in original)

13. Jon Reyhner, leading proponent for the renewal of native languages, argues that

> indigenous language revitalization is part of a larger attempt by indigenous peoples to retain their cultural strengths in the face of the demoralizing assaults of an all-pervasive modern, individualistic, materialistic, and hedonistic technological culture. ("Some Basic" v)

After all, he explains, "Each language carries with it an unspoken network of cultural forces" that shapes "each person's self-awareness, identity, and interpersonal relationships" ("Maintaining" 279). He goes on to argue that "these values are psychological imperatives that help generate and maintain an individual's level of comfort and self-assurance, and, consequently, success in life. In the normal course of events these values are absorbed along with one's mother tongue" (279).

14. Laura Tohe eloquently writes about her movement between her two languages, *Diné bizaad* and English:

My son and I sat on the bed of a late half-light
from the hallway slanted across gray walls.

He spoke of toes and scratches,
and I comforted in the desert tones of our language
we left behind across winter dry plains.

His brown eyes
alive,
      glowing in the shadows with eternal life,
gaze at me,
Feeling the sounds of these words
I so seldom speak.

In this moment caught between languages
    we shared my words
        as if they were secrets
nourished within this half-light.

("Half-Light" 41)

And Acoma sisters Annette Romero, Danielle Victoriano, and Billie Wanya speak freely about their use of their language, Kerésan, which is used at Acoma, Cochiti, Laguna, Santa Ana, Santo Domingo, San Filipe, and Zia Pueblos. The sisters' parents speak Kerésan and use it frequently, but Wanya says, "My mom corrects us and tells us when we're wrong. When she does that, I stop speaking and say, 'O.K., Mom, I won't try.'"

Romero cuts in to say, "Me and my cousin were in Phoenix, and she was the only one I could speak our language with, and we would be laughing. I like talking in our language." She continues with, "When I was younger, I really didn't [speak our language] because I was raised in Idaho, and I wasn't really brought up [to speak our language] until we came back to New Mexico. When I went to live with my grandparents, then I learned" (qtd. in Wanya).

15. Worried, the boy's grandfather came and spoke to him:

"Amoo uh, Nana, because of love for you, your sisters are worried about you not talking, and because of love for you, I have come to you. Perhaps, Nana, it is not time for you yet to speak, but you will when it is time. It is with language you will come about for yourself as a person and as a son of your family. It is with knowledge and words that you will know and express love for yourself and your people. Dzehni neeyah—with language—and with responsibility for yourself and others, you will speak. That is how you will come about as a person. Amoo uh, Nana, nehmahshrou shruuh." Assuring the boy he would come to talk, the grandfather asked him to open his mouth widely, and, reaching into his Levis pocket, he drew out a big, brass door key. He inserted the key into the boy's mouth and said, "Now, Grandson, you will speak." My sister concluded the story by saying, "Ever since then, we haven't been able to keep his mouth shut." (Introduction 7)

Ortiz concludes the vignette by implying that he had been the little silent boy.

16. It's important to keep in mind that Apaches are Athabaskans, as are Navajos and some of the Alaskan indigenous people. Basso's expertise lies with the culture and language of the White Mountain (Western) Apache tribe; he has studied and written about them ever since his first visit to Cibecue, Arizona, in 1959.

17. Calling on the work of Susan Ervin-Tripp and Dell Hymes, Basso defines *situation* as "the location of such a gathering, its physical setting, its point in time, the standing behavior patterns that accompany it, and the social attributes of the persons involved" (*Western Apache* 83).

18. The empirical materials on which this section is based were recorded on tape, with the prior written consent of all Indian parties. The research proposal and design was approved by the Human Subjects Institutional Review Board at the Pennsylvania State University.

19. If memory serves me correctly, Basso paid the informants in his investigation of silence. In his later investigation of Indian place names, he mentions how he paid his informant-guides, mostly in goods:

Dudley and I will catch up our horses and go for a ride. It might last all day, so we will need to take food. Ruth [Dudley's wife] will provide the fresh tortillas. I will contribute two cans of sardines, a box of Ritz crackers, a slab of long-horn cheese, and four bottles of Barg's root beer. Dudley will take me to different places, teach me their names, and tell me what happened at them long ago. Then, maybe, I will understand something. When we get back home Dudley will speak to me in English—'Boy Keez, I'll see you sometime.' Then he will leave me alone to think. In return for these services, he will receive two sacks of flour, two cans of MJB coffee, one sack of sugar, a pail of Crisco, and twenty dollars cash. (*Wisdom* 128–29)

My not paying my "informants" in no way guarantees that what they told me is therefore more authentic or truthful than what Basso's informants told him.

20. Saavedra's wife, Danielle Victoriano, also comes from a long line of well-known Acoma potters. When I interviewed her, she also connected necessary silence with artistic concentration.

21. I asked him if he meant white culture, and he replied, "Yes, white dominated culture."

22. The women identified themselves as three sisters and surely behaved the way three mutually supportive sisters might act. Interestingly, they all told me that Romero was technically a cousin to Wanya and Victoriano, who are biological sisters. When Romero's mother died, Romero began living as a daughter with her mother's sister, the mother of Wanya and Victoriano. Technicalities notwithstanding, these three women are sisters.

23. The Bread Loaf School of English has a summer campus in Santa Fe. During the summer of 2000, it was located on the campus of the Native American Prep School, where Jagles taught and lived throughout the year. The Santa Fe program was directed by Andrea Lunsford, a professor of English at Stanford University, who arrived on campus along with all the other professors and MA students.

24. In another of his early works, *Portraits of "the Whiteman,"* Basso discusses at length the Apache suspicion of white friendships:

> "My friend" [is] an expression that Apaches think Anglo-Americans bandy about in a thoroughly irresponsible way. . . . Whitemen are said to make liberal use of the term when they want something from someone, apparently believing that by professing affection and concern they can improve their chances of getting it. In short, Anglo-Americans pretend to what cannot and should not be pretended to—hasty friendship—and it strikes Apaches as the height of folly and presumptuousness that they do. One of [Basso's] consultants put it succinctly: "Whitemen say you're their friend like it was nothing, like it was air." (48)

25. Basso himself writes that he was "told by adult informants that the young people's reluctance to speak may become even more pronounced in situations where they find themselves alone" ("To Give Up" 218). He was told by "a youth 17 years old" that "it's hard to talk with your sweetheart at first" (219).

These three sisters all registered suspicion about paid informants as did Chino and Todacheene. As I mentioned earlier, I did not pay my informants, so I know that money did not influence their answers. However, I realize that my very presence and my set of questions influenced the situation in ways that I cannot calibrate.

26. Embe (M.B.) was the pseudonym of Marion Burgess, a white woman who taught at Carlisle Indian School and published the Carlisle newsletter, *The Indian Helper.* I am referring to an 1891 edition of *Stiya* housed at the University of New Mexico's Center for Southwest Research. In *Yellow Woman and the Beauty of the Spirit,* Leslie Marmon Silko mentions an 1881 U.S. War Department publication of this book, which I have not been able to locate (162).

Silko's great-grandmother, Marie Anaya Marmon, and great-aunt, Susie Reyes Marmon, both attended Carlisle and received copies of *Stiya* upon their return to Laguna Pueblo. According to Silko, what to do with this book resulted in the only quarrel the two women ever had. Silko's great-grandmother was so offended by the book (she especially detested the wholly inaccurate description of food preparation) that she wanted to burn it. But her daughter-in-law, Silko's great-aunt, wanted to keep the book as proof of the government's lies. Silko's great-aunt asked for and was given the book.

An 1897 issue of *The Indian Helper* featured an interview with Marie Marmon and Mary Bailey Seonia, who were bringing pueblo children to their alma mater. According to the Man-on-the-band-stand (Burgess), the interlocutor of all interviews, Marmon and Seonia were leaders of the successful movement toward white culture:

Mrs. Marmon is a progressive little woman, and has the interests of the Lagunas so much at heart that she seizes every opportunity to help them, and suffers distress of mind when she cannot arrest an influence that is leading her people astray or is hindering their most speedy advancement in the right direction.

Colonel Marmon [a white Ohioan, who had relocated] seconds his wife's efforts, and results show in the superior thrift and intelligence of the Lagunas over the other Pueblos.

"How are the Lagunas getting on?" was the first question asked by the Man-on-the-band-stand through his chief clerk.

"They have improved very much indeed since you were there, in 1889."

"In what way?"

"They have better farms, and the returned students from Carlisle, Albuquerque [Indian School] and other schools have made labor popular. They work upon the Railroad, on their farms and ranches, and the Indian homes look better, especially those who have moved out of the villages."

"Why, I heard that all the returned students had gone back to the old ways."

"It is not so," said Mrs. Marmon with great emphasis. "Most of the boys do as well as they can. Of course they cannot dress as well as they did when they first came home."

"Why not?"

"Well, their clothes soon get shabby and worn out, and it is not so easy to get a new and well-fitting suit as when they were at school."

. . . "Mrs. Seonia, what have YOU to say about the GIRLS? Have they gone back to the old ways?"

"I am sorry to have to report that nearly all the girls have adopted the Indian dress."

. . . "Do you think the dress of an Indian girl speaks much either for or against her character?"

"I believe it does to some extent. My opinion is that an educated girl ought to wear the civilized dress, but if she does not, it is not always evidence that she does not use her education in other useful ways. I have in mind now a young girl who has done much to improve her home, and she is wielding a good influence in her tribe, in many ways, yet she wears the Indian dress. But generally speaking, it is the first step backward when an educated Indian girl puts on the dress of her uneducated mother and friends." (1–2)

I e-mailed the preceding excerpt to Lee Marmon, Silko's father, to ask him how returning Indians might obtain white clothing. He told me that Albuquerque, some sixty miles away by horse, would have been the nearest place to buy cloth or clothing.

27. By the end of the story, however, Stiya converts her parents to white culture: her father no longer participates in the "pagan" Hopi dances; he works shoveling coal for the railroad and saves money for their new house. The family moves from a "filthy room" to a clean three-room adobe, where Stiya and her mother keep house and cook according to Carlisle instruction.

28. Ellis recounts the ritualized silence she met when returning home:

Shiwóyé walked in.

Without a word she crossed the living room floor and gave me a strong hug.

"Hello Shiwóyé," I said.

We gravitated to the kitchen where she poured us each a tall glass of iced tea. We folded the sheets and then she put them away. She returned to the kitchen and watered the herbs sitting on her window sill.

At least ten minutes had passed, and my grandmother had not said a word. I knew it was up to me to begin, so I started to speak endlessly about La Cienega and the ranch. I went on nonstop for twenty minutes. Since my visit was going to be short, I wanted to get this over with right away.

Still Shiwóyé did not speak, which is not that unusual for an Apache. She was following a custom handed down for generations.

I began to prattle on about my case.

Finally she spoke.

"Shiwóyé, shichoo."

The damn had broken. Through my prattling, I had given her time to analyze whether or not my exposure to the outside world had changed me. While it would have been considered rude for Shiwóyé to interrogate me, by my own words I had enabled her to see if my attitudes or views had altered.

It was a ritual we went through every time I returned, just like countless Apache parents welcoming their children home from boarding school. (S. Browning 94–95)

29. The legendary Ira Hayes enlisted in the Marines in 1942 and became one of the elite corps of paratroopers. He and his combat contingent fought at Iwo Jima for four days in one of the bloodiest, fiercest battles of World War II. Six of those men, including Hayes, planted the American flag on a hilltop, which was memorialized in a Pulitzer Prize–winning photograph. Upon his return to the States, Hayes was celebrated as a war hero, yet he drowned his sorrows in silence, isolation, and alcohol, dying at the age of thirty-two (Goldweb).

30. Mihesuah's case in point is *Kiowa Voices,* in which Maurice Boyd interviewed multiheritage Kiowa informants, some of whom later joked to Mihesuah that they had "'made up' songs and stories" because Boyd "wouldn't know the difference" (qtd. in *Natives* 3). These same charges were made against Margaret Mead's research findings, which were published in *Coming of Age in Samoa.*

31. In *Storyteller,* Silko includes a poem about the time ethnologist Franz Boaz entered Laguna Pueblo to collect Laguna stories. Silko's great-grandfather Marmon, a white man from Ohio, told Boaz a peculiar story that revealed nothing of the Indian culture, for, as Silko writes, "the one thing he had to remember" was this: "No matter what is said to you by anyone / you must take care of those most dear to you" (256).

6. Opening Silence

1. Brueggemann's book led the way for other rhetorical projects that use other methods to open silences: James C. Wilson and Cynthia Lewiecki-Wilson's *Embodied Rhetorics;* Sharon L. Snyder, Brueggemann, and Rosemarie Garland-Thomson's *Disability Studies;* and Lennard Davis's *My Sense of Silence* come immediately to mind.

2. Dominick A. Barbara's *The Art of Listening,* Peter Burke's *The Art of Conversation,* Hannah Merker's *Listening,* and Rebecca Z. Shafir's *The Zen of Listening* all offer pathways into a rhetoric of listening—and of silence.

Works Cited

Adams, David Wallace. *Education for Extinction: American Indians and the Board-ing School Experience, 1875–1928*. Lawrence: U of Kansas P, 1995.

"African American Women in Defense of Ourselves." *The New York Times* 11 Nov. 1991. Rpt. in Chrisman and Allen 291–92.

Alcoff, Linda Martin. "The Problem of Speaking for Others." *Overcoming Racism and Sexism*. Ed. Linda A. Bell and David Blumfield. Lanham: Roman, 1995. 229–54.

Alford, Thomas Wildcat. *Civilization, and the Story of the Absentee Shawnee*. As told to Florence Drake. Norman: U of Oklahoma P, 1936.

Allen, Paula Gunn. *Off the Reservation: Reflections on Boundary Busting, Border Crossing, Loose Canons*. Boston: Beacon, 1998.

———. "Problems in Teaching Silko's *Ceremony*." Mihesuah, *Natives* 55–64.

Allison, Dorothy. *Two or Three Things I Know for Sure*. New York: Plume, 1995.

Altman, Karen E. "Bodies of Knowledge." *Quarterly Journal of Speech* 78 (1992): 483–89.

Alvord, Lisa Arviso, and Elizabeth Cohen Van Pelt. *The Scalpel and the Silver Bear*. New York: Bantam, 1999.

Anderson, Jon Lee. "The Reign in Spain." *New Yorker* 27 Apr. and 4 May 1998: 110–19.

Angelou, Maya. "I Dare to Hope." *New York Times* 25 Aug. 1991. Rpt. in Chrisman and Allen 33–35.

Anonymous i. E-mail to the author. 1 Nov. 1999.

Anonymous ii. E-mail to the author. 15 Nov. 1999.

Anonymous iii. E-mail to the author. 10 Nov. 1999.

Anonymous iv. E-mail to the author. 15 Nov. 1999.

Anonymous v. E-mail to the author. 16 Nov. 1999.

Anonymous vi. E-mail to the author. 17 Nov. 1999.

Anonymous vii. E-mail to the author. 19 Nov. 1999.

Anonymous viii. E-mail to the author. 24 Jan. 2002.

Anonymous ix. E-mail to the author. 27 Jan. 2002.

Anonymous x. E-mail to the author. 16 Nov. 1999.

Anonymous xia. E-mail to the author. 1 Feb. 2002.

Anonymous xib. E-mail to the author. 2 Feb. 2002.

Anonymous xii. E-mail to author. 15 Nov. 1999.

Anonymous xiii. Personal interview. 10 Aug. 2000.

Anthony, Carl Sferrazza. "Hillary's Hidden Power." *George* Nov. 1999: 108–17.

Anzaldúa, Gloria. "El sonavabiche." *Borderlands.* San Francisco: Spinsters/Aunt Lute, 1987. 124–29.

Apple, R. W., Jr. "President Blames Himself for Furor Over Nominee." *New York Times* 5 June 1993: A1, A8.

Applebome, Peter. "Where Ideas That Hurt Guinier Thrive." *New York Times* 5 June 1993: A9.

Ardener, Edwin. "The Problem Revisited." *Perceiving Women.* Ed. Shirley Ardener. London: Malaby, 1975. 19–28.

Aristotle. *Politics.* Trans. H. Rackham. Cambridge: Loeb/Harvard UP, 1977.

———. *The Rhetoric and Poetics of Aristotle.* Trans. W. Rhys Roberts and Ingram Bywater. New York: Modern Library, 1984.

Armen, Jean-Claude. *Gazelle-Boy.* Trans. Stephen Hardman. New York: Universe, 1974.

Askew, Anne. *The Lattre Examinacyon of A. Askewe [A Reprint of the Wesel Editions]. The First Examinaciò of A. Askewe (the Lattre Examynacyon.)* Marpurg, Hessen: D. van der Straten, 1546, 1547.

Atkins, J. D. C. *Annual Report of the Commissioner of Indian Affairs to the Secretary of the Interior in the Year 1887.* Washington, D.C.: GPO, 1887.

Bachelard, Gaston. *Water and Dreams.* 3rd ed. Dallas: Dallas Institute, 1999.

Baker, Peter. "Willey Describes Clinton Advance." *Washington Post* 16 Mar. 1998: A1.

Baker, Sidney J. "The Theory of Silences." *Journal of General Psychiatry* 52 (1955): 145–67.

Ballif, Michelle, D. Diane Davis, and Roxanne Mountford. "Negotiating the Differend: A Feminist Trilogue." *JAC* 30 (2000): 583–625.

Barbara, Dominick A. *The Art of Listening.* Springfield: Thomas, 1958.

Barlowe, Jamie. *The Scarlet Mob of Scribblers.* Carbondale: Southern Illinois UP, 2000.

Barnes, Kim. "A Leslie Marmon Silko Interview." 1986. *Conversations with Leslie Marmon Silko.* Ed. Ellen L. Arnold. Jackson: U of Mississippi P, 2000. 69–83.

Basso, Keith H. *The Cibecue Apache.* Prospect Heights: Waveland, 1970.

———. *Portraits of "the Whiteman."* Cambridge: Cambridge UP, 1979.

———. "'To Give Up on Words': Silence in Western Apache Culture." *Southwestern Journal of Anthropology* 26 (1970): 213–30.

———. *Western Apache Language and Culture: Essays in Linguistic Anthropology.* Tucson: U of Arizona P, 1990.

———. *Wisdom Sits in Places: Landscape and Language among the Western Apache.* Albuquerque: U of New Mexico P, 1996.

Bateson, Gregory, Don D. Jackson, Jay Haley, and John Weakland. "Toward a Theory of Schizophrenia." *Behavioral Science* 1 (1956): 251–64.

Bauer, Dale M., and S. Jaret McKinstry, eds. *Feminism, Bakhtin, and the Dialogic.* Albany: State U of New York P, 1991.

Bauman, Richard. *Let Your Words Be Few: Symbolism of Speaking and Silence among Seventeenth-Century Quakers.* Cambridge: Cambridge UP, 1983.

Becker, Robin. "Against Silence." *The Horse Fair.* Pittsburgh: Pittsburgh UP, 2000. 79.

———. "I'm Telling! Secrecy and Shame in One Jewish-American Family." *Prairie Schooner* 71 (1977): 210–22.

Belanoff, Pat. "Silence: Reflection, Literacy, Learning, and Teaching." *CCC* 52 (2001): 399–428.

Berkhofer, Robert F., Jr. *The White Man's Indian: Images of the American Indian from Columbus to the Present.* New York: Random, 1978.

Bianco, Frank. *Voices of Silence.* New York: Anchor, 1991.

Biskupic, Joan. "Lawsuit Against Clinton Can Proceed, Court Says." *Washington Post* 28 May 1997: A10.

Bizzell, Patricia. "Feminist Methods of Research in the History of Rhetoric: What Difference Do They Make?" *Rhetoric Society Quarterly* 30 (2000): 5–17.

Bizzell, Patricia, and Bruce Herzberg, eds. *The Rhetorical Tradition: Readings from Classical Times to the Present.* 2d. ed. Boston: Bedford, 2001.

Black, Edwin. "Secrecy and Disclosure as Rhetorical Forms." *Quarterly Journal of Speech* 74 (1988): 133–50.

Blair, Carole, and Mary L. Kahl. "Revising the History of Rhetorical Theory." Introduction. *Western Journal of Speech Communication* 54 (1990): 148–59.

Blankenship, J., and C. Kay. "Hesitation Phenomena in English Speech: A Study in Distribution." *Word* 20 (1964): 360–72.

Bolick, Clint. "Clinton's Quota Queens." *Wall Street Journal* 30 Apr. 1993: A12.

———. "The Legal Philosophy That Produced Lani Guinier." *Wall Street Journal* 2 June 1993: A15.

Boo, Katherine. "The Organization Woman." *Washington Monthly* Dec. 1991: 44–46.

Bordewich, Fergus M. *Killing the White Man's Indian: Reinventing Native Americans at the End of the Twentieth Century.* New York: Anchor-Doubleday, 1996.

Bourdieu, Pierre. *Distinction: A Social Critique of the Judgement of Taste.* Trans. Richard Nice. Cambridge: Harvard UP, 1984.

———. *The Logic of Practice.* Trans. Richard Nice. Stanford: Stanford UP, 1990.

Boyd, Maurice. *Kiowa Voices.* Linn Pauahty, Kiowa consultant. Fort Worth: Texas Christian UP, c. 1981–1983.

Braithwaite, Charles A. "Cultural Uses and Interpretations of Silence." *The Nonverbal Communication Reader.* 2d ed. Ed. Laura K. Guerrero, Joseph A. DeVito, and Michael L. Hecht. Prospect Heights: Waveland, 1999. 163–72.

Brandenberg, Ruth. *White Women, Race Matters: The Social Construction of Whiteness.* Minneapolis: U of Minnesota P, 1993.

Broaddrick, Juanita. "Key Player: Juanita Broaddrick." Accessed 23 Feb. 2000. <http://www.washingtonpost.com/wp-srv/politics/special/clinton/players/broaddrick.htm>.

Brock, David. "The Fire This Time." *Esquire* Apr. 1998: 60+.

———. "Living with the Clintons: Bill's Arkansas Bodyguards Tell the Story the Press Missed." *American Spectator* Jan. 1994: 18–30.

———. *The Seduction of Hillary Clinton.* New York: Free, 1996.

Browning, Dolly Kyle. "Declaration." Accessed 30 Nov. 1998. <http://cnn.com/ALLPOLITICS/1998/ 03/16/jo.dics/dolly.browning.declaration/001.jpg>.

———. "Sworn Declaration Presented to the House Judiciary Committee on 12/11/98." Accessed 24 Nov. 1999. <http://www.home.inreach.com.dov.kyle.htm>.

Browning, Sinclair. *The Last Song Dogs.* New York: Bantam, 1999.

Brueggemann, Brenda Jo. *Lend Me Your Ear: Rhetorical Constructions of Deafness.* Washington, D.C.: Gallaudet UP, 1999.

Bruneau, Thomas J. "Communicative Silences: Forms and Functions." *Journal of Communication* 23 (1973): 17–46.

Bunyan, John. *Christian Behavior, The Holy City, The Resurrection of the Dead.* 1663. Ed. James Sears McGee. Oxford: Clarendon/Oxford UP, 1987.

Burke, Carolyn G. "Report from Paris: Women's Writing and the Women's Movement." *Signs* 3 (1978): 843–55.

Burke, Kenneth. *Attitudes Toward History.* 3rd ed. Berkeley: U of California P, 1984.

———. *A Grammar of Motives.* 1962. Berkeley: U of California P, 1969.

———. *Language as Symbolic Action.* Berkeley: U of California P, 1966.

———. *Permanence and Change.* 3rd ed. Berkeley: U of California P, 1984.

———. *Perspectives by Incongruity.* Ed. Stanley Edgar Hyman. Bloomington: Indiana UP, 1964.

———. *Philosophy of Literary Form.* Berkeley: U of California P, 1973.

———. *A Rhetoric of Motives.* 1962. Berkeley: U of California P, 1969.

Burke, Peter. *The Art of Conversation.* Ithaca: Cornell UP, 1994.

Butler, Judith. *Bodies That Matter.* New York: Routledge, 1993.

———. *Excitable Speech.* Routledge: New York, 1997.

Bystrom, Dianne G. "Beyond the Hearings: The Continuing Effects of Hill vs. Thomas on Women and Men, the Workplace, and Politics." Ragan, Bystrom, Kaid, Beck 260–82.

Cage, John. *Silence: Lectures and Writings.* Middletown: Wesleyan UP, 1961.

Campbell, Kermit. "'Real Niggaz's Don't Die': African American Students Speaking Themselves into Their Writing." *Writing in Multicultural Settings.* Ed. Carol Severino, Juan C. Guerra, and Johnnella E. Butler. New York: MLA, 1997. 67–78.

Cappella, Joseph N., and Kathleen Hall Jamieson. *Spiral of Cynicism: The Press and the Public Good.* New York: Oxford, 1997.

Carter, Stephen L. Foreword. Guinier, *Tyranny* vii–xx.

Chino, Maurus. Personal interview. 15 Aug. 1999.

Chrisman, Robert, and Robert L. Allen, eds. *Court of Appeal: The Black Community Speaks Out on the Racial and Sexual Politics of Thomas vs. Hill.* New York: Ballantine, 1992.

Cicero. *De Oratore.* 2 vols. Book 3. *De Partitione Oratoriae.* Trans. E. W. Sutton. Cambridge: Harvard UP, 1979.

"A Civil Rights Struggle Ahead." Editorial. *New York Times* 23 May 1993: 144.

Clair, Robin Patric. *Organizing Silence.* Albany: State U of New York P, 1998.

Cliff, Michelle. "Notes on Speechlessness." *Sinister Wisdom* 5 (1978): 5–9.

Clinton, Hillary. *It Takes a Village.* New York: Simon, 1996.

Clinton, William Jefferson. "Deposition." 17 Jan. 1998. Released 13 Mar. 1998. Accessed 3 Feb. 2000. <http://www.washingtonpost.com/wp-srv/politics/special/pjones/clintondep 031398.htm>.

———. "Grand Jury Testimony." 17 Aug. 1998. Accessed 3 Feb. 2000. *Time* online. <http://www.pathfinder.com/time/daily/scandal/testimony/temp.html>.

———. "Transcript of President Clinton's Statement." 17 Aug. 1998. Accessed 3 Feb. 2000. <http://www.salonmagazine.com/news/1998/08/18newsc.html>.

Collins, Patricia Hill. *Fighting Words.* Minneapolis: U of Minnesota P, 1998.

Congressional Record 8 Oct. 1991: Senate 14508.

Crouch, Stanley. "The Huffing and Puffing Military Blues." *Always in Pursuit.* New York: Pantheon, 1998. 102–5.

Dalke, Anne French. *Teaching to Learn, Learning to Teach: Meditations on the Classroom.* New York: Lang, 2002.

Daly, Mary. *Beyond God the Father: Toward a Philosophy of Women's Liberation.* Boston: Beacon, 1973.

———. *The Church and the Second Sex.* 1968. Boston: Beacon, 1985.

———. *Gyn/Ecology: The Metaethics of Radical Feminism.* Boston: Beacon, 1978.

Daly, Mary, in Cahoots with Jane Caputi. *Websters' First New Intergalactic Wickedary of the English Language.* Boston: Beacon, 1987.

Darwin, Thomas J. "Telling the Truth: The Rhetoric of Consistency and Credibility in the Hill-Thomas Hearings." Ragan, Bystrom, Kaid, Beck 190–214.

Dauenhauer, Bernard. *Silence: The Phenomenon and Its Ontological Significance.* Bloomington: Indiana UP, 1980.

Davis, Lennard. *My Sense of Silence*. Urbana: U of Illinois P, 2000.

DeFrancisco, Victoria Leto. "The Sounds of Silence: How Men Silence Women in Marital Relations." *Discourse and Society* 2 (1991): 413–23.

de Laurentis, Teresa. *Technologies of Gender: Essays on Theory, Film, and Fiction.* Bloomington: Indian UP, 1987.

Deloria, Vine, Jr. *Custer Died for Your Sins.* 1966. Norman: U of Oklahoma P, 1988.

———. *God Is Red: A Native View of Religion.* 2d ed. Golden: North American P, 1992.

Dickinson, Emily. *The Complete Poems of Emily Dickinson.* Ed. Thomas H. Johnson. Boston: Little, 1976.

Dilworth, Leah. *Imagining Indians in the Southwest: Persistent Visions of a Primitive Past.* Washington, D.C.: Smithsonian Institution P, 1996.

Dowd, Maureen. "Change of Hart." *New York Times* 22 Mar. 1998: Op-Ed 15.

Drudge, Matt. *The Drudge Report.* <http://www.drudgereport.com>.

Duncan, Hugh D. *Symbols in Society.* New York: Oxford UP, 1968.

Dyer, Richard. *White.* London: Routledge, 1997.

Eastman, Charles. *The Soul of an Indian: An Interpretation.* Boston: Houghton, 1911.

Ede, Lisa, and Andrea Lunsford. "Collaboration and Concepts of Authorship." *PMLA* 116 (2001): 354–69.

———. *Singular Texts/Plural Authors.* Carbondale: Southern Illinois UP, 1990.

Elbow, Peter. "Silence: A Collage." *Everyone Can Write.* New York: Oxford UP, 2000. 173–83.

Elders, Joycelyn, and David Chanoff. *Joycelyn Elders, M.D.* New York: Avon, 1996.

Elshtain, Jean Bethke. *Public Man, Private Woman.* Princeton: Princeton UP, 1987.

Embe [M. Burgess]. *Stiya, A Carlisle Indian Girl at Home.* Cambridge: Riverside, 1891.

Enoch, Jessica. "Women's Resistant Pedagogies in Turn-of-the-Century America: Lydia Maria Child, Zitkala Ša, Jovita Idar, Marta Peña, and Leonor Villegas de Magnón." Diss. Pennsylvania State U, 2003.

Epaloose, Todd. Personal interview. 14 Oct. 1999.

Epstein, Cynthia Fuchs. *Deceptive Distinctions: Sex, Gender, and the Social Order.* New Haven: Yale UP, 1988.

Equal Employment Opportunity Commission. "Guideline on Discrimination Because of Sex." *Federal Register* 45 (1980): 74676–77.

Equal Employment Opportunity Commission Guidelines. 29. Code of Federal Regulations. Sec. 1604.11. 1988.

Erdrich, Louise. "Le Mooz." *New Yorker* 24 Jan. 2000: 74–80.

Faludi, Susan, Susan Brownmiller, Katie Roiphe, Gloria Allred, et al. "We Believe You, Juanita (We Think)." Accessed 3 Dec. 1999. <www.salonmagazine.com/mmwt/feature/1999/03/cov_03feature.html>.

Farmer, Frank. *Saying and Silence: Listening to Composition with Bakhtin.* Logan: Utah State UP, 2001.

[Farrar, Eliza]. By a Lady. *The Young Lady's Friend.* Boston: American Stationers', 1837.

Fausto-Sterling, Anne. "How Many Sexes Are There?" *New York Times* 12 Mar. 1993: A29.

Finkel, Donald L. *Teaching with Your Mouth Shut.* Portsmouth: Boynton, 2000.

Fishman, Pamela. "Interaction: The Work Women Do." *Social Problems* 25 (1978): 397–406. Rpt. in *Language, Gender, and Society.* Ed. Barrie Thorne, Cheris Kramarae, and Nancy Henley. Rowley: Newbury, 1983. 89–102.

Fiumara, Gemma Corradi. *The Other Side of Language: A Philosophy of Listening.* London: Routledge, 1990.

Flinders, Carol Lee. *At the Root of This Longing.* San Francisco: Harper, 1998.

Flowers, Gennifer. "Declaration of Gennifer G. Flowers." Accessed 13 Mar. 1998, 24 Mar. 1998. *Washington Post* online. <http://www. washingtonpost.com/wp-srv/politics/special/clinton/players/ flowers.htm>).

———. *Gennifer Flowers: Passion and Betrayal.* With Jacquelyn Dapper. Del Mar: Dalton, 1995.

Foss, Karen A., Sonja K. Foss, and Cindy L. Griffin. *Feminist Rhetorical Theories.* Thousand Oaks: Sage, 1999.

———. Introduction. Foss, Foss, and Griffin 1–13.

Foss, Sonja, and Cindy L. Griffin. "Beyond Persuasion: A Proposal for an Invitational Rhetoric." *Communication Monographs* 62 (1995): 2–18.

———. "A Feminist Perspective on Rhetorical Theory: Toward a Clarification of Boundaries." *Western Journal of Communication* 56 (1992): 330–49.

Foucault, Michel. *Discipline and Punish: The Birth of the Prison.* Trans. Alan Sheridan. 1977. New York: Vintage, 1995.

———. *The History of Sexuality.* Vol. 1. 1978. New York: Vintage, 1990.

France, Anatole. *The Man Who Married a Dumb Wife.* Trans. Curtis Hidden Page. New York: John Lane, 1915.

Francis, Daniel. *The Imaginary Indian.* Vancouver: Arsenal, 1992.

Franks, Lucinda. "The Intimate Hillary." *Talk* Sept. 1999: 167–74.

Fredericks, Evelyn. E-mail to the author. 18 Jan. 2000.

———. E-mail to the author. 11 May 2000.

———. E-mail to the author. 13 July 2000.

———. E-mail to the author. 18 Nov. 2000.

Gal, Susan. "Between Speech and Silence: The Problematics of Research on Language and Gender." *Gender at the Crossroads of Knowledge: Feminist Anthropology in the Postmodern Era.* Berkeley: U of California P, 1991. 175–203.

Garrow, David J. "Lani Guinier: 'I Was Nominated—and Then the Rules Were Changed.'" *Progressive* Sept. 1999: 28–32.

Gauthier, Xavière. "Is There Such a Thing as Women's Writing?" Trans. Marilyn A. August. *New French Feminisms.* Ed. Elaine Marks and Isabelle de Courtivron. Amherst: U of Massachusetts P, 1979. 162–64.

Gendlin, Eugene T. *Focusing.* New York: Everest, 1978.

Gere, Anne Ruggles. "Revealing Silence: Rethinking Personal Writing." *CCC* 53 (2001): 203–23.

Gerhart, Ann, and Annie Groer. "Chelsea, the Tie That Bonds." *Washington Post* 20 Aug. 1998: B8.

Gigot, Paul. "Hillary's Choice on Civil Rights: Back to the Future." *Wall Street Journal* 7 May 1993: A14.

Gilligan, Carol. *In a Different Voice.* Cambridge: Harvard UP, 1982.

Gilmore, Perry. "Silence and Sulking: Emotional Displays in the Classroom." Tannen and Saville-Troike 139–64.

Gilyard, Keith. "African American Studies." *Encyclopedia of Postmodernism.* Ed. Victor E. Taylor and Charles E. Winquist. London: Routledge, 2001.

———. "Literacy, Identity, Imagination, Flight." *CCC* 52 (2000): 260–72.

———, ed. *Race, Rhetoric, and Composition.* Portsmouth: Heinemann, 1999.

Glendin, Eugene. *Focusing.* 1978. New York: Bantam, 1981.

Glendon, Mary Ann. "What's Wrong with the Elite Law Schools?" *Wall Street Journal* 8 June 1993: A16.

Glenn, Cheryl. *Rhetoric Retold: Regendering the Tradition from Antiquity Through the Renaissance.* Carbondale: Southern Illinois UP, 1997.

Goffman, Erving. "Gender Advertisements." *Studies in the Anthropology of Visual Communication* 3 (1976): 69–154.

Goldstein, Kurt. "The Problem of the Meaning of Words Based upon Observation of Aphasic Patients." *Journal of Psychology* 2 (1936): 301–16.

Goldweb. <http://thegoldweb.com/coices/irahayes.htm>. Accessed 17 Mar. 2004.

Goodman, Paul. *Speaking and Listening.* New York: Random, 1971.

Greene, Alice B. *The Philosophy of Silence.* New York: Richard Smith, 1940.

Guinier, Lani. *Lift Every Voice: Turning a Civil Rights Setback into a New Vision of Social Justice.* New York: Simon, 1998.

———. "The Triumph of Tokenism: The Voting Rights Act and the Theory of Black Electoral Success." *Michigan Law Review* 89 (1991): 1077–154.

———. *The Tyranny of the Majority: Fundamental Fairness in Representative Democracy.* New York: Free, 1994.

————. "Who's Afraid of Lani Guinier?" *New York Times Magazine* 27 Feb. 1994: 40+.

Guinier, Lani, Michelle Fine, and Jane Balin. *Becoming Gentlemen.* Boston: Beacon, 1997.

Guy-Sheftal, Beverly. "Breaking the Silence: A Black Feminist Response to the Thomas/Hill Hearing (for Audre Lorde)." Chrisman and Allen 73–77.

Hampl, Patricia. *Virgin Time: In Search of the Contemplative Life.* New York: Ballantine, 1992.

Harjo, Joy. "Remember." *How We Became Human.* New York: Norton, 2002. 42.

Harvey, David. *Spaces of Hope.* Berkeley: U of California P, 2000.

Hawthorne, Nathaniel. *The Scarlet Letter.* Ed. Harry Levin. Boston: Houghton, 1960.

Hecht, Michael L., Ronald L. Jackson II, and Sidney A. Ribeau. *African American Communication.* 2d ed. Mahwah: Erlbaum, 2003.

Hedges, Elaine, and Shelley Fisher Fishkin, eds. *Listening to Silences.* New York: Oxford UP, 1994.

Heidegger, Martin. *Being and Time.* Trans. J. Macquarrie and E. Robinson. London: SMC, 1962.

Hernton, Calvin. "Breaking Silences." Chrisman and Allen 86–91.

Higginbotham, A. Leon, Jr. "The Hill-Thomas Hearings—What Took Place and What Happened: White Male Domination, Black Male Domination, and the Denigration of Black Women." Hill and Jordan 26–36.

Hill, Anita Faye. *Speaking Truth to Power.* New York: Doubleday, 1997.

————. "Statement of Anita F. Hill to the Senate Judiciary Committee." Smitherman 19–24.

Hill, Anita Faye, and Emma Coleman Jordan, eds. *Race, Gender, and Power in America.* New York: Oxford UP, 1995.

Hinton, Leann. *Flutes of Fire: Essays on California Indian Languages.* Berkeley: Heyday, 1994.

Hogan, Linda. "The Feathers." *Reinventing the Enemy's Language: Contemporary Native Women's Writings of North America.* Ed. Joy Harjo and Gloria Bird. New York: Norton, 1997. 450–54.

Hollis, Karyn. "Liberating Voices: Autobiographical Writing at the Bryn Mawr Summer School for Women Workers, 1921–1928." *CCC* 45 (1994): 31–60.

Holloway, Karla F. C. *Codes of Conduct: Race, Ethics, and the Color of Our Character.* New York: Routledge, 1995.

Holy Bible. Revised Standard Version. Teaneck: Cokesbury, 1962.

hooks, bell. *Talking Back.* Boston: South End, 1989.

————. *Teaching to Transgress.* New York: Routledge, 1994.

Hughes, Langston. "Silence." *The Collected Poems of Langston Hughes.* Ed. Arnold Rampersad. New York: Knopf, 1994. 234.

"Humboldt, Wilhelm von." *Encyclopedia of Philosophy.* 1969. New York: Macmillan, 1972.

Hymes, Dell. "The Ethnography of Speaking." *Anthropology and Human Behavior.* Ed. T. Gladwin and W. Sturtevant. Washington, D.C.: Washington Anthropological Society, 1964. 13–53.

———. "Toward Ethnographies of Communication." Introduction. *The Ethnography of Communication.* Spec. issue of *American Anthropologist* 66 (1964): 6, pt. 2. Ed. J. Gumerz and Dell Hymes.

"Idea Woman." *New Yorker* 14 June 1991: 4+.

Indian Helper 12.48 (10 Sept. 1897).

Isikoff, Michael. *Uncovering Clinton.* New York: Crown, 1999.

Isikoff, Michael, and Evan Thomas. "The Trouble with Willey." *Newsweek* 30 Mar. 1998: 22–29.

Itard, Jean Marc Gaspard (1775–1838). *The Wild Boy of Aveyron.* Trans. George and Muriel Humphrey. Englewood Cliffs: Prentice, 1962.

Jagles, Laura Kaye. Personal interview. 9 Aug. 2000.

Jakobson, Roman. "Signe zéro." *Mélanges de Linguistique offerts à Charles Bally.* Geneva: Georg et Cie. 143–52.

Jamieson, Kathleen Hall. *Beyond the Double Bind: Women and Leadership.* New York: Oxford UP, 1995.

Jaspers, Karl. *Philosophy.* Trans. E. B. Ashton. 2 vols. Chicago: U of Chicago P, 1970.

Johannesen, Richard L. "The Functions of Silence: A Plea for Communication Research." *Western Speech* 38 (1974): 25–35.

Johnston, William. *The Still Point.* New York: Fordham UP, 1970.

Jones, Paula Corbin. "The Paula Jones Deposition." Accessed 6 Feb. 2000. *Washington Post* online. <washingtonpost.com/wp-srv/politics/special/pjones/docs/jonestext 022198.*htm>.

Jong, Erika. *Fear of Flying.* New York: Holt, 1973.

Jordan, June. "Can I Get a Witness?" *Progressive* Dec. 1991. Rpt. in Chrisman and Allen 120–24.

Kahn, Ernest. "Functions of Silence in Life and Literature." *Contemporary Review* 194 (1958): 204–6.

Kalamaras, George. "Meditative Silence and Reciprocity." *Journal of the Assembly for Expanded Perspectives on Learning* 2 (1996–1997): 18–26.

———. *Reclaiming the Tacit Dimension.* Albany: State U of New York P, 1994.

Kaplan, Carla. *The Erotics of Talk.* New York: Oxford UP, 1996.

Kates, Susan. *Activist Rhetorics in American Higher Education.* Carbondale: Southern Illinois UP, 2000.

Katz, Steven. *The Epistemic Music of Rhetoric.* Carbondale: Southern Illinois UP, 1996.

Kemp, Alice Abel. *Women's Work: Degraded and Devalued.* Englewood Cliffs: Prentice, 1994.

Kennedy, Helen. "Beauty Queen Admits to Consensual Sex with Clinton." *Centre Daily Times* 1 Apr. 1998: 7A.

Kramarae, Cheris, and Mercilee M. Jenkins. "Women Take Back the Talk." *Women and Language in Transition.* Ed. Joyce Penfield. Albany: State U of New York P, 1987. 137–56.

Kramarae, Cheris, Muriel Schulz, and William O'Barr, eds. *Language and Power.* Beverly Hills: Sage, 1984.

Kramarae, Cheris, and Paula A. Treichler, with Ann Russo, eds. *A Feminist Dictionary.* 1985. Rpt. as *Amazons, Bluestockings, and Crones: A Feminist Dictionary.* Boston: Pandora, 1992.

Kurzon, Dennis. "To Speak or Not to Speak." *International Journal for the Semiotics of Law* 25 (1996): 3–16.

Lacour, Claudia Brodsky. "Doing Things with Words: 'Racism' as Speech Act and the Undoing of Justice." Morrison, *Race-ing* 127–58.

La Flesche, Francis. *The Middle Five: Indian Schoolboys of the Omaha Tribe.* 1963. Lincoln: U of Nebraska P, 1978.

Lake, Randall A. "Between Myth and History: Enacting Time in Native American Protest Rhetoric." *Quarterly Journal of Speech* 77 (1991): 123–51.

———. "Enacting Red Power: The Consummatory Function in Native American Protest Rhetoric." *Quarterly Journal of Speech* 69 (1983): 127–42.

Lakoff, Robin. *Talking Power.* New York: Basic, 1990.

Laqueur, Thomas. *Making Sex.* Cambridge: Harvard UP, 1990.

Lavelle, Marianne, and Julian E. Barnes. "Staring into the Political Abyss." *U.S. News and World Report* 28 Sept. 1998: 16–20.

Lebo, Joseph R. "Are You Silent?" *Today's Speech* 7 (1959): 3–4.

Leo, John. "A Controversial Choice at Justice." *U.S. News and World Report* 17 May 1993: 19.

Leonard, Mary. "Women Who Accuse Men of Sexual Misconduct Are Often Portrayed Negatively, Prompting Mental Health Experts to Recommend: Don't Complain, Don't File Charges, Just Keep Quiet." *Boston Globe* 22 Mar. 1998: E1.

Lewinsky, Monica. "The Lewinsky Affidavit." (16 Jan. 1998). Accessed 3 Feb. 2000. <http://washingtonpost.Com/wp-srv/politicsspecial/pjones/docs/lewinskyaffidavit.htm>.

———. "Grand Jury Testimony" (6 Aug. 1998). Accessed 17 Mar. 2004. <http://www.washingtonpost.com/wp-srv/politics/special/clinton/stories/m/test080698-ll.htm>.

Lewis, Magda Gere. *Without a Word: Teaching Beyond Women's Silence.* New York: Routledge, 1993.

Lewis, Neil A. "Clinton Selection for a Rights Post May Be Withdrawn." *New York Times* 2 June 1993: A17.

———. "Clinton Tries to Cut Losses after Abandoning a Choice." *New York Times* 5 June 1993: A8.

Lorde, Audre. "Litany for Survival." *The Collected Poems of Audre Lorde.* New York: Norton, 1997. 255–56.

———. "The Master's Tools Will Never Dismantle the Master's House." *Sister Outsider* 110–13.

———. *Sister Outsider.* New York: Quality, 1984.

———. "The Transformation of Silence into Language and Action." *Sister Outsider* 40–44.

Lunsford, Karen J. "Distributed Argumentative Activity: Redefining Arguments and Their Re-Mediation from a Sociohistoric Perspective." Diss. U of Illinois at Chicago, 2003.

Lyons, Scott Richard. "Rhetorical Sovereignty: What Do American Indians Want from Writing?" *CCC* 51 (2000): 447–68.

MacDonald, Scott. "Trinh T. Minh-ha." *A Critical Cinema 2: Interviews with Independent Filmmakers.* Ed. Scott MacDonald. Berkeley: U of California P, 1992.

MacKinnon, Catharine. "Hill's Accusations Ring True to a Legal Trailblazer." *Detroit Free Press* 13 Oct. 1991: 6F.

———. *Sexual Harassment of Working Women: A Case of Sex Discrimination.* New Haven: Yale UP, 1979.

MacLaverty, Bernard. *Grace Notes.* New York: Norton, 1997.

Maclean, Charles. *The Wolf Children.* London: Allen Lane, 1977.

Mann, Thomas. *The Magic Mountain.* Trans. H. T. Lowe-Porter. New York: Modern, 1927.

Mansnerus, Laura. "At the Bar." *New York Times* 3 Sept. 1993: A17.

Maraniss, David. *First in His Class.* New York: Simon, 1995.

Marmon, Lee. Personal interview. 14 Feb. 2000.

———. Personal interview. 5 Aug. 2000.

———. Personal interview. 20 May 2002.

Marshall, Thurgood. "My Dear Mr. President." *New York Times* 28 June 1991: A13.

Martin, Susan Ehrlich. "Sexual Harassment: The Link Joining Gender Stratification, Sexuality, and Women's Economic Status." *Women: A Feminist Perspective.* 4th ed. Ed. Jo Freeman. Mountain View: Mayfield, 1989. 57–75.

Matthiessen, Peter. *In the Spirit of Crazy Horse.* 1983. New York: Penguin, 1991.

Meerloo, Joost. "Contributions of Psychiatry to the Study of Human Communications." *Human Communication Theory.* Ed. Frank E. X. Dance. New York: Holt, 1967.

———. *Conversation and Communication.* New York: International Universities P, 1952.

Mejía, Jaime Armin. "Tejano Arts of the U.S.-Mexico Contact Zone." *JAC* 18 (1999): 123–36.

Merker, Hannah. *Listening.* New York: Harper, 1992.

Merton, Thomas. *Entering the Silence: The Journals of Thomas Merton.* 2 vols. Ed. Jonathan Montaldo. San Francisco: Harper, 1996.

———. *The Seven Storey Mountain.* New York: Signet-American Library, 1948.

Middleton, Joyce Irene. "Kris, I Hear You." *JAC* 20 (2000): 433–43.

Mihesuah, Devon A. *American Indians: Stereotypes and Realities.* Atlanta: Clarity, 1996.

———, ed. *Natives and Academics: Researching and Writing about Native Americans.* Lincoln: U of Nebraska P, 1998.

Miller, Jean Baker. *Toward a New Psychology of Women.* Boston: Beacon, 1976.

Miller, Keith D. "Voice Merging and Self-Making: The Epistemology of 'I Have a Dream.'" *Rhetoric Society Quarterly* 19 (1989): 23–31.

Moffett, James. "Writing, Inner Speech, and Mediation." *College English* 44 (1982): 231–46.

Momaday, N. Scott. *A House Made of Dawn.* New York: Harper, 1966.

Morrison, Toni. *Playing in the Dark. Whiteness and the Literary Imagination.* New York: Vintage, 1992.

———, ed. *Race-ing Justice, En-gendering Power.* New York: Pantheon, 1992.

Morton, Andrew. *Monica's Story.* New York: St. Martin's, 1999.

Murphy, Marjorie N. "Silence, The Word, and Indian Rhetoric." *CCC* 21 (1970): 356–63.

Murray, Tijuana. "Differences and Blurred Visions." *Life Notes: Personal Writings by Contemporary Black Women.* Ed. Patricia Bell-Scott. New York: Norton, 1994. 389–97.

Newman, Maria. "Lani Guinier at Hunter: 'Silence Is Not Golden.'" *New York Times* 2 June 1994: B3.

New York Times 19 Aug. 1998.

Nichols, Bill. "Jones Suit Dismissed." *USA Today* 2 Apr. 1998: A1.

Nomination of Judge Clarence Thomas to Be Associate Justice of the Supreme Court of the United States. (11, 12, 13 Oct. 1991). Hearings before the Committee on the Judiciary—United States Senate (Part 4). 102d Congress, 1st Session. Washington, D.C.: GPO, 1991.

Norris, Kathleen. *Cloister Walk.* New York: Riverhead, 1996.

Nouwen, Henri J. M. *The Way of the Heart.* New York: Harper, 1981.

Nunley, Vorris. "African American Hush Harbor as Rhetorical Tradition." Diss. Pennsylvania State U, 2004.

Oliver, Robert T. *Communication and Culture in Ancient India and China.* Syracuse: Syracuse UP, 1971.

Olson, Barbara. *Hell to Pay.* Washington, D.C.: Regnery, 1999.

O'Neal, Leila Moquino. Personal interview. 16 Aug. 1999.

Ong, Walter, S. J. *The Presence of the Word.* New Haven: Yale UP, 1967.

Ortega y Gasset, José. *Man and People.* Trans. Willard R. Trask. New York: Norton, 1957.

Ortiz, Earl. Personal interview. 10 Aug. 2000.

Ortiz, Simon. Introduction. *Woven* 3–33.

———. "Right of Way." *Woven* 259–60.

———. "What I Mean." *Woven* 326–29.

———. *Woven Stone.* 1992. Tucson: U of Arizona P, 1998.

"Our Stories: Communication Professionals' Narratives of Sexual Harassment." *Journal of Applied Communication Research* 20 (1992): 363–90.

Pagels, Elaine H. "What Became of God the Mother? Conflicting Images of God in Early Christianity." *Signs Reader.* Ed. Elizabeth Abel and Emily K. Abel. Chicago: U of Chicago P, 1983. 97–108.

Patterson, Orlando. "Race, Gender, and Liberal Fallacies." *New York Times* 20 Oct. 1991. Rpt. in Chrisman and Allen 160–64.

Peltier, Leonard. *Prison Writings: My Life Is My Sun Dance.* Ed. Harvey Arden. New York: St. Martin's, 1999.

Pevar, Stephen L. *The Rights of Indians and Tribes: The Basic ACLU Guide to Indian and Tribal Rights.* 2d ed. Southern Illinois UP, 1992.

Peyer, Berndt C. *The Tutor'd Mind: Indian Missionary-Writers in Antebellum America.* Amherst: U Massachusetts P, 1997.

Phelps, Timothy M., and Helen Winternitz. *Capitol Games: Clarence Thomas, Anita Hill, and the Story of a Supreme Court Nomination.* Hyperion: New York, 1992.

Philips, Susan Urmston. *The Invisible Culture: Communication in Classroom and Community on the Warm Springs Indian Reservation.* New York: Longman, 1983.

———. "Participant Structures and Communicative Competence: Warm Springs Children in Community and Classroom." *Functions of Language in the Classroom.* Ed. Courtney Cazden, Vera P. John, and Dell Hymes. New York: Teachers College P, 1972. 370–94.

Picard, Max. *The World of Silence.* 1948. Washington, D.C.: Gateway, 1988.

Plank, Gary A. "What Silence Means for Educators of American Indian Children." *Journal of American Indian Education.* (1994): 3–19.

Pough, Gwendolyn D. "Empowering Rhetoric: Black Students Writing Black Panthers." *CCC* 53 (2002): 466–86.

Powell, Malea. "Rhetorics of Survivance: How American Indians *Use* Writing." *CCC* 53 (2002): 396–434.

Quintilian. *Institution Oratoria.* Trans. H. E. Butler. 1920. 4 vols. London: Heinemann, 1969.

Ragan, Sandra L., Dianne G. Bystrom, Lynda Lee Kaid, and Christina S. Beck, eds. *The Lynching of Language.* Bloomington: Indiana UP, 1996.

Rainwater, Lee, and W. L. Yancey, eds. *The [Daniel] Moynihan Report and the Politics of Controversy: A Transaction Social Science and Public Policy Report.* Cambridge: MIT P, 1967.

Ratcliffe, Krista. *Anglo-American Feminist Challenges to the Rhetorical Tradition(s): Virginia Woolf, Mary Daly, and Adrienne Rich.* Carbondale: Southern Illinois UP, 1995.

———. E-mail to the author. 12 Apr. 2003.

———. Letter to the author. 27 Mar. 2003.

———. "Rhetorical Listening: Identification, Gender, and Whiteness." Unpublished ms.

———. "Rhetorical Listening: A Trope for Interpretive Invention and a 'Code of Cross-Cultural Conduct.'" *CCC* (1999): 195–224.

Reeves, Richard. *President Kennedy: Profile of Power.* New York: Simon, 1993.

Report of Indian Peace Commissioners. (7 Jan. 1868). House of Representatives, 40th Congress, 2d Session, Executive Document No. 97. (Serial Set 1337.11.97).

Reyhner, Jon. "Maintaining and Renewing Native Languages." *Bilingual Research Journal* 19 (1995): 279–304.

———. "Some Basics of Indigenous Language Revitalization." Introduction. *Revitalizing Indigenous Languages.* Ed. John Reyhner, Gina Cantoni, Robert N. St. Clair, and Evangeline Parsons Yazzie. Flagstaff: Northern Arizona UP, 1999. v–xx.

Rice, George P. "The Right to Be Silent." *Quarterly Journal of Speech* 47 (1961): 349–54.

Rich, Adrienne. "Arts of the Possible." *Massachusetts Review* 38 (1997): 319–37.

———. "The Burning of Paper Instead of Children." *The Fact of a Doorframe: Poems Selected and New 1950–1984.* 1975. New York: Norton, 1984. 116–18.

———. "Cartographies of Silence." *The Dream of a Common Language. Poems 1974–1977.* New York: Norton, 1978. 16–20.

———. "Invisibility in Academe." *Blood, Bread, and Poetry. Selected Prose 1979–1985.* New York: Norton, 1986. 198–201.

———. "It Is the Lesbian in Us." *On Lies* 199–202.

———. "North American Time." *The Fact of a Door Frame: Poems Selected and New 1950–1984.* New York: Norton, 1984. 324–28.

———. *On Lies, Secrets, and Silence.* New York: Norton, 1979.

———. "Taking Women Students Seriously." *On Lies* 237–45.

Richardson, Elaine. *African American Literacies.* New York: Routledge, 2003.

Ritchie, Joy, and Kate Ronald, eds. *Available Means: An Anthology of Women's Rhetoric(s).* Pittsburgh: U of Pittsburgh P, 2001.

Roiphe, Katie. "Mothers Who Think: The Willey of Our Discontent." Accessed 20 Aug 1998. <http://www.salonmagazine.com/mwt/feature/1998/03/19feature.html>.

Romero, Annette. Personal interview. 12 Oct. 1999.

Ross, Susan Deller. "Sexual Harassment Law in the Aftermath of the Hill-Thomas Hearings." Hill and Jordan 228–41.

Royster, Jacqueline Jones. "When the First Voice You Hear Is Not Your Own." *CCC* 47 (1996): 29–40.

Rukeyser, Muriel. "Myth." *Breaking Open: New Poems.* New York: Random, 1973. 17.

Rymer, Russ. *Genie, An Abused Child's Flight from Silence.* New York: Harper, 1993.

Saavedra, Kevin. Personal interview. 15 Aug. 1999.

Saint Teresa. *The Complete Works of Saint Teresa of Jesus.* Trans. and ed. E. Allison Peers. 2 vols. London: Sheed, 1950.

Saks, Oliver. *Seeing Voices: A Journey into the World of the Deaf.* New York: Harper, 1990.

Saville-Troike, Muriel. "The Place of Silence in an Integrated Theory of Communication." Tannen and Saville-Troike 3–18.

Schmidt, Susan, Peter Baker, and Toni Locy. "Clinton Accused of Urging Aide to Lie." *Washington Post* 21 Jan. 1998: A1+.

Scott, Blake. *Risky Rhetoric: AIDS and the Cultural Practices of HIV Testing.* Carbondale: Southern Illinois UP, 2003.

Scott, Joan C. "The Evidence of Experience." *Critical Inquiry* 17 (1991): 773–97.

Scott, Joan Wallach. *Gender and the Politics of History.* New York: Columbia UP, 1988.

Scott, Robert L. "Dialectical Tensions of Speaking and Silence." *Quarterly Journal of Speech* 79 (1993): 1–18.

———. "Rhetoric and Silence." *Western Speech* 36 (1972): 146–58.

Sedgwick, Eve. *Epistemology of the Closet.* Berkeley: U of California P, 1990.

Sex and Justice: The Highlights of the Anita Hill/Clarence Thomas Hearings. Film. Presented by Julian Schlossberg and Julian Wishman. Narrated by Gloria Steinem. 1993.

Shafir, Rebecca. *The Zen of Listening.* Wheaton: Quest, 2000.

Sharer, Wendy. *Vote and Voice: Women's Organizations and Political Literacy, 1915–30.* Carbondale: Southern Illinois UP, 2004.

Sheehy, Gail. *Hillary's Choice.* New York: Random, 1999.

Shipman, Pat. *The Evolution of Racism: Human Differences and the Use and Abuse of Science.* New York: Simon, 1994.

———. *Life History of a Fossil: An Introduction to Taphonomy and Paleoecology.* Cambridge: Harvard UP, 1981.

———. *The Man Who Found the Missing Link: Eugène Dubois and His Lifelong Quest to Prove Darwin Right.* New York: Simon, 2001.

———. *Taking Wing: Archaeopteryx and the Evolution of Bird Flight.* New York: Simon, 2001.

———. *To the Heart of the Nile: Lady Florence Baker and the Exploration of Central Africa.* New York: Morrow, 2004.

Showalter, Elaine. "Feminist Criticism in the Wilderness." *The New Feminist Criticism.* Ed. Elaine Showalter. New York: Pantheon, 1985. 243–70.

Silko, Leslie Marmon. "Fences Against Freedom." Accessed 17 June 2000. <http://www.bookwire.com/hmr/Review/silko.html>.

———. "Interior and Exterior Landscapes: The Pueblo Migration Stories." *Landscape in America.* Ed. George F. Thompson. Austin: U of Texas P, 1995. 155–70.

———. *Storyteller.* New York: Arcade, 1981.

———. *Yellow Woman and the Beauty of the Spirit.* New York: Simon, 1996.

Singh, Rev. Joseph A., and Robert M. Zingg. *Wolf-Children and Feral Man* (incorporating *The Diary of the Wolf-Children of Midnapore*). New York: Harper, 1942.

Smitherman, Geneva, ed. *African American Women Speak Out on Anita Hill–Clarence Thomas.* Detroit: Wayne State UP, 1995.

Smith-Rosenberg, Carroll. "Writing History: Language, Class, and Gender." *Feminist Studies/Critical Studies.* Ed. Teresa de Laurentis. Bloomington: Indiana UP, 1986. 1–54.

Snyder, Sharon L., Brenda Jo Brueggemann, and Rosemarie Garland-Thomson, eds. *Disability Studies: Enabling the Humanities.* New York: MLA, 2002.

Soesman, Albert. *Our Twelve Senses, Wellsprings of the Soul.* Stroud, Glos, UK: Hawthorne, 1990.

Sontag, Susan. "The Aesthetics of Silence." *Styles of Radical Will.* New York: Farrar, 1966. 3–34.

Spee, Friedrich. *Cautio Criminalis seu De Processibus Contra Sagas Liber. Ad Magistratus.* Austria: Sumptibus Ioannis Gronaei, 1632.

Spender, Dale. "Defining Reality: A Powerful Tool." Kramarae, Schulz, and O'Barr 194–205.

Starhawk. *Truth or Dare: Encounters with Power, Authority, and Mystery.* San Francisco: Harper, 1990.

Steiner, George. *Language and Silence.* 1958. New Haven: Yale UP, 1998.

Storr, Anthony. *Solitude.* 1988. New York: Ballantine, 1989.

Stout, David. "From a Modest Start to a Threat to the Presidency." *New York Times* 15 Nov. 1998: 34.

Suhor, Charles. "The Uses of Silence." *Council Chronicle* June 1992: 11–12.

Tannen, Deborah. *Talking from 9 to 5.* New York: Avon, 1994.

Tannen, Deborah, and Muriel Saville-Troike, eds. *Perspectives on Silence.* Norwood: Ablex, 1985.

Tavener, John. *The Music of Silence.* Ed. Brian Keeble. London: Faber, 1999.

Thomas, Clarence. "Second Statement from Judge Clarence Thomas October 11, 1991." Chrisman and Allen 22.

———. "Statement of Clarence Thomas to the Senate Judiciary Committee October 11, 1991." Smitherman 25–30.

Thorne, Barrie, Cheris Kramarae, and Nancy Henley, eds. *Language, Gender, and Society.* Rowley: Newbury, 1983.

Todacheene, Andrew. Personal interview. 12 Aug. 1999.

Tohe, Laura. "Half-Light." *No Parole* 41.

———. Introduction. *No Parole* ix–xii.

———. *No Parole Today.* Albuquerque: West End, 1999.

Toobin, Jeffrey. *A Vast Conspiracy.* New York: Random, 1999.

Travis, Molly, and Jamie Barlowe. "Dialogue of the Imaginary." *Women and Language* 18 (1995): 37–40.

Trinh T. Minh-ha. "Difference: 'A Special Third World Women Issue.'" *Discourse* 8 (1986/1987): 11–37.

———. Introduction. *Discourse* 8 (1986/1987): 3–9.

———. *When the Moon Waxes Red: Representation, Gender and Cultural Politics.* New York: Routledge, 1991.

Victoriano, Danielle. Personal interview. 12 Oct. 1999.

Vizenor, Gerald. *Manifest Manners.* Hanover: Wesleyan UP, 1994.

Waas, Murray. "The Other Woman." Accessed 21 Nov. 1998. <http://www.salon.com/news/1998/09/11newsa.html>.

Wagner, Geoffrey. *On the Wisdom of Words.* Princeton: Van Nostrand, 1968.

Wanya, Billie. Personal interview. 12 Oct. 1999.

Washburn, Wilcomb E., ed. *The Indian and the White Man.* Garden City: Anchor, 1964.

Watts, Richard J. "Silence and the Acquisition of Status in Verbal Interaction." *Silence: Interdisciplinary Perspectives.* Ed. Adam Jaworski. Berlin: Mouton de Gruyter, 1997. 87–116.

Watzlawick, Janet Beaven, and Don Jackson. *Pragmatics of Human Communication.* New York: Norton, 1967.

Weber, Max. *The Theory of Social and Economic Organization.* New York: Free, 1969.

Weis, Lois, and Michell Fine, eds. *Beyond Silenced Voices: Class, Race, and Gender in United States Schools.* Albany: State U of New York P, 1993.

Weisberg, Jacob. "The Governor-President Clinton." *New York Times Magazine* 17 Jan. 1999: 30–35+.

Welch, Kathleen E. *Electric Rhetoric.* Cambridge: MIT P, 1999.

West, Susan T. "From Owning to Owning Up: Authorial Rights and Rhetorical Responsibilities." Diss. Ohio State U, 1997.

Whitman, Walt. "I Sit and Look Out." *Leaves of Grass.* Oxford: Oxford UP, 1990. 215.

Wideman, John Edgar. *Hoop Roots.* Boston: Houghton, 2001.

Wieder, D. Lawrence, and Steven Pratt. "On Being a Recognizable Indian among Indians." *Cultural Communication and Intercultural Contact.* Ed. Donald Carbaugh. Hillsdale: Erlbaum, 1990. 45–64.

Willey, Kathleen. "The Kathleen Willey Deposition." 11 Jan. 1998. *Washington Post* online. Accessed 20 Nov. 1998. <washingtonpost.com/wp-srv/Wplate/1998-03/14/1021-031498-idx.html>.

Williams, Patricia J. *The Alchemy of Race and Rights.* Cambridge: Harvard UP, 1991.

———. "Lani, We Hardly Knew Ye: How the Right Wing Created a Monster Out of a Civil Rights Advocate and Bill Clinton Ran in Terror." *Village Voice* 15 June 1993: 15–28.

———. *The Rooster's Egg.* Cambridge: Harvard UP, 1995.

Wilson, Darryl Babe. "Salila-ti Mi-mu d-enn-I-gu." *Advocate* 1. Rpt. in *News from Native California* 7 (1993): 38.

Wilson, James C., and Cynthia Lewiecki-Wilson, eds. *Embodied Rhetorics: Disability in Language and Culture.* Carbondale: Southern Illinois UP, 2001.

Wolf, Naomi. "Feminism and Intimidation on the Job: Have the Hearings Liberated the Movement?" *Washington Post* 13 Oct. 1991: C1.

Wood, Julia, T. "Telling Our Stories: Narratives as a Basis for Theorizing Sexual Harassment." *Journal of Applied Communication Research* 20 (1992): 349–418.

Yost, Pete. "A Hurt Lewinsky Returns to Grand Jury to Tell All." *State College (PA) Centre Daily Times* 21 Aug. 1998: 8A.

Young, Morris. "Standard English and Student Bodies: Institutionalizing Race and Literacy in Hawai'i." *College English* 64 (2002): 405–32.

Index

absolute listening, 156

abuse, 146, 167n10. *See also* sexual harassment

academia: racism in, 43–45; silencing across discourse community, 36–39; silencing in, 33–39, 43–46; top-down silencing in, 33–36; women and silencing in, 33–36, 45–46

action, silence as, 156

action, speech as, 53

African American Women in Defense of Ourselves, 58

"Against Silence" (Becker), 47–48, 51, 70

Alchemy of Race and Rights (Williams), xxi

Alcoff, Linda Martin, 58

Alford, Thomas Wildcat, 127, 140–41

Allen, Paula Gunn, 137, 140, 182–83n5

Alvord, Lisa Arviso, 116

American literature, 51

Angelou, Maya, 168n4

anger, 104, 131–33

Anglo-American Challenges to the Rhetorical Tradition(s): Virginia Woolf, Mary Daly, and Adrienne Rich (Ratcliffe), 152

anxiety, 11–12, 32

aphasia, 12–13

appropriateness of silence, 6–7, 13, 33–35

Ardener, Edwin, 25, 30

Aristotle, 5, 10, 13, 20

articulate groups, 25

"Arts of the Possible" (Rich), 154

Askew, Anne, 2, 104

Athens, 20

audience, 74–75

authority, 30–31; bottom-to-top silencing, 39–41; in male-female relationships,

31–32; use of by peers, 36–37. *See also* academia

authorship, 151

Background, 24–25

Baker, Sidney J., 16–17

Barbara Walters's Fascinating People, 101

Basso, Keith, 17–18, 108, 114, 117, 148, 187n15, 188nn24–25

Bateson, Gregory, 169n8

Bauman, Richard, 158

Becker, Robin, 42–43, 47–48

Becoming Gentlemen (Guinier, Fine, and Balin), 175n37

Belanoff, Pat, 62, 157

Berkhofer, Robert, 108

"Beyond Persuasion: A Proposal for an Invitational Rhetoric" (Foss and Griffin), 156

Beyond Silenced Voices (Weis and Fine), 160

Bizzell, Patricia, 151

black, as term, xxi

Black, Edwin, 79, 80, 81, 100, 175n4

black women, discourse of, 24, 26–28

Blair, Carole, 151

Bleiler, Andrea, 179n31

boarding schools, 114, 126–27, 188–89n26

Bodies That Matter (Butler), xix–xx, 23

body language, 39–41

Bolick, Clint, 66, 67

Boo, Katherine, 61–62

Bordewich, Fergus M., 181n1, 182n4

Bourdieu, Pierre, 27–27, 166n5

Boyd, Maurice, 191n30

Bradley, Ed, 91–92

Braithwaite, Charles A., 159

Brandenburg, Ruth, 163–64n2

213

media: deliberate misreading by, 65–67, 72–
73, 105, 173n23; populist news outlets,
79–80; public view of, 67, 173n23; and
purposeful focus on irrelevant issues,
104–6; racism of, 65–68; and smear
campaigns, 67–68, 73, 173n24; of U.S.
vs. that of other countries, 175–76n5
meditation, 119, 156–57
"Meditative Silence and Reciprocity"
(Kalamaras), 156–57
memories, 147–48
Mihesuah, Devon, 140, 147, 191n30
Mikulski, Barbara, 58, 62
Miller, Jean Baker, 99
Miranda warning, 42
Mitterand, François, 175–76n5
Moffett, James, 156
Momaday, N. Scott, 115–16
Monica in Black and White, 101–2
Morrison, Toni, 50, 51, 57
mourning, 133–37
Moynihan, Daniel, 66
multiplicity of rhetorics, 157–58
Murphy, Marjorie N., 113
Murray, Tijuan, 170–71n12
music, 159
muted groups, 25–28
"Myth" (Rukeyser), 21

NAACP Legal Defense Fund, 72
narrative, 146–47
"Native American," as term, xx–xxi. *See
also* Indians; Real Indian, figure of
Native American Languages Act (1990), 114
negative silence, 16–17
negativity, paradox of, 170–71n12
Nichols, Larry, 82
Nightline, 70–71
nonsubmissive subordinate, 40
nonverbal behavior, 39–41
"nonwhite," as term, xxi, 170n10
nonwhite women: discourse of, 24, 26–28;
double oppression of, 62, 65, 170n11; as
overachievers, 66–67; politics and, 72–
73. *See also* Guinier, Lani; Hill, Anita
"Notes on Speechlessness" (Cliff), 11
Nunley, Vorris, 159

obstruction of justice, 97–98
Oedipus, 21
Off the Reservation (Allen), 143
O'Neal, Leila Moquino, 120, 122, 128, 131,
135, 139, 146
Organizing Silence (Clair), 9
Ortega y Gasset, José, 7, 153
Ortiz, Earl, 120, 121, 125, 130, 133, 135, 139–
40
Ortiz, Simon, 115, 116, 143, 144–45, 186–
87n15
Other: Africanist presence as, 51; Real In-
dian as, 107–8; and scapegoating, 49–51;
silencing of, 23–24, 67–68
overtalker, 38–39

Pagels, Elaine H., 21, 166n1
paraphasias, 11–13
passive resistance, 89–91
Patterson, Orlando, 57–58
Paul, Saint, 2
Peace Commission (1868), 114
Peaches, Mrs. Anne, 114
pedagogical silence, 159–60
Peltier, Leonard, 107, 113
Perdue, Sally, 94
perjury, 97–98, 99, 181n37
personality, silence and, 120, 146
personalization by victims, 61, 71
personal space, 122–23
perspective by incongruity, 104, 154
Pevar, Stephen, 164–65n5
Peyer, Berndt C., 181n2
Philips, Susan, 140, 141–42
Picard, Max, 1, 3–4, 8
Pine Ridge Reservation, 107
Plank, Gary, 140, 141
Playing in the Dark (Morrison), 51
positive silence, 17
postindian, xx, 109, 163n1, 183n6
Powell, Malea, 147
power: and hierarchy of relations, 22, 27–
28, 30, 35; muted groups and, 27–28; of
presidency, 69–70; of Senate Judiciary
Committee, 55–56; speech as, 3
practical sense, 27–28
Pratt, Richard, 114

Cheryl Glenn, an associate professor of English at the Pennsylvania State University, has three complementary areas of scholarly interest: histories of women's rhetorics and writing practices, delivery systems for the teaching of writing, and inclusionary rhetorical practices and theories. Among her publications are *Rhetoric Retold: Regendering the Tradition from Antiquity Through the Renaissance, Rhetorical Education in America, The New St. Martin's Guide to Teaching Writing, The Writer's Harbrace Handbook,* and *Making Sense: A New Rhetorical Reader.* Glenn's rhetorical scholarship has earned her three National Endowment for the Humanities awards, the Conference on College Composition and Communication's Richard Braddock Award, and Best Book/Honorable Mention from the Society for the Study of Early Modern Women.